Republic in Peril

Other titles by David C. Hendrickson:

Union, Nation, or Empire: The American Debate over International Relations, 1789–1941

Peace Pact: The Lost World of the American Founding

The Imperial Temptation: The New World Order and America's Purpose

Empire of Liberty: The Statecraft of Thomas Jefferson

Reforming Defense: The State of American Civil-Military Relations

The Future of American Strategy

The Fall of the First British Empire: Origins of the War of American Independence

Republic in Peril

*American Empire and
the Liberal Tradition*

———◆———

DAVID C. HENDRICKSON

OXFORD
UNIVERSITY PRESS

OXFORD

UNIVERSITY PRESS

Oxford University Press is a department of the University of Oxford. It furthers
the University's objective of excellence in research, scholarship, and education
by publishing worldwide. Oxford is a registered trade mark of Oxford University
Press in the UK and certain other countries.

Published in the United States of America by Oxford University Press
198 Madison Avenue, New York, NY 10016, United States of America.

© Oxford University Press 2018

CIP data is on file at the Library of Congress
ISBN 978–0–19–066038–3

1 3 5 7 9 8 6 4 2
Printed by Sheridan Books, Inc., United States of America

In memory of Whitney deMoraes Hendrickson, 1990–2009.
Tender spirit, sparkling wit. Her radiance never ceases.

Contents

Preface

THIS BOOK ARGUES that American foreign policy needs a return to first principles. Such a renovation in its grand strategy must adapt to new circumstances but should also rest on the philosophical foundations provided by America's Founders and its broader liberal tradition. The argument is similar to one that was made in *The Imperial Temptation: The New World Order and America's Purpose*, a work written with Robert W. Tucker in 1992. That, too, made an appeal from the present to the past, recounted the wise counsel of America's Founders, warned against the bewitchment with force, saw a threat to free institutions and purpose if the belief in force persisted, and invoked William Seward's idea that "all nations must perpetually renovate their virtues and their constitutions, or perish." In 1848, when Seward wrote these words in a eulogy of John Quincy Adams, after the Mexican War had drawn to a close, he saw America "passing from the safe old policy of peace and moderation into a career of conquest and martial renown." That movement was also observable in 1991. It has persisted and even deepened over the past quarter-century.

This book, then, is something of a throwback to *The Imperial Temptation*, but it also functions as a capstone or completion of two earlier studies of mine: *Peace Pact: The Lost World of the American Founding* (2003), and *Union, Nation, or Empire: The American Debate over International Relations, 1789-1941* (2009). These two works, the writing of which rather unexpectedly consumed more than fifteen years, were studies in the intellectual history of American reflection on foreign policy and international affairs. *Republic in Peril* touches their themes in crucial respects. A conclave of Founding Fathers (George Washington, Alexander Hamilton, James Madison, John Adams, and Thomas Jefferson), together with many other American statesmen in ensuing years (Daniel Webster, Henry Clay, John Quincy Adams, Abraham Lincoln, William Seward), are key sources of authority for my argument.

From these esteemed statesmen, along with the European writers on which they drew, do I mainly derive my idea of the liberal tradition. I hope to show that there is merit in this tradition, that we can glean from it the wisdom to seek a better world in the present.

The reason for this focus on the Founders, I have to acknowledge, is partly autobiographical. From graduate school onward, a good part of my scholarly life was spent investigating the life and times of the Founding generation, with a second career as a student of American foreign policy, and I can't quite say where the former left off and the latter began. But such habits undoubtedly matter in forming one's intellectual outlook, settling in like barnacles on the cranium, whether for good or ill the reader may judge.

Observe good faith and justice towards all nations; cultivate peace and harmony with all. Religion and morality enjoin this conduct; and can it be, that good policy does not equally enjoin it?

GEORGE WASHINGTON, Farewell Address, 1796

A nation which does not remember what it was yesterday, does not know what it is today, nor what it is trying to do. We are trying to do a futile thing if we do not know where we came from or what we have been about.

WOODROW WILSON, 1911

Republic in Peril

Introduction

Obama Legacy and Trump Prospect

In disposition and outlook, Barack Obama and George W. Bush could not have been more different. Obama was the consummate pragmatist, coolly weighing the options, always raising difficulties, given to long deliberation; Bush was the crusader, preferring to give subordinates pep talks rather than to pepper them—as Obama did—with questions. Obama's outlook emphasized limits and was tuned to the strains of liberal realism; Bush rejected that view and seemed to think the only limit was the sky. In his response to 9/11, Bush stretched the ambitions of American power to Olympian heights—proposing unquestioned U.S. military supremacy, a doctrine of preventive war, unilateral prerogatives, a vast expansion of America's spying apparatus, and the militarized pursuit of democracy with the aim of ending tyranny and terrorism in the world. Obama, by contrast, was the determined opponent of the crusading impulse, by inclination a stout multilateralist, and always attuned to the unintended consequences likely to ensue from rash decisions. On the strength of his early opposition to the Iraq War, he had bested Hillary Clinton for the 2008 Democratic nomination. His supporters saw in his candidacy a promise to end the wars and to bring profound change to the Bush foreign policy.

Eight years later, when his presidency came to an end, the contrast between the hopes of 2009 and the grim realities of 2017 was manifest. Obama did certain things in foreign policy that Bush would never have done, such as reaching an agreement with Iran and beginning to normalize relations with Cuba; in other respects, however, he continued and even advanced the objectives of the previous administration:

- Obama proved no less committed than Bush to a doctrine of U.S. military supremacy. Though Pentagon expenditures declined with the drawdowns in Iraq and Afghanistan, total military expenditures in Obama's two terms exceeded those under his predecessor.

- Obama continued and even expanded the policies of unlimited surveillance that Bush had introduced, drawing back in only a few celebrated instances. (He pledged, after the Snowden revelations, to stop tapping the cellphones of allied leaders, but would not make a similar pledge for their staffs or their larger governmental apparatus.)

- Obama adopted a more strident posture in East Asia, vigorously contesting China's strategic policies, a change symbolized by Secretary of State Hillary Clinton's 2011 bid for the leadership of an anti-Chinese coalition, followed by the "pivot to Asia" and the Trans Pacific Partnership.

- Obama presided over a renewed Cold War with Russia over Ukraine, in which the U.S. State Department, led by Assistant Secretary Victoria Nuland, worked to facilitate the overthrow of the elected government of Viktor Yanukovych, provoking civil war, Russian intervention, and the return of overt hostility between old Cold War rivals.

- Obama promised steps to rid the world of nuclear weapons, but he acquiesced in plans to modernize the U.S. strategic arsenal, at an expected cost of $1 trillion over thirty years, and bowed to the stout opposition of the national security complex in refusing to endorse a "no-first-use" policy toward nuclear weapons.

- Obama greatly expanded the use of drones in targeted assassinations against radical Islamists in Pakistan, Yemen, Somalia, and Libya.

- Obama greatly expanded arms sales, especially in the Middle East, authorizing $115 billion to Saudi Arabia alone, and supported the Saudis in their illegal intervention in Yemen.

- Most remarkably of all, Obama continued Bush's strategy devoted to the armed overthrow of autocratic governments in the Middle East. Bush had done this in the name of ending terrorism and spreading democracy; Obama did it in the name of humanitarianism and preventing atrocities. His administration intervened in Libya's civil war and smashed its state apparatus in 2011, throwing Libya (and North Africa generally) into chaos and opening a vast new front in the war on terror. From the beginning of the Syrian rebellion, the United States called for Bashar al-Assad's removal and gave diplomatic cover—and considerable military aid—to so-called moderates seeking the overthrow of Assad. Secretary of State Clinton gave the green light to Saudi Arabia, Qatar, and Turkey to send arms to the Sunni jihadists fighting Assad, much of which ended up in the hands of ISIS and the Nusra Front, al-Qaeda's affiliate in Syria. After the rise of

ISIS and its seizure in 2014 of vast territory in eastern Syria and western Iraq, Obama committed to a war to destroy the Islamic State, making the removal of Assad a secondary objective, but the policy of overthrow contributed very much to the grim outcome, as the anarchy unleashed by Syrian rebellion provided the circumstances in which apocalyptic groups like ISIS would thrive. Syria fell into the worst of all human conditions, civil war.

In nearly all these actions, Obama was criticized by most Republicans for doing too little; undoubtedly, John McCain or Mitt Romney, his Republican opponents in 2008 and 2012, would have done more. And there is a real sense in which Obama was expansive about U.S. ends but cautious about U.S. means. He signed on to a strategy of overthrow in Libya, Syria, and Ukraine, but then proved reluctant to get more fully involved, somehow managing at most points along the arc of crisis to be both engaged and detached. But the larger pattern is clear. Despite the promises of 2008, there was more continuity than change in the Obama administration's approach to foreign policy. He departed from the Bush policy in some respects, especially toward Iran and Cuba, but in most respects he confirmed the precedents that Bush had set.

Obama was philosophically disposed to resist this tendency toward greater U.S. intervention abroad. In the main, however, he did not resist it. Why this is so is a question that will doubtless occupy historians for many years. Though Obama was a conscientious objector to what he called "the Washington playbook," whereby increased toughness and the hegemonic presumption are the solution to international conflict, he conformed to rather than strayed from the playbook in many of his administration's most consequential actions.[1]

That Obama failed in crucial respects to reorient U.S. foreign policy, despite having at the outset an intention of doing so, is dispiriting. It suggests the power of the machine over the man. John F. Kennedy liked to tell the story about how he discovered the limits of presidential power, after learning that an explicit order he had given had been ignored. The bureaucracy, he realized, is adept at subverting pronounced challenges to its way of doing things. The president is figurehead, mascot, and sometime decision maker, but the great wheels of state are not easy to divert from their accustomed course. As Obama too would learn, vested interests and familiar ideologies have a way of proving more consequential.

This book is a study of those vested interests and familiar ideologies. Its centerpiece is not so much the outlook of a Bush or an Obama but of "the official mind"—one that is determined to live on even as these presidents fade into the mist.[2] Obama was certainly right in identifying a "Washington playbook," a way of interpreting the world and America's role in it that has exerted profound importance over foreign policy. Its central proposition is that it is impossible to have a liberal world order without having hostile relations with Russia, China, and Iran. In her gut instincts and core beliefs, Hillary Clinton was the perfect embodiment of this consensus. Even Donald Trump will be greatly constrained by it, may even be swallowed by it. Whoever occupies the Oval Office, the playbook's customary rules constitute the milieu and structure of political forces within which the president must think and act. Individual presidents may matter greatly for good or ill in particular circumstances, but the permanent government and its supporting array of institutions—think tanks, news media, and corporate interests—remain crucial in understanding the American approach to the world. To change this official mind—and change it must—we must first better understand its origins and character.

Though both vested interests and regnant ideologies are vital in arriving at a satisfactory explanation of America's role in the world, it is not easy to judge accurately the relative weight of the two. John Maynard Keynes famously struggled with that difficulty in his *General Theory*, and what he said about the power of economic ideas is just as true of ideas concerning security. "Practical men, who believe themselves to be quite exempt from any intellectual influences, are usually the slaves of some defunct economist. Madmen in authority, who hear voices in the air, are distilling their frenzy from some academic scribbler of a few years back."[3] Keynes wanted to show the power of ideas as against the "vested interests"; the sway of the latter he thought "vastly exaggerated compared with the gradual encroachment of ideas." His discussion is very pertinent to U.S. foreign policy today, where powerful domestic interests are vested in the conflicts the United States prosecutes abroad. The importance of this national security interest, I will be arguing, deserves far more attention than it has received, but in the end one cannot deny the thrust of Keynes' observation affirming the importance of ideas. The ideas of the security establishment do reflect a sort of "distilled frenzy"—incubated in the laboratories of the 1930s, synthesized and mass-produced during the Cold War, then set free in the post-Cold War era of unipolarity and the war on terror—that continues to exert profound influence.

That larger consensus, formed in a bygone age, needs a thorough interrogation. America's foreign policy and national security strategy of the last twenty-five years—the template by which it has managed the international order—became badly out of kilter over time. Its purposes and methods require a fundamental reordering. The present work tries to describe how the nation arrived at that awful pass, and proposes ways of getting out. Because this book is critical of the pretensions and objectives of the U.S. national security state, it will doubtless be perceived as anti-American in some quarters. To this I say, the nation is a compact between the dead, the living, and the yet unborn. I suggest further that the dead have something of great value to offer us today. The change in policy I recommend draws greatly from American precedents and can be seen as a distillation of what was once termed "Americanism" (evoking a nation that tries to live by the creed).

I should like to emphasize, however, that recalling the old American tradition is not an exercise in nostalgia, but in philosophy; its objective is to inform contemporary debates with the strains of the liberal Enlightenment, not to wallow in nativism. The Founders' science of international politics, a blend of what are known today as liberalism and realism, reveals truths often forgotten by today's policymakers and academicians. Among other insights, they saw the dangers military power posed to a regime devoted to republican liberty, understood the need for balance in both domestic and foreign affairs, and embraced a pluralist conception of the society of states. They saw the law of nations as authoritative, but shrewdly advanced the interests of their country, and knew that one could do that through law and not in defiance of it. Holding their own state to its obligations, they believed, was just as important as holding other states to theirs.

The ideas of the Founding generation about the purposes of foreign policy and the nature of international order are not irrelevant at all, but more often incisive and bracing in their challenge to contemporary predilections and orthodoxies. Despite the enormous difference in circumstances between their day and ours, most commentators would acknowledge that the essentials of the American Creed were laid out by the Founders; it should not seem incongruous or hidebound to turn to them in hours of perplexity, as these undoubtedly are. Ultimately, the great questions of foreign policy are philosophical in character, concerning the right ordering of the commanding values of American civilization in confrontation with the problem of insecurity. In this important inquiry into the fundaments of the American purpose and the bases of American security, the progenitors of our civil religion may surely lend a hand.

The Americanism I seek to recover, alas, is worlds apart from the "Americanism" that Donald Trump has touted. Trump is undoubtedly a work in progress, and an inevitable theme of his presidency will be the ease with which he breaks his promises. But which ones? No one can be sure of that. Whereas Hillary Clinton adopted a campaign rhetoric almost indistinguishable on national security questions from the second George W. Bush administration, Trump threw riotously into question basic elements of the foreign policy consensus, one held tenaciously by the security elites hitherto dominant in both political parties. Though unique in manifold respects, his electoral victory was weirdly symbolic of a worldwide trend toward aggressive and populist nationalism. In Poland and Hungary, in China and Russia, in India and the Philippines, in little 'ole England and the U.S. of A.—just about everywhere, in fact—nationalism has rekindled its old appeal, breathing fire against a malign outside world.

In his life before the presidency, Trump was all about the abolition of traditional limits; he had risen upward by defying convention in the name of celebrity. His campaign for the presidency violated many elementary decencies, as if inhabiting a world in which the appropriate and the ethical had ceased to be relevant categories, and only a tawdry instrumentalism remained. Equally disappointing, though admittedly less shocking, was his inability to articulate a coherent alternative to America's globalist policies. That such an alternative is needed is a key assumption of the present work.

Trump styled his movement as an insurgent American nationalism that would always put America First, as Pat Buchanan did in his presidential bids in 1992 and 1996. Trump, however, did not counsel a reduction in military spending or a withdrawal from America's alliances, as did Buchanan, but rather saw the alliances as arrangements between a superpower protector and deadbeat dependents, who should pay up or shove off. In one respect, Trump's proclaimed desire to extract rents from "allies" is directly contrary to the ethos of the "liberal world order," but in another respect it simply intensifies an existing trend (lately taking the form of the U.S. Congress legislating for the world, because the world has a dollar-based financial system). Clearly, however, Trump's attitude was worlds apart from "isolationists" and the "America Firsters" of yore, all of whom would have recoiled from an empire of tribute.[4]

Trump's campaign message was most contradictory in its approach to the Greater Middle East, the overwhelming destination for the use of U.S. military power over the last generation. An ostensible critic of the 2003 Iraq War and the 2011 intervention in Libya to overthrow Muammar el-Qaddafi—of regime change and nation-building—he also called for a war to eradicate "radical Islamic terrorism," in which cause he seemed to include not only the Islamic State and its widespread franchise but also, at a minimum, Iran, Hezbollah, Hamas, and the Houthis. Trump rightly labeled the 2003 Iraq

War as a disaster, but then added the thought that, having mistakenly done the deed, the United States ought to have seized Iraqi oil fields as compensation for the misadventure (which would have united Sunni and Shia and Kurd, really the entirety of the Muslim world and the free world, against us, which is no mean feat). From the beginning of his electoral campaign, he lambasted the Iran nuclear agreement as "one of the worst deals ever made," placing himself in alignment with the neoconservatives he otherwise denounced, but he bad-mouthed the Saudis, too. He argued more broadly to remove restraints on U.S. airpower in targeting terrorists and their families, intimating that the real flaw in U.S. strategy in the region was insufficient zeal in the disproportionate and indiscriminate use of force. Trump called it a scandal that trillions of dollars were squandered in Middle Eastern wars, consuming resources that might have been used to rebuild America's crumbling infrastructure, but his stated aspirations in the region pointed toward a similar calamity. In the age-old conflict between internationalism and isolationism, engagement and withdrawal, maximalism and minimalism, Trump thus cut a wildly erratic figure in his campaign. A critic of globalism and neoliberalism, he presented himself not as a non-interventionist but as an assertive nationalist, not an isolationist but a unilateralist. Against anything like universalism, he wanted even more from the world than did Hillary Clinton, who so well reflected establishment thinking.

When Trump was elected, the shocking result was widely seen as potentially revolutionary, upending America's role in the "liberal world order." A few months of his presidency, however, indicated that no revolution in policy was impending. Trump being Trump, no one could be sure, but what was on offer in the domain of national security were mostly ideas that Republicans had championed for two decades. If Obama represented continuity with George W. Bush's second administration, Trump's initial forays represented continuity with Bush's first administration. The belligerent posture toward North Korea and the menacing language toward Iran featured in Trump's first months in 2017 were replays of Bush's first months in early 2001. Twenty years ago, the Republicans were working to sabotage the Agreed Framework that Clinton achieved in 1994 with North Korea; in the early 2000s, they proceeded to tear it up for good, making far more likely North Korea's march to a bomb. The general attitude—that anything that works for North Korea is *ipso facto* bad for us—is nothing new at all. In the Republican Party, the same attitude toward Russia, China, and Iran has been dominant for a generation. Having them (but not only them) as enemies has long been the first article of Republican faith.

Trump's reversals of position on foreign policy became legendary in his first 100 days, but the flip-flops had in common a movement toward traditional Republican verities. In his first acts as president, Trump brought into his national security coterie many men and women of a decidedly militaristic outlook. He then attached his belligerent nationalism to highly ambitious objectives across Eurasia. Obama had been weak; he would be strong. NATO, previously obsolete, became vital again. While Trump continued intermittent gestures of conciliation toward Russia (provoking frenzied opposition from the Washington establishment), his responsible officials adopted a Russia policy even tougher than Obama's; they, at least, seemed to understand that a hawkish stance toward Russia might be a bludgeon against Trump's Democratic adversaries, forcing his enemies to applaud him. In the Greater Middle East, Obama's supposed timidity was replaced by escalation in numerous theaters (Yemen, Syria, Afghanistan, Iraq), with Iran re-emerging as the focus of evil against which U.S. policy was directed. At the beginning of Trump's administration, China made for a while a curious journey from foremost adversary to dragooned partner, but the prevailing U.S. tone in East Asia—do as we say, or else—was identical with his Republican predecessor's first months.

Bush, to be fair, did appoint as secretary of state a skilled and experienced diplomat in Colin Powell; Trump seems to lack such a balance wheel. And the Bush people understood the value of constancy, of meaning what you say and saying what you mean, whereas Trump has appeared as a sort of boneless wonder defined by his erraticism. Unfortunately, it surely matters that Trump knows he has a reputation to live down in that regard. In all probability, he believes that the steely use of force will help repair it. In overall cast of thinking, Trump seems more of a militarist than any previous U.S. president; his illiberal policies for large-scale deportations and incarceration at home are of a piece with that trait. Though he could be a force for foreign policy restraint in some respects (an outcome desired by the Rust Belt constituency that put him over the top), the greater likelihood is that the non-interventionists among his supporters will end up feeling swindled.

Even during his 2016 campaign, Trump gave plenty of warning that his inclinations ran more toward domination than reciprocity, more toward imperialism than isolationism, more toward militarism than pacifism. Toward both domestic and foreign rivals, bullying rather than sweet reason quickly emerged as the dominant calling card—that, and an uncanny knack for saying (or tweeting) things that were unseemly, unfitting, and unbecoming.[5]

Gung-ho for additional military spending and nuclear modernization in his campaign, he went further once in office, proposing a "hard-power" budget that bolstered armaments across the board and ruthlessly excised anything suggestive of a humanitarian purpose or that sought preparedness against non-military dangers. It was obvious from Trump's campaign that he had little regard for diplomacy, the first principles of which he seemed to have discarded, but not apparent that he would seek once in office to discombobulate and marginalize the State Department. (Trump seems not to have realized that the military officers he lionizes are in their strategic outlook nearly identical with the civilian diplomats he despises. "Who knew?" he may ask one day.)

John Adams, in one of his early missives on American foreign policy, called for a posture in which it would be the duty and interest of the United States to be friends of all the powers of Europe, and enemies to none, whereas Trump's vision, with its omnidirectional abuse against foreign nations, has seemed perilously close to "enemies to all, friends to none." Also alarming for his conduct of foreign policy is that Trump, like academic "neo-sovereigntists" and nativists of the Tea Party, seems hostile to the very idea of international law, suggestive as it is of restraints on national self-assertion. The Founders, by contrast, believed that a central purpose of America, in James Madison's words, was to seek "by appeals to reason and by its liberal examples to infuse into the law which governs the civilized world a spirit which may diminish the frequency or circumscribe the calamities of war, and meliorate the social and beneficent relations of peace."[6]

Trump's presidency highlights the Madisonian hypothesis that political institutions must be judged by their capacity to protect the people against the most problematic rulers. Institutions should be commodious for good times, but built to survive the bad times, on the theory that enlightened statesmen will not always be at the helm. So far as "national security" is concerned, this may prove to be a case of the blind checking the blind, with reason hardly in a position to prevail, but the Trump phenomenon undoubtedly poses a severe test for American political institutions and world order. That a man with his notorious personal failings should hold the most powerful office in the world suggests the peril of accumulating so much power in that office. Executive discretion, pronounced on many fronts, exists most completely in the use of force and in the conduct of the nation's foreign policy. The imperial presidency, now entrusted to Trump, may turn out to be the most profound legacy of the "liberal world order."[7]

America, Liberalism, and Empire

Among the master symbols of American civilization, none are more important than empire and liberty. From George Washington's journey to the
Monongahela River in 1754 to George W. Bush's conquests in Mesopotamia
in 2003, observers have puzzled over the relationship between our thirst for
dominion and our attachment to freedom. When Patrick Henry argued in
1788 against the "great and splendid empire" he espied in the vision of the
Constitution's architects, he set that in opposition to the liberty that was
America's original resolution: "If we admit this Consolidated Government it
will be because we like a great splendid one. Some way or other we must be a
great and mighty empire; we must have an army, and a navy, and a number of
things: When the American spirit was in its youth, the language of America
was different: Liberty, Sir, was then the primary object."[8]

Some variation on Henry's theme has been played on every subsequent
occasion in which the use of force figured—1798, 1812, 1818, 1830, 1846, 1861,
1898, and on to the wars of the American Century.[9] As much as these debates
might be dismissed as belonging to another age, without relevance to our globalized world, they express views that go to the core of the nation's purposes
and convictions today. The relation America bears to liberalism and imperialism, to use the modern terminology, is of intense interest in the contemporary
world, but in a fundamental sense it has always been such.

Despite its centrality, the relation between empire and liberty is not easy
to characterize. It is certainly complex. The debate over it can rise to great
heights of eloquence; it can fall into the labyrinths of obscurity. Both imperialism and liberalism (and their cognates) have a multiplicity of meanings,
employed in a multiplicity of contexts. Liberty, instantiated in "the American
system," referred to "written constitutions, representative government, religious toleration, freedom of opinion, of speech and of the press," as a Kentucky
ally of Henry Clay put it in 1822.[10] But it has also signified collective freedom,
especially independence from foreign rule, and the freedom reflected in the
integrity of the nation's political institutions.

Empire is an especially slippery concept, tending toward domination in
theory but in practice displaying relaxations that concede much freedom to
the periphery. While empire is typically defined in terms of alien control and
domination, nearly all successful empires relied on indirect means of control.
They usually required the co-option of local elites. They were often patchwork
and incoherent affairs, with no clear delineation of the lines of authority. As
Edmund Burke famously said, describing a world in which "seas roll, and

months pass, between the order and the execution," the first rule of empire was that it couldn't control everything. "The Sultan gets such obedience as he can. He governs with a loose rein that he may govern at all; and the whole of the force and vigour of his authority in his centre is derived from a prudent relaxation in all his borders. Spain, in her provinces, is, perhaps, not so well obeyed as you are in yours. She complies too, she submits, she watches time. This is the immutable condition, the eternal law, of extensive and detached empire."[11]

Burke reminds us that political structures have been called empires, and figured long in the mind as such, that do not comport with any simple portrait of sheer domination. Burke is one of a handful of great theorists of the empire of liberty, and his admonitions on how to run the British Empire, c. 1775, are not irrelevant to the administration of American Empire today.[12] Describing the relation England should bear to its American colonists, he wanted "to keep the sovereign authority of this country as the sanctuary of liberty, the sacred temple consecrated to our common faith." As long as England did this, the more friends among the colonists it would have. "The more ardently they love liberty, the more perfect will be their obedience. Slavery they can have anywhere. It is a weed that grows in every soil. They may have it from Spain; they may have it from Prussia; but, until you become lost to all feeling of your true interest and your natural dignity, freedom they can have from none but you."[13] Burke's grand solution to the colonial crisis— keeping Parliament's sovereignty but conceding the particular issues in the dispute, in the name of peace—fell on deaf ears in 1775, but something of its spirit lived on in the "union of the empire" Americans built for themselves. George Washington spoke with pride of the "stubendous *fabrick* of *Freedom* and *Empire*" created by the American Revolution, one that would be an asylum for the oppressed peoples of Europe.[14] Jefferson wrote of an "empire of liberty" and an "empire for liberty," neither of them having in their minds' eye a system of domination. These expressions evoke themes that stubbornly resonate to this day.

But empire had a more sinister meaning, even at the time, signifying an apparatus of power and arbitrary rule that had gone beyond its just limits, and this darker side has been its more usual connotation in political speech over the last two centuries. As John Adams put it on the eve of the American Revolution, in the course of arguing that the British Empire was not an empire at all, but a limited monarchy: an empire is "a despotism, and an emperor a despot, bound by no law or limitation but his own will: it is a stretch of tyranny beyond absolute monarchy."[15]

Historians have increasingly recognized that American rule, as it played out over time, meant the dispossession of and domination over disparate peoples, a key attribute of the move from continental to hemispheric to global empire. Judging the overall record, it might fairly be said that the United States was most imperial with respect to the peoples of color on its progressively expanding continental and oceanic frontiers (e.g., Indians, Africans, Mexicans, Filipinos, Vietnamese, Iraqis); it was least imperial in its approach to the European system and in its own internal organization (which accorded equality and internal autonomy to the new states of the expanding union). That there is an internal as well as external aspect of the question, however, complicates any easy summation. There might be domination within, as well as domination without, an imperial relation not only to other peoples, but also to one's own people. The federal union, as perfected in 1787 by the Constitution, was intended by its framers to operate as an antidote to the ills of the European state system, widely seen as having given an unconditional surrender to the theology of force. The new federative system created at Philadelphia, truly a new order of the ages, was anti-imperial in vital respects, and dedicated to peace. But it also as the price of union consolidated domestic slavery in the Southern states—a system of domination, wrote Frederick Douglass, "one hour of which was worse than ages of the oppression your fathers rose in rebellion to oppose."[16] The Southern states, in the years before the Civil War, were no less inveterate in describing schemes to interfere in their "domestic institutions" as an imperial project par excellence. "Call it imperialism, if you please," Northern abolitionists answered; "it is simply the imperialism of the Declaration of Independence, with all its promises fulfilled."[17]

If empire is about domination, liberalism is about resistance to domination, in the name of right. Within every liberal, resistance to unjust domination runs deep, and just about all Americans are liberals in this sense. It should come as no surprise that there is a long tradition of anti-imperialism in American political thought. Walter Lippmann could write, in 1944, that "the American antipathy to imperialism . . . is organic in the American character, and is transmitted on American soil to all whose minds are molded by the American tradition."[18] The appeal to anti-imperialism, however, does not resolve the problem, but rather restates it, as nominal opposition to imperialism has been part of the justification *for* every major American war, just as it has figured in all the dissents *against* them. Faithful to an anti-imperialist ethos, one set of Americans have wanted to stay away from war; another set of Americans, those who urged war or the threat of war, insisted they were being faithful to that same ethos. In this curious interplay of rival anti-imperialisms, the relation between empire and liberty is central—and is so for both sides of the argument. The anti-imperial thread in American political thought bespeaks enduring (though clashing) commitments that go to the core of the national purpose.[19]

In U.S. foreign policy and the theory of international relations, this argument among nominal anti-imperialists—some in favor, other opposed, to force or the threat of force—is the most important and enduring antagonism. Unfortunately, the opposition is very inadequately captured by conventional categories in international relations and indeed of political thought more generally, since the two key schools, realism and liberalism, have thinkers on either side of the question. The colloquial terminology of "hawks" and "doves," who differ mightily in their estimations of the utility and morality of force, gets to the central antagonism better than these conventional categories. Though hawks and doves differ strongly over the use of force, they are invariably, in their own rhetoric and self-imaginings, fierce anti-imperialists themselves. One side says you need empire to preserve or promote liberty; the other warns that the embrace of empire and force is in crucial respects a bargain with the devil, with liberty imperiled in the pursuit.

I am of the latter school. The argument in these pages is that America's zeal for anti-imperialist projects abroad has created a new imperialism of its own that is expansive and provocative of conflict. America's role over the last 70 years is often justified as building an "anti-imperial" world, that is, a liberal world order that is "rule-based" and in which American dominance is critical to avoid the predations of opposing despotic empires.[20] This widely accepted account ignores the degree to which the United States got in the habit of violating the rules, rather than upholding them. It fails to appreciate that the "liberal order" has itself undergone great change, significantly expanding its geographical reach and abandoning rules (like non-intervention and sovereignty) that were once central to it. The pluralist conception of the society of states, once closely identified with liberalism, became over the last generation a shadow of its former self, displaced by doctrines of indispensability and exceptionalism and revolutionary overthrow that have given the United States a wide remit to intervene in the affairs of other nations. The pattern of rule-breaking and support for revolutionary upheaval abroad, especially marked in the last fifteen years, raises a question about America's fidelity to liberal ideals. It also raises a question about its provision of "world public goods"—that is, systemic benefits to the global order from which all states profit, an advantage often touted on its behalf.

Those who emphasize the anti-imperialism of the U.S. record in foreign policy especially fail to take adequate account of the phenomenon whereby the United States not only defeated and dismantled adversary empires but also acquired, in the act of defeating them, many of the characteristics once deemed obnoxious in these enemies—powerful standing military establishments, a pervasive apparatus for spying and surveillance, a propensity to rely on force as a preferred instrument of policy, and a disdain for popular opinion or legislative control in matters of war. The institutions of the U.S. national security state are essentially problematic from the standpoint of liberal traditions. As George Washington observed in his Farewell Address, "overgrown military establishments" are "inauspicious to liberty" under any form of government and "are to be regarded as particularly hostile to republican liberty."[21] Over the past quarter century, the overgrown military establishment and national security apparatus maintained by the United States have become threatening to domestic liberty and international freedom—that is, to both the "liberties of individuals" and "the liberties of states."[22]

Among both critics and supporters, American foreign policy has been indelibly identified with the maintenance of a liberal world order. The customary practice has been to accept whatever the United States has done, or whatever rule it has promoted, as "liberal." If the American vision of world order has had flaws, it has then followed that these flaws must be ascribed to liberalism. In fact, however, liberalism's abundant resources are better deployed in a critique of the U.S. vision of world order. The most cogent critique of the U.S. role arises from within the liberal tradition, not outside of it.

What, then, is the relation between American Empire and the liberal tradition? The national security elite sees them in a tight alliance; I see them as standing increasingly in mortal contradiction. The empire, I contend, threatens liberty, despite having been built on its foundation, recalling the history and predicament of Republican Rome. "The history of Roman historiography," notes J. G. A. Pocock, is the history of "the problem of *libertas et imperium*, in which liberty is perceived as accumulating an empire by which it is itself threatened."[23] My argument, in a nutshell, is that this has become the central problem of American history, if not yet perhaps of American historiography. This was so even before the age of Trump; it is a clear and present danger now.[24]

Returning to older conceptions of liberalism—a renovation in foreign policy that looks back to first principles—is key to escaping the contradictions of America's current role. Measured by contemporary understandings, these conclusions will doubtless appear radical, but they are in their essence a conservative defense of America's first and greatest tradition, the liberal tradition consecrated by the Founders and still worthy of our esteem and affection. This grand tradition gives us the light to see a better future, if we will but follow it.

Plan of Work

On the death of Hugh Trevor-Roper, the great British historian, his ten commandments on writing were presented at his memorial service, having previously circulated "in *samizdat*." First among his commandments was the following: "Thou shalt know thine own argument and cleave fast to it, and shalt not digress nor deviate from it without the knowledge and consent of the reader, whom at all times thou shalt lead at a pace which he can follow and by a route which is made clear to him as he goeth."[25] In that spirit, I offer the following guide to the questions taken up in and conclusions reached in the following chapters. Many surprises remain in store, *Mesdames et Messieurs*, but this is the gist.

Chapter 1 ("Liberal Hegemony") analyzes America's relationships with its allies and dependents, those states within its system. Its main purpose is to understand what this "free world complex" has become, describing its justification and contours in preparation for a critique of its claims. We examine, especially, the often repeated claim of officialdom and its supporters: that the United States has been distinguished among other Great Powers in its commitment to following the rules, that it has enforced the rules to which it voluntarily adheres, making its role unique and exceptional in the history of statecraft. I subsequently show that the United States has rather consistently violated the rules. By way of example, official U.S. attitudes toward the Ukraine crisis, the right of secession, the Non-Proliferation Treaty, the surveillance state—together with its history of illegal military interventions—throw into grave question the conception of the U.S. role as that of honest broker and "umpire" of the system. Rather than operating as a rule-based system, the great alliances rest on the distinction between friends and enemies. That aspect gives to the (strong) protector and the (weak) protected a relationship that cannot be adequately understood in terms of the neutral application of principle. Who benefits most from that arrangement? Who is using whom?

Chapter 2 ("Universal Empire and Westphalian Ruins") argues that the American idea of world order now predominant, and repeatedly called liberal, has in signal respects displaced an older view, also once called liberal, that embraced a pluralist conception of the society of states. The unipolar or supremacist conception that gained paramountcy in the twenty-first century, resting on "the most powerful military in the history of the world," routed the older understandings of international law, as reflected in both the public law of the old European system and the "revised Westphalianism" of the United Nations Charter. I argue that on the issue that liberalism most cared about in the past—how to tame the war system?—the norms of the older pluralism reflect an understanding of the route to international peace superior to the global interventionism that displaced it.

To understand the stakes of this controversy, we need to go back to the Enlightenment's critique of Rome, for the modern law of nations, as it was termed in the eighteenth century, arose in conscious opposition to Roman precedents. In signal respects, American ideas for mastering the state system have strongly recalled these Roman ambitions. What Machiavelli called "the Roman method" of expansion bears a striking resemblance to what we can call "the American method" of expansion. Both are distinguished by their search for enemies to fight, peoples to liberate, and protectorates to create. The eighteenth-century publicists of the law of nature and of nations—who, as Patrick Henry said, "held up the torch of science to a benighted world"— projected a different system, undertaken in conscious opposition to Roman precedents.[26] Balance rather than dominance; independence rather than uniformity; plurality rather than the universal state—such was the normative order of the European society of states as it was described by publicists and statesmen, and as it was defended against would-be aspirants to universal dominion—themes especially pronounced in the Anglo-American tradition of foreign affairs.[27] However different the United States may be from Republican Rome in certain particulars, the Westphalian and Enlightenment critique of Roman aspirations serves nicely as a critique of contemporary American policy. The "Westphalian peace" or "Westphalian principles," so named after Europe's Peace of Westphalia in 1648 that ended the religious wars, are not defined entirely consistently by scholars, but the central conception, as Henry Kissinger has noted, relied "on a system of independent states refraining from interference in each other's domestic affairs and checking each other's ambitions through a general equilibrium of power."[28] In neither respect has the United States, in its essential strategic and foreign policy doctrines, conformed to these requirements. It has rejected the balance of power in the name of "full spectrum dominance." It has rejected the non-intervention norm in the name of democracy, human rights, and counterterrorism.

The merits of a pluralist order, embraced by the American Founders, were once understood in the United States, even among earlier liberal internationalists in the twentieth century, but such ideas were essentially abandoned in the era of American unipolarity. Westward the course of right reason once took its way, but no longer, as I would summarize the overall pitch of the chapter. Time's noblest offspring took a wrong turn. At the end of the chapter, I recommend the Golden Rule—a foundational liberal principle—as the key underpinning of a prudent and ethical foreign policy.

Chapter 3 ("Public Bads in the Illiberal World Order") queries the often pronounced view that U.S. military power provides indispensable "public goods," without which the liberal world order would collapse. Without the U.S. role, we often hear, the open world would again become closed. This often expressed characterization and justification of the U.S. world role see global commerce and the world trading and financial system as underwritten by superior U.S. military power.

U.S. actions under Bush and Obama belied these commitments. With its bevy of sanctions and its pronounced tendency to subordinate commercial interests to strategic calculation, the United States often acted to undermine the liberal order it ostensibly upheld. It produced public bads as well as public goods. Though the commitment to openness was an often touted feature of U.S. policy in the last quarter century, the national security state came increasingly to close doors that financial, energy, and manufacturing interests wanted left open. Many other domains of policy have conformed to the same pattern, including the injury the NSA did to Internet security and to the information technology companies. I advance the view that many vaunted U.S. contributions to public goods have been illusory, and that a retrenchment of U.S. military ambitions is in no wise incompatible with maintaining an open world economy. The U.S. Navy's insistence on its right to go "up the gut" in sensitive areas—the Yellow Sea, the South China Sea, the Black Sea, the Persian Gulf—is more provocative than peace-inducing; it is absurd to make these operations the litmus test for the survival of world commerce and of "all we hold dear back home." It is, on the contrary, this advanced strategic posture that most threatens ideas of openness, creating conflicts where there need be none.

U.S. foreign policy has been driven by the outlook and supposed necessities of the national security state rather than by imperatives of "openness." Policy has responded much more to the imperative of making the world dangerous for our enemies than either making it safe for American businesses or ensuring public goods. The preeminence of the security caucus in the politics of Washington has reflected the predominance of the "praetorians" over the "plutocrats"—a new configuration of oligarchical power seldom appreciated among observers. It also helps explain the overall pattern of a policy—ostensibly liberal—that so often has seemed at cross purposes with itself, more intent on illiberal means than liberal ends.

Chapter 4 ("Taps for Republican Liberty") shows how broken are the promises of early American internationalism and why the national security state holds peril to liberal and republican values. The promise of liberal internationalism, according to Woodrow Wilson and Franklin Roosevelt, was that it would ward off tendencies toward domestic militarism; instead, the consequence of America's world project was to entrench them. The cure for ridding the world of militarism, which all the early internationalists wanted to do, was to ingurgitate 50 percent of it ourselves. The doctor saved the patient, but she herself grew sick.

I trace the process by which this occurred using the thought of James Madison, John Calhoun, and Joseph Schumpeter, each of whom offered classic analyses of the way in which war and the warfare state profoundly influenced historical development and the character of political institutions. To liberal thinkers, the encounter with the war system was almost certain to deform domestic institutions. I ask readers to consider that what the Founders warned against has, in fact, taken place. The proper view of this development is obstructed by hosannas for the greatness and specialness of the members of the U.S. armed forces, a rhetoric whose evident purposes are to suppress criticism of the wars that America fights and to funnel more funds to the Pentagon.

The national security state is the core of American Empire. The share taken by the national security portfolio in federal finances leads those with an interest therein to organize in lobbies, devote keen attention to their causes, and make financial support conditional on political compliance. And so we have a situation of "domestic capture," and not of this or that economic sector, but of the government itself. Ironically, this security apparatus does poorly at precisely the thing it is supposed to do: provide security. Instead, U.S. forces have been strung out over the globe as guardians of peripheral interests or liberators in waiting, risking war for objects remote from "national security."

The most imposing alternative to the system of collective defense, pursued since the late 1940s under American leadership, is the system of the previous century that it displaced, known by its architects and advocates as a system of neutrality, non-intervention, and non-entanglement. Though this policy did seek to isolate the United States from the frequent wars that had disturbed the European system, American leaders also saw neutrality as a progressive principle. For them, it was a form of what would later be called internationalism. Neutrality, that is, was a conception of the society of states—a way of managing conflict—quite as much as later ideas of collective security or collective defense were for their successors in the twentieth century. Neutrality sought the isolation of conflict, whereas collective defense, which has prevailed since 1947, insists that aggression anywhere is a threat to the peace everywhere; it universalizes conflict.

The respective pretensions of these two schools of thought are brought into focus at the end of this chapter. My argument is that the critics of neutrality were right in the great dispute of the 1930s, when collective action against Hitler's Germany was undoubtedly required, but that this should not be considered a victory for every time and place. A system of neutrality would today better suit the objective of international peace than the U.S.-led sanctioning state relentlessly concerned with punishing transgressions, real and imagined, the world over. The debate highlighted here is almost forgotten, but it is the biggest and most important division in American theories of international order. Those looking for the *ultima ratio* of the American regime must navigate the rapids of this crucial argument.

Chapter 5 ("The Renovation of American Foreign Policy") describes a new foreign policy and grand strategy for the United States, what I call "a new internationalism." This requires above all a rethinking of the U.S. attitude toward force. Americans should question the role of their military establishment as the nation's primary interlocutor with the world. I describe an alternative that is non-interventionist in crucial respects but that falls well short of isolationism. It seeks instead to recast America's relations with its principal enemies while maintaining the friendships at the core of its alliances in Europe and East Asia.

Such a recasting requires not only a different distribution of military burdens within these alliances but also a reorientation of America's military strategy. This would move away from the forward deployments that are a key part of America's contemporary posture. It would also move away from strategies looking toward the annihilation of the enemy's armed forces, focusing instead on "attrition" and emphasizing the historic utility of a maritime strategy. It would repudiate America's plans to spend $1 trillion in modernizing its strategic nuclear forces and instead adopt a "no-first-use" policy regarding nuclear weapons. It would refocus America, Russia, and China on what remains one of their most important responsibilities: seeking to defuse the dangers posed by the massive nuclear arsenals built during the Cold War (together with the new dangers posed by their antagonism in cyberspace).

Under the imprint of a new internationalism, America would accept the primacy of domestic over foreign policy. Its normative rock, concerning the rights of war and peace, would be pluralist rather than "solidarist" or "universalistic." Seeking to reduce threats to itself, it would be far less profligate in holding out threats to others.

A new internationalism would also reconsider the "forever war," America's unending and unsuccessful "war on terrorism." More than any other factor, it is the fear of terrorism that sustains public support for a large U.S. military apparatus. Especially since the 2001 attacks on the World Trade Center and the Pentagon, public justification for the U.S. role in the world has focused on this fear. The results achieved by the use of force in pursuit of "ending terror," however, have been almost uniformly counterproductive. Considered in the gross, they have detracted from rather than enhanced the goal of diminishing the threat from terrorism (one which, in the nature of things, cannot be ended altogether). It was, in fact, the spectacular display of U.S. firepower in the 1991 Gulf War, with its enormous human cost for Iraqis, that fueled in Osama bin Laden the desire to perpetrate the attacks of 2001 (just as revenge had prompted the unsuccessful terrorist attack on the World Trade Center in 1993). From that great U.S. triumph in 1991 dates the emergence of America's terrorism problem in its modern form. Subsequently, U.S. support for the overthrow of governments in Iraq (2003), Libya (2011), and Syria (2011-?) gravely exacerbated the problem of terrorism, by creating the circumstances in which Al-Qaeda in Iraq, ISIS, and the Al-Nusra Front have thrived. After the war against ISIS in Iraq and Syria, America needs to prepare for strategic disengagement from the Greater Middle East. The United States should give up the targeted assassinations, delivered by drones, that have become a hallmark of its interventionism—so attractive because of their technological wizardry, so destructive in their political effects.

A new internationalism would especially reconsider U.S. relations with Iran, Russia, and China (worst, next worst, and worst to come, in the demonology of the national security state). It would base relations with these states on the recognition of their vital interests. It would surrender and condemn the idea that it was the U.S. intention to overthrow them. It would treat them as possessing the rights that all nations have to self-protection. It would restore an older conception of diplomacy based on the peaceful resolution of disputes for the version now so much favored (and so much influenced by ugly practices of the twentieth century) that sees communication with foreign governments as the occasion for propaganda and the issuing of threats. It would acknowledge, as sensible diplomacy has always acknowledged, the zones of vital interest possessed by other great states, but would justify this not as the concession of a sphere of influence to others, but as the acceptance of a sphere of limitation on ourselves. It would base policy on the Golden Rule, seeking to understand the national and political rights of rivals as having equal weight—in the eyes of God and of the law of nations—with our own.

A new internationalism is also required to deal with an array of global challenges that are of great moment but have been given short shrift in Washington's allocation of resources. The specter of relentlessly increasing temperatures, making for climate change and food insecurity; the danger of widespread pandemics, overleaping borders and imperiling public health and world commerce; the alarming state of the world's oceans, facing an increasingly hazardous future (for them and for us)—these challenges require national exertion and international cooperation. They raise problems in which all the world's nations are vitally interested, but which cannot be successfully addressed without widespread collaboration among "the influentials."

Economic affairs display the same embedded interdependence. The international financial system is a fragile thing; no nation can maintain its prosperity separately, and the management of the world economy requires international negotiation and treaties if it is to avoid hard times. Even if the Washington consensus of the free movement of goods and capital is modified in critical respects, as I believe it should be, the objective should simply be that the United States would address its persistent deficits in trade and would again have an industrial policy and a labor policy, as enjoyed by all its principal economic competitors. It ought not signal withdrawal from the world economy.

America's highly militarized form of internationalism is often justified as a necessary underpinning of other forms of international engagement, but in a critical respect it is deeply at odds with them. Competing for the slender share of discretionary funds within the federal budget, the security sector has feasted, while other sectors have endured famine. One sort of engagement with the world, led by the spear, has flourished; another sort of engagement, requiring patient diplomacy and the commitment of nonmilitary resources, has floundered. This disjunction needs to be overcome instead of being exacerbated, as Trump and the Republican Congress seem intent on doing.

Frustrated by America's globalist aspirations in the 1960s, George Kennan once distinguished between those who conduct foreign policy in order to live, and those who live in order to conduct foreign policy. Kennan's observation reminds us that the maladies from which American foreign policy has suffered are not unprecedented. They did not arise simply in the current

generation (though it is also true that policy over the last 20 years has exhibited these traits on a yet larger scale and theater). Kennan's remark suggests
that American statecraft needed then and needs today to return to the classic understanding whereby American statecraft was guided by the primacy of
domestic over foreign policy, recognizing that the first obligation of a nation's
rulers is to the security, prosperity, and freedom of its own citizens. It would
conduct foreign policy in order to live. But Kennan also understood that a
nation would presume too much of its own virtue if it sought to govern the
world. To restrain one's ambitions, in recognition of the rights of others, is a
contributor to international order, not an abdication from it.

The global ambitions reflected in what is styled a program for "national
security" are not, strictly speaking, unaffordable for a rich nation, but they
are very costly. In the first decade and a half of the twenty-first century, those
ambitions became most magnified just when U.S. budgetary and trade deficits
began to hemorrhage. Six years into an expansion from the troughs of 2009,
the federal budget deficit stood at over $500 billion, with annual expendi-
tures for "national defense" (if fairly counted) at over $1 trillion. Projections
over the next ten years (assuming no change in policy, no wars, and no financial crisis) show a cumulative deficit of $8.6 trillion. Trump's stated program
of massively increasing military expenditures and massively decreasing taxes
would blow that figure open. The U.S. share of world output, 22 percent in
1991, has fallen to 16 percent and is on track to be roughly 15 percent in 2021.[29]

On any realistic calculation, a retrenchment of foreign policy ambitions
is an indispensable part of addressing what Eisenhower called "the Great
Equation"—reconciling the needs of national security with the imperatives
of domestic welfare and liberty. But it is not the unaffordability of "national
security" expenditures that drives the argument of this book. Were "defense
spending" truly necessary, the case for it would be unassailable. Defense, as
Adam Smith once observed, "is of much more importance than opulence."
The much deeper problem is that U.S. ambitions have detracted from rather
than contributed to international order and the security, liberty, and prosperity of the American people. The global commitments and doctrines of the
U.S. national security state have compromised rather than bolstered these primary goals. That needs to change.

The American national security state—the most powerful of all the
power states in world history—is the nerve center of American Empire. It

has prospered under enmity with adversaries and friendship with allies, but its interests are not those of the people it ostensibly represents. It was built on "theories" of world order remote from the patriotic sentiments that sustain those who serve within the security complex. Like the British mercantile system that Adam Smith criticized at the outset of the American Revolution, the partial benefits accorded by America's world hegemony accrue to but a small portion of the nation and mask a more general burden shared by all.

I

Liberal Hegemony

Officialdom

According to what may be termed the official narrative, one broadly shared by Democratic and Republican officials over the last 25 years, the key element that has made the United States stand out as exceptional in its world role is that it is bound by rules. America has enforced the "rules of the game." Its role is necessary to uphold a liberal international order. It assumed this role because the United States has a stake in the preservation of the system and also because there is no one else. The collective action problem attending the organization of a disparate range of countries into a cohesive confederation requires a hand on the tiller. American leadership is that hand. Of course, the predominance of American power within the "liberal world order" raises a question of legitimacy, and that is where the U.S. role as rule enforcer comes in. In committing itself to liberal principles, it represents something much larger than itself. No defender of the liberal world order would say that we should do these things simply for ourselves, though they insist that our long-term interests are deeply served by actions in support of the liberal world order. Instead, American power has been seen as simply the linchpin for a broader idea of world order that, apart from a few rogues, unites the international community on behalf of widely shared norms and values.

Something like that has been the official narrative, the one propounded by Obama, Clinton, and (more or less) the two Bushes. Of course, they prevaricated a bit on the balance between universal values and national interests, always making sure when speaking to a domestic audience that direct American national interests—always invoked, never defined—were not forgotten but were ever present in their calculations. The American people, it might be said, have been offered the ends of Wilsonian internationalism through powerful appeals to Jacksonian nationalism. To this double-barreled appeal, they have a known inclination to submit. The term "Jacksonian," coined by Walter Russell Mead, refers to the bellicose nationalism, highly conscious of honor and fair play, but tough as nails, that the Scotch-Irish especially brought to the land of the free. World order doesn't concern them. But they have often been willing to fight for some idea of it.[1]

American leaders have gotten round the sometime conflict between interests and values by insisting that they are essentially the same thing. This view has taken many different forms; probably the most discussed recent example—articulated by Clinton, Bush, and Obama—is the proposition that America has an interest in promoting democracy because democracies don't fight one another. Another example is the importance of the norm forbidding aggression; it is important to nip that in the bud, the conventional thinking says, because if you wait, it will be too late: from the wound not cauterized will emerge a direct threat to American national security. Our attachment to the norm goes beyond our national interest, but is ultimately identified with it. Within this golden circle, which reconciles the narrowest interest with the grandest ideals, it is believed that America needs to be "active and engaged throughout the world" because the country has "been a positive force for stability and order, which as a continental nation with global interests is in our national-security interest." In light of America's record in defeat of fascism and communism, "we are the indispensable, exceptional nation, and we have burdens that come from indispensability and exceptionalism." Those are the words of Tom Cotton, Republican senator from Arkansas, but Hillary Clinton has said the same. That puts them squarely within the "post-World War II bipartisan consensus" on American foreign policy.[2] Though there are differences in the approach to foreign policy of the two main parties, they also share a great deal in common. Over the past two generations, to be sure, Democrats running from association with McGovernism or "Carterism" could not entirely escape the suspicion of play-acting in their imitations of Republican hawkishness, but this interpretation of late seems too cynical by half. Hillary Clinton did not repudiate McGovernism for electoral convenience. She repudiated it out of conviction.[3]

In the rhetoric of American presidents and the admiring portraits of many academics, American purposes in the world have had a very attractive aspect about them. If we did not like to hear this story—the one in which our leadership and commitment to various great ideals and principles invariably make the world a better place—we would not have repeated it over and over again. In his recounting of American leadership, President Obama followed in his predecessors' footsteps. His true bottom line, he said at West Point in May 2014, was that "America must always lead on the world stage. If we don't, no one else will. The military that you have joined," he told the cadets, "is and always will be the backbone of that leadership." Declaring that he believed in American exceptionalism devoutly, he insisted that "what makes us exceptional is not our ability to flout international norms and the rule of law; it is our willingness to affirm them through our actions." His national security strategy in 2010, by the same token, held that the United States "must pursue a rules-based international system that can advance our own interests by serving mutual interests."

In this liberal world order, the United States has encouraged the peaceful settlement of disputes; has upheld fundamental principles like the defense of territorial integrity and the freedom of navigation; and has built a cooperative international system. Having tasted the evil fruit of isolationism, the world bore witness in the 1930s to the havoc that American abstention could cause. That havoc reached America's shores, giving the United States a vital stake in the evolution of a peaceful international system. "America will always be a world leader," affirmed Hillary Clinton in 2009, "as long as we remain true to our ideals and embrace strategies that match the times. So we will exercise American leadership to build partnerships and solve problems that no nation can solve on its own, and we will pursue policies to mobilize more partners and deliver results." The purpose of American leadership was to "overcome" what the experts called "collective action problems," but that she called "obstacles to cooperation." Rejecting past approaches, Clinton held, "It does not make sense to adopt a 19th century concert of powers, or a 20th century balance of power strategy." The rejection of concert and balance sits closely alongside the claimed indispensability of U.S. leadership. As Clinton observed, "Just as no nation can meet these challenges alone, no challenge can be met without America."[4]

Among political scientists, John Ikenberry has provided, in his *Liberal Leviathan* (2011), the most theoretically sophisticated defense of the American system. The Western-oriented system created by the United States is "open, integrated, and rule based." A product of "farsighted U.S. leadership," the postwar American system meant "the creation of universal institutions that not only invited global membership but also brought democracies and market societies closer together." The U.S. "built an order that facilitated the participation and integration of both established great powers and newly independent states." Ikenberry emphasized that American power was indispensable to the formation of this system, originally centered on the West, and argued that the system continues to need a "Leviathan" in the business of enforcing rules (while holding out the probability that this will become a more collective Leviathan over time). "The United States," he wrote, "has been one of the most successful order-building states in world history because it has combined the exercise of its power with the championing of rule-based order."[5] Ikenberry's account closely follows (and in some measure perhaps inspired) the understanding of American political elites.[6] Many other articulations of this view exist. It has been the consensus view of American officialdom.[7]

Trump has risen by defying rules rather than respecting them; he seems the least convincing spokesman imaginable for a rule-based order. Among the celebrants of the liberal world order criticized herein, Trump's victory was uniformly received as a body blow to their worldview. How can there be a liberal world order without a liberal at the head of it? After his electoral victory, each side in the great foreign policy battle dimly entertained the possibility that Trump would incline in their direction, though it was also obvious that he would do whatever he did in his own inimitable way, often in defiance of the rules. It is grim indeed that his history is above all marked by that trait. For it is one thing to object to the content of a rule-based order, querying the reasonableness of the rules to be enforced; quite another to dispense with the idea of a rule-based order at all. That way lies madness.

Rule Maker, Rule Breaker

A power that conducts itself according to widely accepted rules is a responsible international citizen. Following rules may be theorized as a rational choice for maximizing interest, but it also betokens respect for justice. Typically, though not always explicitly, the claim has been advanced to establish the legitimacy of the American role. But though rule-following may indeed be the only route to the satisfaction of interest and the provision of justice, saying is not the same as doing. Unfortunately, the American record regarding rule-following is in recent memory not a happy one. In the era of unipolarity beginning in 1990, it may be ventured, the United States made new rules for the international system, but in the course of doing so broke many old ones. Its attitude toward rule-following became a caricature of a once-proud tradition. Even in the economic arena where the IMF, World Bank, and WTO come into play, "rule-following" does not tell the whole picture, but in the security arena, especially, it became widely at variance with the reality. Let us consider a few examples from recent crises.

One such example is the role played by the United States and its European allies in the 2014 Ukraine crisis, the result of which was an abrupt worsening of relations between Russia and the West. U.S. support for the Maidan demonstrations against the elected president Victor Yanukovich showed a cavalier disregard of elementary democratic rules. Ukraine had a constitution; a vote for the presidency was scheduled for February 2015, only a year away. However corrupt Yanukovich's administration may have become, the command of democratic constitutionalism was to wait for the regularly scheduled elections to seek his ouster. To do so through street demonstrations that turned to violence entailed a radical change in Ukraine's government and the bringing to power of nationalistic forces that were anathema to the Russophones in Ukraine's East. This—together with the serial violations of the constitutional provisions regarding impeachment—was a clear violation of basic democratic principles, about which the partisans of "democracy promotion" were uniformly silent. By virtue of the support that outside Western powers gave to Maidan before, during, and after the February 22 revolution (with U.S. officials caught plotting the composition of the new government two weeks before the old government fell), it was also a violation of the norm forbidding external intervention in the internal affairs of other states. This cavalier and aggressive stance, conspiring in the overthrow of a government outside electoral means, bears direct responsibility for the evil consequences that followed. In the Ukraine crisis, the United States did not follow the rules. Its actions were an aggressive push into an area of vital Russian interest, abetted by means that violated both Ukraine's constitution and international law. When Russia annexed Crimea in response and gave unacknowledged support to the rebellion in Ukraine's southeast, the West charged Russia with a massive violation of the most elementary rule of a rule-based order. But it ignored its own previous violation of such rules.[8]

The West's policy in the Ukraine crisis must also be considered against the double standards employed with regard to the right of secession. Since Woodrow Wilson's day (indeed, since the American Civil War), there has existed in international society a profound tension between the general norms of sovereignty and territorial integrity, investing in states the right to suppress separatist movements within their own territory, and the right of national self-determination, the latter based on the idea that every nation should have its own state. Somehow, as Wilson said, the interests of the population concerned had to be balanced with "the equitable claims of the government whose title is to be determined."[9] But it is difficult to see a balancing of equities in the rules elaborated by the West over the last 25 years. We learned, successively, that it was legitimate for the Slovenians, Croatians, and Bosnians to secede from Yugoslavia, but not legitimate for the Bosnian Serbs to secede from Bosnia nor for Serbia to repress Kosovo's struggle for independence. It was legitimate for Eritrea to secede from Ethiopia and for South Sudan to secede from Sudan, but not legitimate for South Ossetia to secede from Georgia or for Crimea to secede from Ukraine. Taking an impartial view of the right of self-determination, it would be difficult to arrive at these serial conclusions.

Or take American policy toward non-proliferation. Iran has had a set of rules imposed on it that are far different from those applied to Israel and India, both non-signatories of the Non-Proliferation Treaty (NPT). One might justify this posture in relation to exigent security requirements, but it is very difficult to see it as an application of neutral principles. The signatories of the NPT are forbidden from cooperation with non-signators, a stipulation clearly violated by the U.S.-India nuclear agreement. The United States has never punished Israel's transgression against it in developing nuclear weapons—Israel swore it wasn't doing so, even while it did—or officially acknowledged Israel's surreptitious theft of enriched uranium from a U.S. facility, or even conceded that non-proliferation negotiations in the Middle East might rightly take note of the Israeli capability. These double standards find a complement in the threat to bomb Iran's nuclear facilities in the absence of a satisfactory agreement and in the use of the Stuxnet virus to sabotage Iranian nuclear facilities, both of which plainly violated international law.[10] The nuclear agreement with Iran in 2015 makes these double standards less blatant than they once were, a credit to the Obama administration's diplomacy, but the harsh domestic reaction in the United States to the agreement also shows the continuing U.S. antagonism toward a "rule-based" approach to non-proliferation. The basic principle, instead, appears to be that Israel should retain its nuclear monopoly in the region.[11]

Perhaps the most egregious case of American rule-breaking lies in its espionage activities. When Edward Snowden publicly revealed the secrets of the National Security Agency (NSA), the United States was reminded of central principles of international law by two stateswomen, Angela Merkel of Germany and Dilma Rousseff of Brazil. The Snowden revelations of a "global network of electronic espionage," noted Rousseff, "have caused indignation and repudiation in public opinion around the world." The indiscriminate interception of the personal data of citizens, the penetration of Brazil's diplomatic missions and its corporate enterprises, constituted "a breach of International Law" and "an affront to the principles that must guide relations among [states]. . ... The right to safety of citizens of one country," Rousseff said, "can never be guaranteed by violating fundamental human rights of citizens of another country." "This is like the Stasi," Merkel exclaimed. That the United States should treat its faithful allies in this fashion was really incomprehensible to the Germans, and they struggled to decide whether it was the stupidity and arrogance of the surveillance, or the betrayal and ingratitude that it manifested, that most disturbed them. But they widely considered it a deep corruption of the faith that America once taught them.[12]

That the U.S. espionage program violated fundamental human rights is hardly ever registered in the domestic debate in the United States, despite America's vaunted support of a universal standard in that regard. Even stalwart defenders of American personal liberties often profess indifference with regard to the rights of foreigners. The American people could care less. In fact, however, these programs have violated universal human rights and crossed far beyond justifiable measures for targeted surveillance. The power to drill down into all the personal communications of just about everybody on the planet—such is the astonishing aspiration of the NSA—is an immense power.[13] To belittle the rights violated—or to ignore the obvious potentialities for blackmail resulting from such practices—is offensive to centuries of Anglo-American jurisprudence identifying the protection of an individual's personal papers and effects as immune from indiscriminate search, understandings adopted by much of the world in the Universal Declaration of Human Rights (Article 12) and the International Covenant on Civil and Political Rights (Article 17). Even were this power exercised with respect to principles of justice, every other state and people would have a right to presume otherwise. The official U.S. defense that "everybody else does it" and you would be naïve to think otherwise is palpably absurd. What other states have access to the entirety of the world's information flows? That this universal panopticon was constructed in secret is a pertinent commentary on the importance the security elite has placed on transparency, just as it also discloses the real value placed on partnership with allies.

These examples, unfortunately, do not cover the entire ground. The United States has conducted a wide variety of military interventions that on their face have been violations of international law. Over the last 30 years, the clearest cases were Grenada (1983), Nicaragua (1984), Panama (1989), Kosovo (1999), Iraq (2003), and Libya (2011). As we will see in Chapter 2, its policy stands in contradiction with "Westphalian norms," not in support of them. It has given strong support for, or otherwise ignored, violations of basic rules by its allies, especially in the Middle East. Israel has plainly violated the international law of occupation in building permanent settlements in the West Bank; its punishment was an aid package worth $38 billion over ten years.[14] Saudi Arabia intervened illegally in Syria and Yemen; its punishment consisted in U.S. servicing of the $115 billion in arms authorized to be sold to the Saudis during Obama's presidency, a figure likely to be increased by Trump. I forbear to detail further evidence of U.S. torture, drone attacks, kidnappings, and official lying as unnecessary to establish the point. Unless we are to understand the basic rule of this "ruled-based" system to be that the United States is free to dispense with the rules when it wants to, or can just make them up as it goes along, one cannot say that America has acted in accordance with the rules. Across wide domains of action, the only rule plainly visible is

> . . . the good old rule
> . . . the simple plan,
> That they should take, who have the power
> And they should keep who can.[15]

Friends and Enemies, Protector and Protected

The propensity to seek a separate set of rules for me and thee stems in large part from human nature. Certainly, the United States is not alone in this proclivity. "No man is allowed to be a judge in his own cause," wrote James Madison, "because his interest would certainly bias his judgment, and, not improbably, corrupt his integrity. With equal, nay with greater reason," Madison held, "a body of men are unfit to be both judges and parties at the same time."[16] If we add the novel condition of unipolarity that arose after 1990 to the inveterate tendency for national egotism to induce narcissism and hypocrisy,[17] we have perhaps a sufficient explanation for U.S. rule-breaking. Perceived self-interest and cultural filters prompted a biased judgment; unipolarity prevented others from effectively sanctioning the behavior of a superior power.

But there is a further reason for the tendency arising from the nature of the American alliance system. In theory it is a "rules-based" set of relationships, but in practice it has been based on the distinction between friends and enemies. In such a system, you are supposed to be good to your friends and tough with your enemies. Indeed, being tough with your enemies is often the litmus test of whether you are good to your friends. That distinction is an old one in political thought. It suggests that the American alliance system has been a form of "negative association," whose central feature is cooperation against a common enemy.[18] The Romans brought its ethos to a sort of perfection within the regnant code of the day. Throughout "the whole Roman History," wrote John Adams in 1777, "Nothing was too good for a Friend or too bad for an Enemy."[19] While American elites would not be so bold as to declare the latter, they have adhered to something like it in practice; and while the American people would not be too keen on the former notion, they have acquiesced in the declarations of American leaders that the security of the United States and that of its allies is "indissoluble" and "unbreakable." As a practical matter, the principle of thwarting enemies and supporting friends has been fundamental to the alliance system and far more important than the application of impartial rules.

Ikenberry emphasizes that this liberal order has hierarchical characteristics, and his explication of this point deserves scrutiny:

> In critical respects, the order is organized around superordinate and subordinate relationships. States have differentiated roles and capacities. Several leading states—Japan and Germany—do not possess the full military capacities of traditional great powers. Rules and institutions in the global system provide special roles and responsibilities for a leading state. Although a formal governance structure does not exist, power and authority is informally manifest in hierarchical ways. The United States is situated at the top of the order and other states are organized below it in various ways as allies, partners, and clients. Second, the order is marked by the pervasiveness of liberal relationships. At least in the Western core of this order, other liberal democratic states engage in reciprocal and bargained relations with the United States. The order is organized around an expanding array of rules and institutions that reduce and constrain the prevalence of power politics. The United States shares governance responsibilities with other states. In these various ways, the American-led order has characteristics of a hierarchy with liberal features.[20]

While it is certainly true that the free world complex has had both hierarchical and liberal characteristics, there remain several problems with Ikenberry's overall characterization. First, it conflates the Western alliance system with the "global system," though states outside the Western alliance comprise about three-quarters of humanity and are far larger in number than the 50-odd states within the U.S.-led free world complex. In his *Clash of Civilizations*, Samuel P. Huntington, like Ikenberry, insisted that the Western

alliance was not an empire "but rather a compound of federations, confederations, and international regimes and organizations"; unlike Ikenberry and
other liberal internationalists, he did not presume that this represents "the
international community" or "the global system."[21]

A second problem is that, within the alliance, the key exchange has not
been the commitment to impartial rules but, as we have emphasized, allegiance in exchange for protection. The United States has in the past granted
this protection freely, and it has seen its job as organizing its allies to better
confront such enemies. If the workings of this exchange have often appeared as
a form of power politics within the alliance, they have done so yet more often
from the vantage point of those outside its institutions. In security affairs, it
has been for the better prosecution of adversarial relations with enemies that
American leaders have usually appealed for "international cooperation."

In most cases, America has been front and center in the confrontation. Its
doctrine of leadership has rested on the vital importance of U.S. credibility,
understood to mean that it cannot lose in a trial of wills without putting the
whole edifice at risk. Allied interests became U.S. interests, over which the
United States extended the mantle of its protection. Since it did not see itself
as being able to threaten abandonment without grossly sacrificing its credibility, the United States forfeited considerable influence over its dependents
(with the compensating advantage to the security establishment that it would
remain indispensable). These protectorates have not necessarily obeyed, and
their consent has sometimes been passive, but they have been simultaneously
dependent on and emboldened by the American guarantee. This condition,
as Barry Posen has noted, may give rise to "reckless driving" on their part,
assured that the insurance is paid up. Because of the dogma of American
leadership, their vital and no-so-vital interests have been annexed to those
of the United States; those interests, in the most important but neglected
aspect of this "transmission belt," then become closely identified with the
nation's honor. Once engaged, America must stand firm as if the interest were
its own.[22]

These considerations are crucial in understanding the potential expansi-
bility of the Western order, a question to which Ikenberry has devoted close
attention. Though he sometimes has written as if this Western-led order had
become already "the international order," he also projected its further expansion, in which it embraces rather than repels other rising powers. "The more
this order binds together capitalist democratic states in deeply rooted institutions; the more open, consensual, and rule-based it is; and the more widely
spread its benefits, the more likely it will be that rising powers can and will

secure their interests through integration and accommodation rather than through war. And if the Western system offers rules and institutions that benefit the full range of states—rising and falling, weak and strong, emerging and mature—its dominance as an international order is all but certain."[23] This is indeed an attractive vision, but problematic if considered in relation to America's actually existing alliances, based more on the distinction between friends and enemies than such neutral principles as "defense against aggression" or "territorial integrity." The effective decision rule is to thwart Russia on behalf of European allies, to thwart China on behalf of Asian allies, to thwart Iran on behalf of Israel and Saudi Arabia. Understanding it thusly, it is evident why the West has not invited adversarial states to join its security groupings. The very purpose of the club is to exclude them. It is also evident that, if expansion does occur, it would almost certainly take the form in each theater of enlistment in a coalition against America's putative adversaries—for example, Ukraine and Georgia against Russia; Vietnam or other Southeast Asian states against China; whoever can be signed up to fight the complex of enemies in the Middle East (e.g., ISIS, Al-Qaeda, Hezbollah, Bashar al-Assad, Iran). Ikenberry writes of cooperation as a sort of free-floating good in which everybody can share, and would that it were so, but, in the alliance system built by the United States, security cooperation with allies has had as its purpose the thwarting and obstruction of enemies. Punctuated by various periods of détente (that of the 1990s outdoing the first iteration in the 1970s), such has been the enduring reality since the late 1940s.

The American alliance system has been multifarious, with special relationships and institutional configurations in each region that make generalizations hazardous. The multilateral structure of the North Atlantic Treaty Organization (NATO) was never the same as America's legacy hub-and-spoke system in East Asia. The ferocity of its enmities has also differed according to region: the relationship with China, though deeply troubled, also has had compensating elements of inextricable economic interdependence that make for co-existence. Somewhat ironically, the free world complex is most "liberal" because of what its components are, not what they do in foreign policy. As free states respecting the panoply of liberal democratic values in their domestic competences, the nations of Europe and East Asia have been natural allies of a state that (mostly) respects the same. So, too, it has been true, as Ikenberry notes, that "at least in the Western core of this order, other liberal democratic states engage in reciprocal and bargained relations with the United States." That has especially been the case when the relationship has approximated equality, as in the economic diplomacy between the U.S. and the European Union (EU). But concerning the issues that security policy must adjudge, the idea of liberal partnership has often been more false veneer than true fact. To understand the exchange in terms of a relationship between (strong) protector and (weak) protected helps illuminate the dynamics at play much better than understanding these relationships as a manifestation of open, consensual, and rule-based decision-making. Despite the inequality of power between the consumers and providers of this collective good (security), Ikenberry's conceit, as of officialdom generally, has been that the relationship has been conducted as if it were between equals. That, presumably, is what is meant by saying that "the order is marked by the pervasiveness of liberal relationships." But the actual structure of power and influence within these alliances has not often corresponded with the portrait of partners and allies reaching consensus round a round table.

Consider, for example, Poland's motives in sending forces to Iraq and Afghanistan. The official view would see it as a manifestation of a solidarity of aims, but in reality, it was Poland doing something it did not wish to do in exchange for the promise of American protection against Russia. The bitter (and secretly recorded) comments of then Polish Foreign Minister Radoslaw Sikorski in early 2014, complaining that Poland had sucked up to the United States and had done so to assuage its fear of abandonment, but without any confidence in the success of the maneuver, attest to such a tendency.[24] This is not to deny that allied pressure for American intervention and "maximalism" has sometimes exercised real influence. Britain and France did so in importuning for intervention against Muammar el-Qaddafi in Libya in 2011, a step opposed by the Pentagon. America's oldest allies put themselves—and the United States—in a situation where they would have been left high and dry without U.S. munitions and logistical support. France went to war before the United States did, offering to withdraw its planes while in the air but apparently not having previously consulted the United States before launching them in the first place.[25] On balance, however, it has seldom happened (though it happened here) that the U.S. national security establishment has been brought into war against its inclinations. In the Ukraine crisis, then Assistant Secretary of State Victoria Nuland's dismissive taunt—"Fuck the EU"—reflected the old neoconservative instinct that the United States was to tell the Europeans what to do, not listen to them.[26] Here, we find another example, and this in its most hallowed multilateral venue, where there seems considerably more hegemony than liberalism, more dominance than equality, in the system of liberal hegemony.

Probably the most dramatic illustration of an attitude among U.S. officialdom worlds apart from the language of "partnership" and "friendship" with allies is the widespread NSA surveillance of allied leaders. The scale of U.S. surveillance on allied governments, especially toward Germany, France, and Japan, has been simply astonishing. The documents released by WikiLeaks on the U.S. surveillance of Japan (of a piece with that toward other governments) "demonstrate intimate knowledge of internal Japanese deliberations on such issues as: agricultural imports and trade disputes; negotiating positions in the Doha Round of the World Trade Organization; Japanese technical development plans, climate change policy, nuclear and energy policy and carbon emissions schemes; correspondence with international bodies such as the International Energy Agency (IEA); strategy planning and draft talking points memoranda concerning the management of diplomatic relations with the United States and the European Union; and the content of a confidential Prime Ministerial briefing that took place at Shinzo Abe's official residence."[27] Such intimate surveillance of all and sundry reveals a decidedly unfriendly and even sinister posture. By casting a deeply cynical eye on trust, by in effect insisting on unbounded loyalty, the spying apparatus introduces a source of deep corrosion to the friendship that once existed.[28]

It would be a mistake to regard this as simply an intelligence agency run amok, because the scope of the targets selected means that a great many departments and agencies of the U.S. government have made use of this intelligence and have been deeply complicit in the corruption of diplomatic principles that it represents. The principle of such surveillance is not new—the U.S. government spied on partner states in San Francisco when negotiating the UN Charter in 1945—but the *scale* of it is fundamentally different.[29] While these new totalizing modes of surveillance seem to have gotten underway in the late 1990s, they were greatly expanded in 2001 by the Bush administration, under cover of the war on terror and the Patriot Act.

Other states, it is true, spy on their friends, but the U.S. has invested by far the most resources in building the worldwide infrastructure for the surveillance state. So far as spying on allies is concerned, it seems the most illiberal of the free world's Leviathans. Responding to the uproar caused by the Snowden revelations, President Obama agreed not to tap the cellphones of allied leaders, but he refused to offer that pledge to their staffs. National Security Advisor Susan Rice, in a stormy meeting with German officials, told them that the United States was unwilling to carve out an exception for Germany because all other allies would demand the same.[30] This response made clear that such surveillance was to be a permanent feature of the U.S. government's

posture to its "friends," ratified by both Republican and Democratic administrations. It is difficult to imagine anything that would be more inconsistent
with the public commitment to open, consensual, and rule-based decision-
making. But as the old saying goes, you value what you save in a crisis.

One decisive new development in the U.S. alliance system has been the
integration of arms acquisition under the auspices of the United States, creating a powerful network of interdependencies. This interlocking structure has
been built up over the last generation, and did not characterize procurement
practices for most of the Cold War. Arms exports have emerged as of vital
importance to the Pentagon. It is the network of U.S. alliances that enables
America to dominate the market in arms exports, at more than 50 percent
of the world total, a significant change from the Cold War period, when
the Soviets contended for leadership in this dubious category.[31] WikiLeaks'
release of State Department cables showed much agitation from U.S. embassies to purchase American arms. Foreign governments were informed just how
important this was as a demonstration of the friendship between them and
the United States. That U.S. embassies have become promotional outlets for
U.S. arms sales reflects the critical significance of such sales for the Pentagon.
The modernization programs of the U.S. armed forces are economically unvi-
able without large-scale foreign purchases. Military officers and civilian contractors have reasoned about this in the same way as Hollywood moguls—it
is the foreign market that makes or break the economics of film-making, just
as it is the foreign market that makes or breaks a new weapons system. The
ability to add foreign markets to Pentagon acquisitions has provided leverage for arms merchants to convince legislators that these arms programs are
affordable and will create jobs in their states and districts. This pattern of
advantage and influence has constituted a powerful structural support, gener-
ated by internal incentives, for the maintenance of a wide network of foreign
allies and arms sales.

While many observers have seen the American-led order as being essentially continuous as between the Cold War and post-Cold War epochs, a
fundamental change occurred in the structure of U.S. alliances after the collapse of the Soviet Union, especially in Europe. It is not merely that NATO
expanded—a gross violation of the pledges made to Mikhail Gorbachev when
he accepted the unification of Germany—but that its expansion changed
the structure of power and influence within the alliance, diminishing "old
Europe" and heightening the influence of the new entrants from Eastern
Europe. Those collateral effects of expansion also increased U.S. influence
by virtue of the greater dependence of the new states on America, a classic

example of the "scale effect."[32] Despite this enlargement of strength from twelve new members, which on the theory of states in union ought to have increased Europe's contribution, there emerged in the last decade a big change in relative expenditures as between the United States and its allies, with the United States supplying recently some 72 percent of total NATO expenditures, as compared with the 60 percent average during the Cold War. Though U.S. military expenditures had fallen 35 percent from Cold War levels by 1997, a decline that almost kept pace with Europe's demobilization, the disparity grew sharply in the next decade when U.S. spending surged and Europe's stayed flat or declined. Though this growing disparity was largely attributable to America's newfound ambitions in the Greater Middle East, it could not fail to affect the locale of effectual decision-making within the alliance.

In its chief characteristics, then, the Western security order has not been one in which the United States blindly followed the rules, but one in which it has proven quite flexible and versatile in its application of the rules. The rules have been applied quite sternly to adversaries, but flaccidly or not at all to allies and its own conduct. Whereas in the immediate post-Cold War, the United States seemed genuinely interested in integrating its great power adversaries, Russia and China, into the Western-led order, it became crystal clear in the last decade that they were outside it. The pattern of influence within the alliance has hardly corresponded with the idealized portraits; this is so even with respect to economic arrangements, which also became more exclusivist in the early 2000s and were increasingly used by the United States to enforce sanctions against adversaries and allies alike.

The Neoliberal Economic Order on the Ropes

Though "liberalism" has long been seen as informing the American-led economic order, the content of that doctrine has undergone significant change over the past six decades. The General Agreement on Tariffs and Trade (GATT) was established after World War II and reduced tariffs through successive "rounds" of negotiation in subsequent decades. The World Trade Organization, GATT's successor, was established in the 1990s. Both the GATT and WTO were and are deemed exercises in liberalism, but the labeling obscures the degree to which their underlying purposes have shifted. The post-World War II Bretton Woods order embedded protections for labor that were abandoned in the post-1990 dispensation, which greatly favored capital.[33] In either guise, the rules of the liberal economic order were basically made by the Western powers; for most of the rest, admission to the club has meant submission to the rules. A symbol of this is the some 80,000 pages of the *acquis communitaire* that new members of the EU have had to sign as a condition of entry. A similar bargain was offered to the weaker states in joining the WTO.

Though rule-based in some respects, the international financial institutions have also represented Western interests. It has often been difficult to perceive the uniform rule the International Monetary Fund (IMF) follows in its bailouts and bail-ins, save that it has been an instrument of the West's foreign policy. The IMF has been clearly swayed by geopolitical criteria in its handling of the Ukraine crisis; its actions in many locales have broken rules it set for itself.[34] Despite diminished U.S. contributions, the IMF remains effectively dominated by the U.S. Treasury Department and the U.S. Federal Reserve Bank. Save your friends (especially their creditors), and let your non-friends freeze, is a better summation of IMF-Fed-Treasury actions than an account based on rule-following.

One set of rules appears ironclad; that is the principle that debtor countries, like Greece, must pay their debts and must submit to external control of their domestic legislation to secure outside relief. The approach by the troika (EU Commission, European Central Bank, IMF) in Greece was nothing new; it was another among a host of structural adjustments imposed on other countries as a condition of aid from the IMF or World Bank. In the Grecian case, that solution looked irrational because it promised to increase Greece's debt-to-GDP ratio, when policy had to be directed toward reducing it. But even if we stipulate the unlikely hypothesis that such rule-based policies were suitable as a remedy, promising long-term benefits,[35] structural adjustment programs have inevitably entailed a concomitant loss of self-governance by the weak. The surrender, under the imprint of necessity, of the right of autonomous decision-making is a key loss from a liberal republican perspective. If the rules were uniformly applied—a big if—one might say that these programs are illustrative of a rule-based order, but an impartial view must note that many weaker states and peoples see this as an onerous order bearing hard upon them and operating only with their forced consent.

Despite these objections, it has been in international economic institutions and policies that we are most likely to find the traits that liberal internationalists identify with following the rules. After 1990, the prospect for the universalization of the Western-led order seemed bright, as reflected in the growth of trade with the former Communist bloc, the abandonment of protectionism in the Global South, and the creation of the WTO (along with the admission into it of China in 2001 and Russia in 2012), all pointing to a larger integration of the global economy. But the renewal of hostile relations between Russia and the West in 2014, when added to already frigid relations with China and Iran, has shown how distant that prospect of universality really is.

Even before Trump, the 1990s aspiration had unraveled. Efforts to reform the WTO (the Doha Round, begun in November 2001) dissolved into side agreements. Obama looked toward the intensification of trade cooperation and regulatory harmonization across the Atlantic and the Pacific, leaving the Russians and the Chinese out. China, leading the BRICS nations, proposed a set of financial institutions to run parallel with the West's, including the Asian Infrastructure Investment Bank, the Asian Bond Fund Initiative, the New Development Bank, and the Chiang Mai Initiative (entailing currency swaps). Much of the momentum behind these initiatives derived from the unwillingness of the U.S. Congress to approve the 2010 IMF reform plan. This would have given China and other developing powers a greater say in the running of the IMF, a reasonable step to reforming the institution but where the American leadership role, not for the first time, fell apart in Congress.

Heightening these tendencies against the universality of the liberal capitalist order have been recent innovations in the use of economic sanctions. The United States has been much more aggressive recently in employing the dollar-based financial system as an instrument to achieve political/strategic aims.[36] The economic embargo against Iran, enforced by U.S. threats against noncompliant allies, has been the most dramatic instance of this; another is the $9 billion judgment in 2014 against the French bank BNP Paribas for handling accounts for Cuba, Sudan, and Iran, followed by lesser settlements with other European banks. The growing exploitation of dollar hegemony against allies is a general departure from norms widely prevalent previously; it has made a hash of previous notions of sovereign immunity. It is also deeply inconsistent with the interests of American financial centers. Nevertheless, the extraction of rents from allies has become since the early 2000s a growing propensity of the American state. Trump seemingly wants to make that exchange more blatant than it has ever been, but the tendency is not so unusual. Secretary of State Clinton, in her first major statement on foreign policy in 2009, offered the same idea in her injunction to "pursue policies to mobilize more partners and deliver results."[37]

The desire to mobilize more partners and get results was also on display in Obama's push for the trans-Atlantic and trans-Pacific trade agreements— known as the Transatlantic Trade and Investment Partnership (TTIP) and the Trans-Pacific Partnership (TPP), the latter signed by twelve nations on

October 5, 2015. These have been invariably styled as "free trade" agreements, but in fact their dominant feature was the extension into allied states of U.S.-style regulatory practices. Touted by the Obama administration as offering strong protections for labor and environment, skepticism was warranted on the point, as the dominant thrust of past agreements has favored capital over labor. The TPP's provisions regarding arbitration were intended to take a whole slew of corporate practices off the legislative agenda and into arbitral boards tightly constrained by corporate rights. The extension of copyright and patent protection made the benefits impressive to Hollywood and Silicon Valley—to the entertainment-industrial complex and the biotech- and info-tech-industrial complex; it would also have been beneficial to U.S. corporate agriculture, intent as ever on breaking down barriers to exports. However these advantages are weighed, it is striking that allied states were attracted to the bargain; for some, at least, this can only be explained as an outcome of their security dependence on the United States. The TPP and TTIP, now cashiered by Brexit and Trump's victory, were intended as payoffs to corporate interests at home, a way of leveraging security dependence in order to distribute benefits to domestic supporters and giving those domestic supporters an incentive to support the security state.

The renewal of cold war with Russia since 2014 has further confirmed the diminishment of the global trading regime. Sanctions remain in the saddle and ride diplomacy, having emerged as all-purpose punitive measures short of war, the thrust of which is deeply antithetical to the provisions of the WTO. In the years before the Ukraine crisis, with the EU in the throes of economic stagnation, it was widely feared that the euro would break down. The U.S.-led economic sanctions on Russia, of much greater consequence to the European than the American economy, battened European economic prospects even further; about half of European opinion has considered these sanctions a public bad rather than a public good, an imposition of U.S. hegemony.

Instead of a deepening of "globalization," bringing nearly all the world's economies into a single integrated trading and financial system, the Obama years saw the outlines of a bifurcated or bipolar economic realm, pitting the West or the "trilateral world" against the BRICS, each of them competing for the new "third world." (Whether India is of the chasers or the chased is a pivotal question. Whether the West survives as a coherent entity is another.)[38] It is highly likely that those fearful of Western sanctions and intervention will be drawn into this alternative order, and they will be larger in number the more that the financial system is used to pursue U.S. strategic ambitions. The emergence of a nascent bipolarity in international financial institutions represents a distinct upending of the globalist aspirations that developed in the 1990s. Domestically, the readiness to exploit dollar hegemony for strategic aims has also shown the superior power of the national security establishment over financial and energy oligarchs. The latter's interests were seriously wounded by the sanctions against Russia; it did not matter.[39]

U.S. depictions of the "liberal world order," fashioned after the Washington consensus of low barriers to trade and the movement of capital, invariably assume that it is intrinsically the best, a judgment that won widespread acceptance in America after the communist model collapsed. But many of the features of that neoliberal world have seemed both inequitable and precarious. Its emergence was closely associated with widening inequalities of income and wealth in the United States and played a key role in generating downward pressures on America's middle class. It also made for huge trade deficits, neglecting the long-term importance of maintaining America's productive capacity in balance with its consumption. Oil apart, the trade gap in goods and services was in recent years the highest on record.[40] By the end of 2016, the U.S. net international investment position—measuring a country's external financial assets and liabilities, "what it owns" in relation to "what it owes"—had fallen to minus $8.1 trillion, from minus $2 trillion at the end of 2007. That steep drop shows few signs of slowing down.[41]

The neoliberal world economic order has also become closely associated with massive increases in public and private indebtedness. Even with an explosion of such indebtedness after the Great Recession, growth has been anemic. A system predicated on growth, when the sources of growth are hard to find, is vulnerable to crisis. The $80 trillion increase in global debt outstanding—from $145 trillion on the eve of the 2008 financial crisis to $225 trillion in 2016—is far larger than the $16 trillion of GDP growth over the same period (which saw world GDP rise from $63 trillion to $79 trillion).[42] This is in the class of those things that can't go on forever, and bespeaks a day of reckoning to come. State expenditures in the U.S. fund present consumption and (apart from military-related items) starve research and development. Wondrous depictions of the liberal world order that ignore these unpleasant developments, all of which predated Trump, lack persuasiveness. Instead of "rule following," the neoliberal economic order of the last generation rested on a series of gambles by U.S. elites whose unanticipated consequences came to look distinctly unattractive.

Who-Whom?

The confederal ideal of union among like-minded republics—condemned to hang together or hang separately—has deep roots in American history. It was coeval with the foundation of the republic. It deeply informed conceptions of internationalism in the first half of the twentieth century.[43] "We are persuaded by necessity and by belief," said President Eisenhower in 1953, "that the strength of all free peoples lies in unity; their danger, in discord." That was, he reiterated in 1957, the one truth that "must rule all we think and all we do. The unity of all who dwell in freedom is their only sure defense." Citing Hiawatha, Secretary of State James Baker said the same: "All your strength is in union; all your danger is in discord."[44]

Much of the argument over America's system of alliances has fallen between two rival images—between those who have claimed it is more like an empire than a union, and others who have insisted that it is more like a union than an empire. The ambiguity is captured in Ikenberry's depiction of a "Liberal Leviathan." The union is embodied in the system of alliances and in subscription to a "rule-based" system. The empire (a.k.a. the U.S. national security state) inheres in America's global military commands and its outsized military spending and surveillance apparatus. These rival conceptions, it should be apparent, have been deeply interdependent for officialdom: the union of states embodied in the free world complex has needed a hand on the tiller to resist the natural tendency of confederations to fall apart. It found that hand in the security guarantee provided by empire. The empire, on the other hand, has needed the legitimating function that the union provides. Allies give tangible support to the proposition that the United States acts not for itself but for the international community.

For those who saw a species of constitutionalism in the formation of the postwar international institutions linking the United States with its principal allies, the idea that the allies might provide a source of real restraint on America's apparatus of power was not unreasonable. Their role would be what the international relations specialists call "soft balancing" (criticism and dissent) rather than "hard balancing" (involving secession from the alliance). In this understanding, as Obama articulated it, "multilateralism regulates hubris."[45] To join with others in a common enterprise, in theory at least, gives them a voice in the management thereof, controlling the imperial temptation.

In its early days, the Atlantic alliance was undoubtedly marked by the spirit of union and by the corollary liberal elements of cooperation and partnership, with postwar leaders in Europe and America forming a real fraternity of spirit. Underpinning it, too, was a larger allegiance among America and its Western allies to liberal democratic values, forged in opposition to totalitarianism and diminishing the significance of the disparity in power (very great at the outset). In the third world, however, the alliance system featured a more disorganized grouping of clients and protectorates, much less agreement on values, and a U.S. policy more aggressive than in Western Europe. America's record of order-building on the periphery was far less impressive than its creative acts at the center, often leaving simple destruction in its wake.[46]

The global expansion and consolidation of the U.S. position after the end of the Cold War subtly transformed the nature of the union. Less and less after 1991 did this system resemble the ideas of alliance held by the early architects of internationalism; it became top heavy with empire. Early conceptions of internationalism lacked such an outsized role for the United States. Eisenhower, for example, saw America's role in Europe as vital but temporary, yielding ultimately a more balanced division of responsibility within NATO. Walter Lippmann had called during the Second World War for "a concert of free nations held together by a realization of their common interests and acting together by consent." The growth of U.S. military might in the post-Cold War era, together with the expansion of U.S. commitments, made the alliance system more closely resemble the alternative that Lippmann also espied, but dreaded: "one military empire ruled from one capital." [47]

Given these changes, the promise of allies as a sort of senate never really lived up to the implied promises; over time, their role became more like the contemporary British House of Lords, a group of very distinguished personages with no institutional whack. American leaders have so many allied voices to listen to and appease that no one ally can claim, on virtually any point, a right to get its own way, and American opinion has for more than two decades been emphatic on the idea that allies could have a voice, but never a veto, on the U.S. use of force. Nor were allies necessarily interested in restraint. More often of late, the security blanket provided by the United States has emboldened them to take provocative stances in the expectation of U.S. support. Georgia did it in 2008 with its invasion of South Ossetia. Britain and France did it in 2011 by agitating for intervention in Libya. Poland did it in the Ukraine crisis; China's neighbors have done it over disputed territorial waters. Israel—and, increasingly, Saudi Arabia—do it as a matter of course.

The chief objection to considering America's allies as components of an empire is that they have generally been very well treated. If an empire, it has been to them a largely benevolent empire. Their dependent relationship, it is true, has come at a price, whether that is measured in terms of their loss of autonomous decision-making, their subjection to financial sanctions via the edict of the U.S. Congress, or their humiliating status as targets of America's surveillance state. The indictment of former British Prime Minister Tony Blair as "America's poodle" is representative of a degradation or diminishment that most every ally has felt at one point or another (though Blair certainly did his level best to outdo everybody on that score, fully earning his sobriquet). Despite these costs and irritations, American protection—an easy subsistence under the "security umbrella"—undoubtedly carried with it signal advantages. It allowed Europe to put its internal security rivalries, focused on the German problem, into a sort of oblivion, relying on the American gendarme to maintain the security order. The arrangement is intimately associated with Europe's peaceful rise from the ashes after World War II, leaving Europeans loath to contemplate any fundamental change. In East Asia, the same sense of dependence on U.S. power has existed, leading allies to support American objectives in other parts of the world even against their own inclinations, but also seeking to elicit U.S. support in their competition with China. With respect to America's principal alliance relationships, it is not at all clear how to answer Lenin's famous question—Who-whom? That is, it is often not clear who is taking advantage of whom. One could argue the case either way.[48]

A different, indeed unique, pattern is presented by U.S. policy in the Middle East. This has been driven partly by oil but more importantly by Israel's strategic demands and insecurities, with Israel's mortal adversaries (Iran, Hezbollah, Syria, Hamas, especially) becoming America's as well. Israel's prominence in Washington decision-making, and its broader support in the American political system, make it an anomaly in America's alliance relationships, though no less important for that. This peculiar relationship recalls Benjamin Franklin's observation, apropos the incorporation of Scotland in Great Britain, that whereas the Scots feared "that the whale would swallow Jonas," the reverse had occurred: "Jonas had swallowed the whale." Bill Clinton gave expression to a similar anomaly when he exclaimed to his staff, after first meeting with Benjamin Netanyahu in 1996: "Who's the superpower here?"[49]

Israel has had enormous uses for U.S. power, but the U.S. has had little to no use for Israeli power, making it a relationship unlike any other. Israel is not a "means" for Americans—the security and survival of the Jewish state are ends in themselves—whereas American power is very much a means for Israel. In a few instances, like the secret training of Guatemalan paramilitary forces in the 1980s, Israel has been a "means" for the U.S., but it is not a "means" in the Middle East. Rather, Israel is invariably urged by the U.S. to stay out of military conflicts when the U.S. is trying to organize an Arab coalition.

Israel's diplomacy "out of area" is also often discordant with U.S. objectives. It did not, for instance, impose sanctions on Russia in 2014 after the Ukraine crisis; it sells arms to China and other states where the U.S. has imposed a weapons ban.

The importance of the Israel lobby is difficult to measure, in addition to being somewhat risky to explore (as candid explanations seem rather consistently to elicit charges of anti-Semitism). On matters directly concerning U.S. policy toward Israel and the region, the lobby is certainly powerful, yet not all powerful. The lobby doesn't decide great matters of state (though it certainly wants to). It is best thought of as constituting a critical influence on the milieu in which issues related to Israel and the Middle East play out, the political force field that presidents and other political officials must navigate, at peril to their careers if they misstep.

Every American president since Harry Truman has encouraged a peace between Israel and the Palestinians, but serious pressure on Israel has not been a feature of U.S. policy since the administration of George H. W. Bush, who held up loan guarantees to Israel in the early 1990s. Obama's diplomacy pressed for serious change in the Israeli negotiating posture, but in the end rewarded Israel with a ten-year $38 billion aid package. Obama was influenced while in Chicago by a strain of liberal Judaism that counseled Israeli concessions to the Palestinians.[50] The president, however, backed away from any confrontation with Netanyahu over Israeli settlements in the Occupied Territories because there was only political loss to be had by provoking a showdown, with the likely prospect of small or non-existent gains. He felt he had to try, because most of his predecessors had tried, but as the event showed had little confidence in success. He faced an unbreakable domestic phalanx opposed to serious U.S. pressure on Israel. Obama probably believed that only a total cutoff of U.S. economic and military aid would conceivably work, and he had no chance of pulling that off domestically and no assurance that the Israelis would budge, even were the aforesaid miracle to occur. That the United States was not prepared to threaten anything was apparent from the outset of the negotiations led by Secretary of State John Kerry, launched in July 2013, giving them a farcical and "doomed to fail" aspect from the beginning. Kerry brought nothing to the table but reasons that the Israelis had previously rejected and were determined to reject again. And that is what happened less than a year later, with the talks breaking down in late April 2014, followed by heated recriminations between the two governments.

The demonstration by Israel of the strict limits to American influence was then followed by the Iran agreement in 2015, which demonstrated the limits to Israel's influence. Obama won that showdown with the lobby because it raised an issue of war and peace on which the Joint Chiefs of Staff had generally given as firm a thumbs down as they can muster, given their obligation to obey the president's orders as commander in chief. In essence, they insisted that it was not a good idea at all unless absolutely necessary, and even then with no assurance of permanently accomplishing the objective, requiring far more resources and producing potentially catastrophic casualties for the Iranians that would lock the United States in a protracted and costly war. Bush stood down from war with Iran in 2008 because of that opposition. Strictly speaking, war was not the alternative if Obama's negotiations failed, but if the U.S. walked away from an agreement with Iran—supported, too, by the other major world powers—it would leave the Iranian program with far less international supervision and control than would be possible in an agreement. Pressures to bomb Iran, on the supposition of a failure of the negotiations, would then be directly back on the table. That made it a question of reason of state. The lobby does very well with Congress, but encounters stiffer resistance from the U.S. military brass, who get a sort of veto power when they might be left holding the bag. Israel and its friends cannot prevent the United States from selling weapons to Saudi Arabia (about which in any case Israel sees certain advantages, as the Saudi antagonism is directed toward their common enemy, Iran); but Israel can and always has received compensating arms packages that ensure Israeli military superiority over any Muslim coalition. The U.S. security complex wins both ways in gaining more arms sales, so has no interest in stopping this particular game.

The pattern of influence thus resembles the proverbial Mexican standoff, as they used to call it in the westerns: the U.S. can't make Israel do anything that Israel doesn't want to do with respect to any question of security, even though the United States pays a lot of Israel's bills. Theoretically, the paymaster should call the tune, but is blocked by powerful political obstacles from doing so. Israel and its sympathizers in America, on the other hand, do have power to move the U.S. government, but fall well short of puppeteer status. True, the lobby can force Congress into quite the marionette show, with ritual demonstrations of loyalty demanded and given, but nothing approaching this influence has existed within the executive branch or its agencies, much more sensitive than the Congress to other-than-Israeli foreign opinion and their own interests. The political heft of the lobby, however, cannot be gainsaid, in what has been the most important region for the use of U.S. military power since 1991. Politically, the hold of the lobby has always been stronger over congressmen than presidents, because congressmen can be isolated—punished or rewarded—at election time in more direct ways. But the overall lesson for U.S. politicians is straightforward: on issues of intense concern to Israel, you'd better have an excellent reason to trifle with its supporters.[51]

Despite the political importance of Jewish opinion in shaping views of the Middle East, and also of Jewish money in American elections, what ultimately matters for U.S. policy is not the Jews but the vast millions of Protestants, Catholics, and non-believers who sympathize with the Israeli position as against the Palestinians. Much of that affinity, in turn, has been driven by the memory of the disastrous Palestinian adoption of terrorism—a course that, as intended, drew attention to their plight, but also brought their cause profound moral discredit. That sentiment survives increasingly disproportionate uses of force by Israel. Polls taken during the Gaza War of 2014 showed that 57 percent of Americans believed Israel's actions in Gaza were justified, with 40 percent opposed. In 2009, the approval rate was 63 percent. (The margins are closer in Gallup polling, with a late July 2014 poll showing a 42-39 split on whether Israel's actions were justified and—disturbing for Israel—a 25-51 split among people aged 18 to 29.) In a Brookings poll of late 2016, 46 percent of Americans believed the U.S. should impose sanctions on new Israel settlements, nine points higher than the previous year (with 27 percent opposed and the rest neutral). Nevertheless, Americans sympathize with Israelis far more than they do with Palestinians, by a whopping 54 to 19 margin in the latest Pew survey.[52]

Though some polls do raise a question about the depth of support for Israel among the broader public, few politicians have seen any advantage in challenging the pro-Israel consensus in Washington, even if this requires the suppression of humanitarian sympathies for the weaker party deprived of its just rights. Would this change if U.S. media began to develop a more even-handed portrait of the Israeli-Palestinian conflict? Probably it would, though it seems likely that attitudes in the public at large are driven more by fear of Arabs or Muslims (and their association with terrorism) than by sympathy for the Jews.

The structural nature of the U.S.-Israeli relationship is thus unique in crucial respects: there's really nothing else like this pattern of influence in the other alliances, multilateral and bilateral, of the United States. Israel's influence, and its potent domestic support, are also very different in character from that exercised by foreign statesmen and diplomats (e.g., Winston Churchill and Konrad Adenauer) in the 1940s and 1950s. Other foreign lobbies deploy a similar type of power over issues of intense concern to them, but nobody has done it with such tenacity and resources as the Israel lobby, and in a region where issues of war and peace have been central (as they have not been, e.g., in Cuba or Ireland). All this heavy interaction—with deep dependencies but also opportunity for bitter rancor—unfolds in the absence of any formal treaty between the two countries pledging mutual support if attacked. Yet Israel is frequently called by U.S. politicians "our most important and critical ally."

America's other formal and informal allies in the Middle East—Turkey, Saudi Arabia, and the Gulf states—do not deploy anything like the influence that Israel does in Washington, but they have gained from the U.S. connection even as they have aggressively pursued policies difficult to square with America's declared interests. In the two years that elapsed after President Obama announced a military campaign to degrade and destroy ISIS (in August 2014), Turkey, Qatar, and Saudi Arabia gave greatly expanded aid to the Syrian branch of Al-Qaeda, Jabhat al-Nusra—that is, to the very organization that plotted the 9/11 attacks.[53] Turkey viewed its Kurdish rebels— especially the PKK but including the Kurdish YPG militia units that fought against ISIS in northern Syria in conjunction with the United States—as a worse threat than ISIS, and devoted approximately 90 percent of its military effort against the Kurds. Saudi Arabia launched an illegal external intervention into Yemen that gravely exacerbated the humanitarian crisis in that country and that was directed against the Houthis rather than AQAP (Al-Qaeda in the Arabian Peninsula), against whom the U.S. has been conducting a drone war of assassinations for many years. America's alliances in the Middle East have certainly been predicated on the distinction between friends and enemies; nowhere does the public ideology of acting on the basis of neutral principles seem more far-fetched; nowhere, too, does the public language of "allies," assuming as it does a commonality of aims, seem more absurd.

Complaints over allied burden-sharing have long been uttered by American politicians and officials, but never more stridently than in the 2016 presidential campaign. Sharply breaking from the security consensus, Trump insisted that America had gotten a rotten deal from its alliances, giving much while getting little in return. He intimated that he would make protection conditional on further allied contributions. Among America Firsters, an expression Trump endorsed, the traditional response to unequal burden-sharing was to propose a withdrawal from America's alliances, but Trump's resolution was very different. Instead, he proposed a massive new investment in U.S. armed forces, though such a buildup could only be justified as a way of shoring up America's global military position—hence, the protection of the very allies he excoriated as deadbeats. What Trump most seemed to want was not the abandonment of the alliances but their explicit reformulation as relationships of avowed U.S. protection to be repaid in tangible benefits—the geopolitical version of the protection racket. Trump was condemned by conventional opinion for that view, though it simply goes further down a road—the extraction of rents from allies—that has already been traversed by the U.S. national security state. It is remarkable that Trump, so unconventional in other respects, should illustrate that tendency in his outlook.

In the classic exchange justifying monarchical rule, obedience is given in return for protection. While there has seemed considerably more protection than obedience at play in America's relationships in the Middle East, this exchange has closely approximated the main alliance relationships across the Atlantic and the Pacific. The allies in Europe and East Asia have chafed under this restriction, but have mostly observed it. The expectation that this dependence would decline as Europe and Japan recovered, a prediction often indulged in the post-World War II period, proved misplaced. Whether Trump will change this relationship—demands for subordination invariably also produce compensating movements for independence—is one of the "known unknowns" of his presidency. If he does, it would mark a dramatic change from the past decade: under Obama, Europe's and East Asia's sense of dependence on the United States actually heightened. The Europeans, despite some unpleasantness, worked cordially with Obama and greatly preferred him to Bush, accepting that the American role in Europe was indispensable. Under the Obama administration, Japan enlisted the United States in its "rule-based" competition with China over the Senkaku/Diayou islands and conceded long-standing U.S. demands to integrate its forces into the U.S. military posture in East Asia. Under Shinzo Abe's leadership, Japan was also ready to compromise the traditional protection of its agricultural sector; its motives for supporting the Trans-Pacific Partnership were closely tied to its security dependence on the United States.

Given the relatively good deal that America's allies have enjoyed under the protection of the United States, "hegemony" rather than "empire" has long been the most apt description of this relationship. Though not without some tendencies pointing toward imperial domination, America's alliance relationships have, in the main, been an instance of "leader and followers" rather than "ruler and ruled."[54] In its unconditional extension of a security umbrella over allies, America has been very liberal in the older meaning of that term—that is, generous to a fault—but it has been less liberal on the score of rule-following and equal partnership. It has been decidedly illiberal in other practices, especially in its fondness for nearly unlimited surveillance and its use of the dollar-based financial system to impose discipline on friends and enemies alike.

While America's wishes and practices have borne hard upon the allies some of the time, its close allies (Europe, Japan, South Korea) have been at all times conscious of the utility of American power in dealing with their security problem. Not without misgivings, they have generally calculated that they are safer within the U.S. system than outside it. If they have felt on some occasions like the proverbial battered spouse, bitter over injuries received but conscious of the practical incapacity to exit, they have at other times seen themselves as valued partners grateful that they have a voice. While not without elements of forced submission over its long history, the relationship has been largely one of voluntary acquiescence. This facet of the American position in the world, however, does not acquit the United States of the charge of imperialism. That aspect has been most pronounced not in relation to America's allies, but in relation to America's adversaries.

2

Universal Empire
and Westphalian Ruins

Toward Universal Empire

The most striking feature of imperial ambitions over the last 20 years may be found in the national security doctrine of the George W. Bush administration. Announced in 2002 in an address at West Point and further elaborated in his national security strategy, the doctrine set forth a combination of claims that reflected a desire to dominate the system of states. The United States, Bush held, intended to maintain and even extend its position of military dominance of the international system, one that would render competitive efforts to "balance" against American power fruitless. He combined this with a doctrine of preventive war, holding that the possible acquisition by hostile powers of weapons of mass destruction justified the use of U.S. force against them. A third doctrine, most fully elaborated at Bush's second inaugural in 2005, made it the objective of the United States to seek an "end of tyranny" in the world and identified that as a fundamental requirement of America's national security. While Bush was careful to add that this objective was not primarily to be sought through the use of force, he did not rule out the use of force for this purpose, and, of course, both the wars in Afghanistan and Iraq had the "extension of liberty" as one of their primary aims. The Bush administration made clear that neither the UN Security Council nor allied states could claim any sort of veto over those decisions, and imposed the stern test of being either with the United States or "with the terrorists." In secret, Bush also vastly expanded Washington's intelligence apparatus, hoping to create a universal panopticon.

There is no mistaking the fact that Bush was far more zealously committed to these ambitions than his successor, though it also true that Obama
was generally loath to directly repudiate them. In crucial respects, as we
saw earlier, Obama confirmed the essential strategic claims of the preceding
administration, despite the cautiousness of his embrace. He affirmed the vital
imperative of maintaining U.S. military superiority. He continued to build
the panopticon. He embraced regime change and the strategy of overthrow,
though with less vigor than Bush, and for different purposes. And although he
prohibited torture and sought to bring U.S. conduct within the scope of the
laws of war, he authorized the expansion of the global battlefield, to include
Pakistan, Yemen, Somalia, Syria, and Libya, with the purposes of the war to
be defined by the executive. Obama spoke, as did the rest of Washington, in
a reverential tone of Bush's expansion of NATO, which brought the Baltics
and the Balkans into the fold—another of those areas where initiatives boldly
advocated and pushed through by Bush in the revolutionary moment of
2002 became, a dozen years later, fixed and unquestionable axioms of the
Washington establishment. Confessedly, Obama was a far more moderate
character than Bush, and really did want to stay out of new wars; that a fellow
pacifically inclined should use force as often as he did speaks volumes about
the weight of the Washington consensus.

The complex of attitudes to which Obama accommodated, but that he
didn't fully share, has remained wedded to notions of indispensability, exceptionalism, and superior power. The supremacist ideas making up this outlook
achieved predominance after 9/11, but they were all adumbrated in the early
1990s, most especially by Charles Krauthammer, whose seminal essay "The
Unipolar Moment" attracted wide attention and coined a phrase. Less well
known is an earlier essay by Krauthammer, which he concluded with the following appeal: "If the new age dawns and some new national purpose is to be
offered and sold to the American people, I suggest that we go all the way and
stop at nothing short of universal dominion."[1]

Universal dominion is indeed an apt expression for the aspirations
announced by Krauthammer, instantiated by Bush, and tremulously followed
by Obama. The frustration encountered by U.S. uses of force, especially
in the last decade and a half, may make the idea of universal empire seem
absurd: there is a yawning chasm between the dominion inhering in superior U.S. military power and the repeated disutility of its uses of force, a gap
between its renowned superiority in the arts of destruction and the actual
utility of its military operations.[2] The liberation of Baghdad, in Andrew
Bacevich's pungent expression of 2004, "punctured the illusion that the

world's sole superpower has reserves of power to spare. It doesn't, not militarily, not financially and not morally. Iraq has shown how narrow the margin is between global hegemony and imperial overstretch."[3]

Under Obama, the persistence of American ambitions alongside the diminishment of American strength emerged as the most paradoxical aspect of the U.S. position. It seemed that the former tendency had to yield to the latter, but in the main it did not. In keeping with public opinion, Obama had a more restrained attitude in the actual use of force, especially as compared with the hawks, but in his first term he "surged" into Afghanistan and greatly escalated drone strikes. He also accepted the principle that commitments once made must be sacredly observed, ratifying many of his predecessor's policies. The idea behind the American Century—that the United States could creatively shape the world's direction—was greatly diminished after 2003 by the failure to achieve the objectives originally set forth in these multiple wars. It is now yet more burdened by the specter of Trump. Withal, American Empire remains, and expenditures on it are set to grow. There has proved to be a great deal of ruin in it.[4]

It is a fundamental and little remarked feature of America's larger strategic position that these expansive ambitions took root at a time of undisputed U.S. military superiority, but have been pressed forward as the world grows increasingly multipolar.[5] We will return to that disjunction in a later chapter; for now, I want to try to understand that aspiration in relation to competing conceptions of international order. The aspiration to dominate the state system has been unprecedented in some respects, because it has been prosecuted in novel technological circumstances (unimaginably destructive nuclear arsenals, the revolution in precision guidance, new domains of competition like space and cyberspace). In the American self-understanding, of course, it has been unprecedented especially because of the nobility and selflessness of U.S. purposes, in which there has been an entire coincidence between U.S. objectives and international order. But the U.S. bid for mastery *does* have precedents. One might even take the view that U.S. overreaching, given its great power, is the most normal thing in the world, considering the past history of Great Powers and the careers of expansion on which they embarked. As the TV commercial says, "It's what they do."[6]

The term "universal empire" is not in common usage today—"global hegemony" is more likely to come from the keyboards of critical writers, and Krauthammer's "universal dominion" is something of an embarrassment even for neoconservatives—but it was in widespread currency during the long emergence of the European state system. I like the older term because it gives us imaginative access to a critique of the phenomenon that was once part of the American consensus and that speaks to certain enduring issues. Up until the profoundly interdependent and globalized age of the twentieth century, the term usually did not connote the literal domination of the earth, but rather dominance and mastery over a wide swath of peoples (who should otherwise, by virtue of proximity or interaction, form a system of states).[7] Above all, it meant any situation in which one monarchy or state was in a position to give the law to the others.

"Universal empire" is thus a very different phenomenon than "empire" as such, a distinction seldom made in the critical literature on America's world role. Whereas empires are common in international history—the predominant form before the emergence of the modern state—much rarer is the attempt to dominate the state system. "Empire," in a commonly accepted definition, means political control that is exercised by one political unit over another distinct people; "universal empire" means control over the state system as a whole. More simply, empire is ruling over other peoples without their consent, while universal empire is ruling over the society of states without its consent. Both are exercises in domination, which is usually the key attribute that users of the label have in mind, but they are very different in significance. European international history from the Renaissance to the twentieth century is essentially organized around the story of the successive bids for domination or mastery of the state system and of the countervailing coalitions those bids provoked in the name of the balance of power and "the liberties of Europe." As Martin Wight summarized the record of that half millennium, "Every dominant power aspires, by giving political unification to the whole of international society, to become a universal empire." Every attempt to do so, as he also noted, provoked resistance.[8] The U.S. quest for dominance of the state system has raised the same issues as these previous attempts, while outdoing them in the notable respect of being the first to actually be global in its reach. The opposing pluralist claims today go under the names of a "polycentric system," "multipolarity," or "sovereignty," but they are in their basic propositions very old. Recalling the idea of "universal empire" gives us imaginative access to the long debates—and impressive critiques—attending the rise of inordinate power within the old Westphalian system.[9]

The debate has taken a wide variety of forms over time, involving a vast array of actors and labels, but the core issue is between "pluralism" and "liberal solidarism" (to use the terminology of the English School of International Relations). Pluralism is roughly equivalent to what has been called "Charter liberalism" and has close affinities with "Westphalian principles," based on the balance of power and non-intervention in the internal affairs of other states. Liberal solidarism is identifiable with the claims of humanitarian interventionists, democratic liberationists, and "anti-pluralist" liberals. This solidarist doctrine achieved preeminence in the American-led unipolar order of the last quarter-century. Both viewpoints (paradigms, ideologies, systems of thought) are closely identified with rival conceptions of international law, each of which developed distinctive interpretations of the rights of war and peace.

The Westphalian peace was closely associated, first, with respect for sovereignty and non-intervention in the internal affairs of other states, and second, the avoidance of a situation in which one power would be in a position to dominate the rest, which was the core meaning of "the balance of power" or "a general equilibrium of power."[10] Though the "balance of power" is often identified with realism, the classical writers on the law of nations recognized that a system of international law depended on the balance, and were quite emphatic about the probable dangers posed by attempts to overturn it.

The UN Charter made for certain innovations in the received body of international law. In keeping with the League of Nations covenant and the Kellogg-Briand Pact of 1928, it outlawed offensive war. The license previously given in international law to colonialism was sharply abridged, the UN's foundational principle being the self-determination of peoples. With the Security Council, the UN system projected a concert among the Great Powers, rather than the balance of power, for preserving international peace and security, but even this was traditional in certain respects, harkening back to the quadruple alliances in the years after the Treaty of Utrecht, the Congress of Europe after the Napoleonic Wars, and the League of Nations Council. Though novel in certain respects, the Charter also built on long recognized norms of the society of states and the law of nations, and thus represented an attempt to reform Westphalian principles rather than uproot them. Nothing in the Charter was to abridge the inherent right of states to order their own affairs and to provide for their own defense.[11]

Both these ideas—the need for checks and balances, the duty of non-intervention—once occupied honored places in the American political lexicon, but no longer. Whether we take the "full spectrum dominance" aimed at in the 1990s, or George W. Bush's declaration that the United States intended to keep a military superiority over rivals so complete that they would abandon any thought of competition with America, or Obama's pledge to maintain U.S. "military superiority in all areas: air, land, sea, space, and cyber," it is clear that "the balance of power" is not and has not been for a long time an adequate depiction of American objectives. Hillary Clinton and Donald Trump disagreed about nearly everything in their 2016 presidential race, but they did not disagree about the vital importance of maintaining America's undisputed military superiority.

To make "the expansion of freedom in all the world . . . the urgent requirement of our nation's security," as Bush II did at his second inaugural, is also distinctly contrary to Westphalian or pluralist ideas of world order. In the last fifteen years, especially, the United States has reversed and overthrown previous public commitments to the society of states, above all the norm forbidding external intervention. Obama seemed to promise a rejection of that policy in his 2008 campaign—was that not why he had opposed the Iraq War?—but he did not follow through. No sooner was Iraq put on the back burner than Libya, Syria, and Ukraine flared up, and in each case the United States supported the side that wanted to overturn an existing government by violent means. This bold and forward policy was quite contrary to the traditional liberal understanding, which counseled fidelity to international law. In no way should these innovations be considered as exemplifying a "Westphalian" approach; they stand four-square against it. They upended the law of aggression, with its prohibition on preventive war. They have also upended the traditional international law of civil war, which once counseled abstention to outsiders; now that law seems to give virtually unlimited license to external intervention in support of internal revolution. These new rules are not merely "post-Westphalian." They are "contra-Westphalian."

In its dealings with international rivals, the American position has been invariably distinguished by the absence of reciprocity—that is, by an unwillingness to accord to other Great Powers respect for their vital interests. That proclivity is strongly reinforced by a cultural tendency that divides the world into "good guys" and "bad guys"; to confuse them is the sin of sins in foreign policy discourse. In America's diagnosis of foreign conflict, it often seems driven more by its own internal cultural understandings (or misunderstandings) than by an objective assessment of external threats. America's sometimes missionary zeal, its resentments against others, its religiosity produce a style of foreign policy that acts out a script driven by the way Americans understand conflict, in which their enemies assume common features. The propensity is hardly unique to the American people; its collective egotism and its vast capacity for enmity are in many respects characteristic of the nations from time immemorial. But America's great power gives this proclivity far-reaching significance and entrenches it in standing institutions.

For those of this mindset, "seeing things from the other side" makes America complicit with evil, with the lash of perceived conscience encouraging myopia. There are exceptions, of course, but a large swathe of the media is given over to making out prosecutorial indictments against adversary states. That characteristic, pervasive in political culture, suggests that America needs enemies and would be lost in its identity without them. Indeed, it has often seemed to care more for its enmities than its friendships; the norm of consulting with allies has trouble withstanding the force of a sacred mission. Even its imperialism, of which it is for the most part blissfully unconscious, is largely a residue or incident of nationalism and its blinkered perspectives. Call it the cultural contradictions of American internationalism, chief of which is the antagonism between the disinterested internationalism America has preached and the biased nationalism it has exhibited.[12]

This great cartographic division of the world into good guys and bad guys makes it virtually impossible for America to put itself in the shoes of others. If we do so, it is easy to see why Russian, Chinese, or Iranian nationals would see U.S. claims as encroaching on their zones of vital interest and as depriving them of essential national rights. Would the United States, they ask, bear to have deployed against it the advanced military positions that the United States deploys against them? Would it submit to bases by a foreign power in its "soft underbelly" in Central America and the Caribbean, undertaken for the purpose of ensuring America's strict observance of international law within the Western Hemisphere? Would it accept restrictions on its rights to technological development, or interference in its internal affairs?

In a democratic world, it would surely seem to matter that, on the points on which the United States has disputed with Russia, China, and Iran, it has confronted preponderant majorities in each of these countries who in no wise stand in opposition to their government's viewpoint. Washington has wanted to style its enmities as conflicts between democrats and despots, but these are conflicts among nations. It has seen the popular majorities in the nations arrayed against it as the product of a controlled press manipulated by autocrats, but these contrary views have arisen much more fundamentally as a grievance of offended nationalism. They would be there even if these states became what America is not: perfect democracies. The United States has been very solicitous with regard to its own national rights, but not at all attentive to the rights of adversaries; indeed, it has scarcely regarded such rights in any other light than as a smokescreen for illegitimate interests or a lie to cover misdeeds. The default U.S. assumption has been that its adversaries are "unjust enemies," stripped of the protection that the law of nature and of nations once provided them.[13]

The pluralist understanding needs a second look. In the new world order that arose after 1991, it was displaced by new doctrines allowing unprecedented intervention for six or seven different reasons, not coincidentally carried out by a state that had acquired the predominant role in the international system. Rather than ordering the international system, these interventions have destabilized it. But there is available an older view, once closely associated with liberalism, that was far more restrictive about when force could legitimately be used; the purpose of this chapter is to trace its origins and show its merits. Resting on the ground of sovereignty, non-intervention, and the balancing of power, the pluralist understanding points most convincingly away from the scourge of war, the *summum malum*. Its norms offer a superior route to a peaceful international system. Though strongly supported by reason, its merits are also confirmed by experience, a point that ought to count, but does not count, with contemporary American conservatism, especially its hitherto dominant neoconservative variant, which has looked on these older rules with disdain. Contemporary American realists should also take heed, as the political realism they defend is far more consonant with the old international law than is often supposed, even by realists themselves. The restrictions on the use of force inherent in the UN Charter, once closely identified with liberalism, fit today's realist prescriptions as the hand fits the glove. [14]

Rome and America

The idea of universal empire inevitably evokes comparisons to ancient Rome, which after its defeat of Carthage was put in a position where it could gain mastery of the known world. It was a model for its successors, but an antimodel to those who built the Westphalian system, founded on maxims opposite to Rome's. Great as are the differences in objectives and sensibilities by which Rome and America were thrust into a position of dominance, the course of Roman expansion after the defeat of Carthage bears comparison with the methods of the Americans after the defeat of its imperial adversaries. The Romans, notes Richard Tuck, often saw their interests as in alignment with those of oppressed citizens elsewhere and made appeal to that solidarity:

> Rome's mission, in the famous words of Vergil, could be thought of as "parcere subjectis and debellare superbos" ("to spare the oppressed and bring down the proud," *Aeneid* VI.852). Rome's status during its

expansion into the Eastern Mediterranean as the only republic left in a world of military despotisms undoubtedly contributed to its self-image as a liberator, freeing the subject peoples of Greece and Asia from the despotic descendants of Alexander's generals (though, as the ruthless destruction of Corinth in 146 BC testifies, Rome could in practice be even more tyrannical to the Greeks than the Kings of Macedon or Pontus had ever been). Rome certainly felt free to respond to appeals for help from populations engaged in struggles against their rulers or in war with their neighbors, and to some extent its entire imperial expansion was driven by a succession of such responses.[15]

This depiction of Roman expansion in the second century B.C.E. suggests a remarkable parallel with American expansion of the last 70 years. Unlike Rome, America has not made provinces, but both histories feature the incorporation of former enemies as protectorates and the cultivation of insurgents against despotic enemies. Neoconservatives and liberal hawks may fairly be seen as defining America's mission as that of liberating the oppressed and detonating despotic rule, and they have driven American expansion (or tried to) on the old Roman road. Even when this expansion entails catastrophic consequences, as occurred with the U.S. invasion of Iraq in 2003, the "liberated" come to feel a dependency on the "liberators." Iraq desperately wanted to escape this dependency, but it has thus far been unable to do so; loath to accept U.S. ground forces, it still has need of U.S. airpower, advisors, and military equipment. It is a disturbing fact that America's method of expansion— simultaneously looking for enemies to fight and protectorates to create—runs parallel to the road marked out by Rome.

The writer who most memorably conveyed the logic of Roman expansion was Niccolò Machiavelli, at the beginning of the modern age. The sense of wonder with which Renaissance writers viewed antiquity is itself wonderful; they were enthralled by it. When the range of ancient works was discovered and digested, writes the historian John Hale, Renaissance thinkers wanted to live in the past rather than in their own time. The newly reawakened spectacle of antiquity was all the more fascinating because it presented "the wholeness of a completed cycle, from obscurity through world empire to barbarian chaos."[16] Machiavelli was amazed that this rich experience had hardly been taken account of by contemporaries, and in the tale of Rome's ascent, he saw the remedy for Italy's difficulties. The analysis of this question in his *Discourses on Livy* bears striking similarities with the American predicament in the world today.

Of the three methods for expansion that ancient practices suggested, Machiavelli argued that Rome's example was undoubtedly the best. He rejected and treated scornfully the practice of Athens and Sparta, who followed cloistered policies toward those they conquered—making them subjects, not citizens—and who treated foreigners with disdain. Rome, by contrast, both broke its enemies and welcomed them, giving it a population base far superior to the other ancient republics. The Romans, Machiavelli marveled, could put 200,000 men into the field, Athens and Sparta only 20,000. While Machiavelli condemned the Athenian and Spartan method as absurd, he was far more respectful of the principle of confederation. He called this "the Tuscan method," which was "to form a confederation of several republics, neither of which had any eminence over the other in rank or authority." Though conceding real advantages to the confederal course, Machiavelli was ultimately most enthralled by the Roman method, which he saw as based on making "associates of other states; reserving to themselves, however, the rights of sovereignty, the seat of empire, and the glory of their enterprises." Machiavelli's depiction of Roman expansion emphasizes a peculiar combination of confederal and imperial principles, but the real secret of the Roman method, in his view, was that Rome's "associates (without being themselves aware of it) devoted their own efforts and blood to their own subjugation." Once Rome's associates realized the trap into which they had fallen, it was too late. "From associates they were degraded to subjects."[17]

This combination of imperial and confederal principles—oddly mixing the conceptions of domination and reciprocity—suggests a strong parallel with the international order of the last 25 years. At least toward its allies, America has been much more beneficent than Rome; at the same time, its rule, like that of Rome, has represented a sort of halfway house between confederation and empire, partaking curiously of both, fully embracing neither. The leaders of this peculiar construction have seemed conscious of the fact that neither mode of proceeding by itself can offer a solution to the problem of international order, so they have clasped both of these contradictory ways while also repelling either when inconvenient. The free world complex has justified itself through the appeal to confederal principles, holding that its normative claims are identical to international society as a whole, but its efficient power, which prevents the confederation from falling apart, has resided in the U.S. national security state.

Machiavelli's glorification of early republican Rome was not shared by his successors in Western political thought. Indeed, they repudiated it. As the new European society of states emerged from the detritus of 1648, but especially so after the Treaty of Utrecht in 1713, it defined itself against the Roman experience of universal empire, proffering a new mode of existence among nations. This new civilization, based on commerce, religious toleration, and the balance of power, saw Rome as its chief competitor, and imagined itself in conscious opposition to it. Balance rather than dominance; independence rather than uniformity; plurality rather than the universal state—such were the leitmotifs of the European society of states as it was described by publicists and statesmen. However different the United States may be from Rome in certain particulars, the Westphalian critique of ancient Rome is also a critique of American policy over the last quarter-century.

The case against *Monarchia Universalis* was advanced by a remarkable group of Spanish writers, including Vitoria, Las Casas, and Soto, in the sixteenth century, but the American Founders imbibed the critique from a host of Enlightenment thinkers in the eighteenth century.[18] Montesquieu, Vattel, Hume, Robertson, Burke, and Gibbon all considered the theme, and were as one in regarding universal empire as, in Hamilton's words, a "hideous project." The prevention of a situation in which any one power could give the law to the others was thought by these classic writers to be a necessary underpinning of international society, and they all looked with dread on any aspirant to universal dominion. Whether in Western constitutional thought or among the publicists of the law of nations, it was axiomatic that any situation of unbounded power held peril for the maintenance of both order and liberty. In the late seventeenth century, the French prelate Fénelon articulated what would soon emerge as its organizing principle: "It is not to be expected, among men, that a superior power will contain itself within the bounds of an exact moderation, and that it will not employ its force to obtain for itself what advantages it can, by oppressing the weaker. Or if this power should happen to be for some time harmless in the hands of an excellent prince, who could bear such prosperity so well, the wonder, 'tis likely, would cease with his reign." Fénelon could not believe "that a people who had it in their power to subdue their neighbours, would abstain from it for any considerable time." Such power would inevitably be abused; a prince who did not do so would be "the ornament of history, and a prodigy not to be looked for again."[19]

Universal empire did not necessarily connote direct rule over subject provinces. Hamilton called the conduct of revolutionary France toward Great Britain a "copy of that of Rome toward Carthage," aimed at destroying "the principal obstacle to a domination over Europe," but he acknowledged that France did not intend "to reduce all other nations formally to the condition of provinces. This was not done by Rome in the zenith of her greatness. She had her provinces, and she had her allies. But her allies were in fact her vassals." Juridical niceties, Hamilton was saying, could not settle the question of whether any state aimed at universal empire. Control that was not expressed in terms of formal sovereignty could nonetheless be practically effective and certainly threatening if it represented a bid for mastery of the state system.[20]

While conceding that universal empire had a certain irresistible and sirenlike appeal, Enlightenment writers believed that the enterprise would inevitably recoil upon its authors. Universal empire was deemed not only a menace to others but also a threat to its possessors. Montesquieu doubted that Louis XIV, accused "a thousand times . . . of having formed and pursued the project of universal monarchy," had really done so; but had the Sun King been successful in the pursuit of that objective, Montesquieu held, "nothing would have been more fatal to Europe, to his first subjects, to himself, and to his family." "Enormous monarchies," Hume wrote, "are, probably, destructive to human nature; in their progress, in their continuance, and even in their downfall, which never can be very distant from their establishment." Hume traced out, as had Montesquieu, a natural process by which aggrandizement turned on itself: "Thus human nature checks itself in its airy elevation; thus ambition blindly labours for the destruction of the conqueror." Rousseau reached a conclusion very similar to that of Hume: "If the princes who are accused of aiming at universal monarchy were in reality guilty of any such project, they gave more proof of ambition than of genius. How could any man look such a project in the face without instantly perceiving its absurdity?"[21]

A special venom was reserved for the universal dominion of Rome—"whose passion was to command, whose ambition was to subject everything, who had always usurped, who usurped still"—in Montesquieu's words.[22] Machiavelli had made the ways of early republican Rome a sort of instruction manual for modern princes and peoples, but the Enlightenment rejected Rome's mad ambition to dominate and saw grievous consequences as ensuing from it. Hobbes announces his philosophic enterprise, in the preface to De Cive, by excoriating those whom Machiavelli had celebrated: "What sort of animal was the Roman People? By the agency of citizens who took the names Africanus, Asiaticus, Macedonicus, Achaicus and so on from the nations they had robbed, that people plundered nearly all the world."[23] Whereas Machiavelli glorified early republican Rome for perfecting the ways of military expansion, Hobbes made the people of Rome the villain of the piece. A century after Hobbes, William Robertson also lamented the awful consequences following from the Roman conquest, which left the conquered peoples losing "not only the habit but even the capacity" to think for themselves: "The dominion of the Romans, like that of all great Empires, degraded and debased the human species."[24]

Of all these various bids for universal empire over the last 500 years, the one bearing the closest analogy in ideological complexion to that of twenty-first-century America is that which occurred in conjunction with the French Revolution and the wars that erupted in its train. It has it all: a universal and revolutionary creed, a strategic doctrine of preventive war, a declared will-ingness to liberate foreign peoples from tyranny, and a military machine that had discovered sources of power hitherto unknown.[25] The essential features of this colossal power were limned by Alexander Hamilton in the late 1790s, when he charged that France was making "hasty and colossal strides to univer-sal empire." Revolutionary France, in Hamilton's estimation, had "betrayed a spirit of universal domination; an opinion that she had a right to be the legislatrix of nations; that they are all bound to submit to her mandates, to take from her their moral, political, and religious creeds; that her plastic and regenerating hand is to mould them into whatever shape she thinks fit; and that her interest is to be the sole measure of the rights of the rest of the world." Here, in capsule form, are all the essential symptoms of the dread disease, the historic checklist for detecting the malady of universal empire. Altogether familiar to denizens of the twenty-first century is the charge that Hamilton brought against France, for it was the same charge brought against the Bush administration and has not disappeared today. Hamilton traced this spirit to "the love of dominion, inherent in the heart of man," reasoning that "the rul-ers of the most powerful nation in the world, whether a Committee of Safety or a Directory, will forever aim at an undue empire over other nations." "The spirit of moderation in a state of overbearing power," as Hamilton nicely sum-marized the point, "is a phenomenon which has not yet appeared, and which no wise man will expect ever to see."[26]

No comparison between the United States and Rome can ignore the profound differences that exist between antiquity and "postmodern" times. In the ancient world, "war paid" in a way that it has ceased to do in recent times. As a world power, Americans have not despoiled the wealth of defeated nations, enslaved captives, and annexed territory for settlement, as the Romans did. Nor does its officer corps and all volunteer force—troubling though their status is—threaten the kind of subversion of the republic that Caesar effected when he crossed with his legions into Italy.[27] There remains, withal, a profound similarity in the aspiration that one leading state should play the indispensable role in creating and sustaining a *Pax Universalis*, and a yet more remarkable similarity in the method of finding peoples to liberate, enemies to fight, and protectorates to create. Even the historians of Rome and America argue about their respective experiences in similar ways: the historiographical debate over the motives and context of expansion, for both Rome and America, counterpoises a thirst for dominion against a series of prudent defensive steps against aggressive enemies.[28]

Ultimately, the defense of the American position in the world, whether considered as a liberal hegemony or an illiberal empire, as repudiating or embodying Roman precedents, has rested on the contribution it makes to the maintenance of peace. Its claim to fame has been that its actions "uphold the peace" in Europe, Asia, and elsewhere, preventing the kind of conflagration that befell the world in 1914 or 1939. But here, the record is mixed, with historic achievements fading with each year into the distance, new sins multiplying. America's contribution to upholding the peace after 1945 was quite positive in Western Europe and Northeast Asia, where it helped rebuild its former enemies. It behaved responsibly in fashioning the post-Cold War settlement in Europe. During the Cold War, however, its interventions in the third world probably brought more anarchy than order. And over the last fifteen years, especially, its formula for "peace upholding" came to require continuous war. In the new features it has assumed for the whole of the post-Cold War period, but especially since 2002, it is a war-provoking formula. This is so, I would assert, exactly in proportion to the U.S. departure from pluralist principles. Hillary Clinton may argue that "balance" and "concert" are misguided notions drawn from an archaic past, but they are, in fact, the building blocks of world order that no stateswoman should despise. Non-intervention, too, as Daniel Webster said, is indispensable to the preservation of the world's peace, and the rules contained in traditional international law prescribing non-intervention as a duty are far superior to the broad range of rationales for intervention accepted in the West today.

Revolution, Intervention, and the Law of Nations

Like the argument between dominion and preponderance on the one hand, and balance and concert on the other, the debate over intervention has a long history. Some years ago, the historian Gary Bass published a work, *Freedom's Battle*, that explored the development of humanitarian intervention in the nineteenth century, successively analyzing European (mostly British) debates over intervention in Greece (1820s), Syria (c. 1860) and Bulgaria (c. 1877-88)—with each case significantly featuring, in addition to its humanitarian aspects, a conflict between the crescent and the cross. Bass' evident purpose, handsomely accomplished, was to show that humanitarian intervention had a history that didn't simply begin in the 1990s.[29] Not to be outdone, two British historians subsequently showed that humanitarian intervention has an even larger range of precedents, stretching back four centuries. "The modern phenomenon known as 'humanitarian intervention,'" they wrote, "is like a river formed from the combination of several different tributaries: these include confessional solidarity, opposition to 'tyranny', abolitionism that transcended race, and a belief in a variety of values, including liberty, civilization, democracy, and (eventually) human rights. A complete analysis of intervention must incorporate the long-term history and must begin, not in 1990, nor in 1945, nor even in the 1820s, but in the late sixteenth century."[30]

These are excellent points, but one might legitimately wonder why we should stop at the late sixteenth century. It was surely a feature of the European interventions into the *Regnum Italicum* that began in 1494, and then grew in ferocity throughout the early and mid-sixteenth century, that they were attended by rhetoric emphasizing the high purposes of the intervening powers. As John Adams would later remark, accurately summarizing the historical record: "Power always sincerely, conscientiously, *de tres bon foi*, believes itself right. Power always thinks it has a great soul, and vast views, beyond the comprehension of the weak; and that it is doing God service, when it is violating all his laws."[31] Machiavelli's age was not lacking in such examples, as the Florentine often had occasion to observe. Contending with the high purposes and low motives of the European powers as they made Italy their battlefield was the commanding political predicament of Machiavelli's life (he died in 1527). The phenomenon, as previously noted, was hardly unknown in antiquity.

It is especially interesting that the complex of questions with which we wrestle today, involving humanitarian intervention, regime change, and religious conflict, drew the attention of the founders of international law. Two key aspects of their discussion remain highly relevant today—whether there is a right of revolution by an oppressed people, and whether outside powers have the right (or duty) to intervene to put an end to acts that shock the moral sense. The absence of reflection on these questions in the United States is probably due not so much to a lack of interest in such questions, but to a much deeper sense among the elites that they have already been decided and are no longer open to serious discussion. Of course, people living under dictators have a right of revolution, Americans would say; of course (says the elite), the United States has a right of external intervention, for any among a half a dozen reasons (saving strangers, deposing drug lords or tyrants, fighting terrorists, promoting democracy, forcibly preventing nuclear proliferation) that have been urged in the last quarter-century. The widespread acceptance of such ideas has seemingly left "inexpediency" as the only remaining ground of opposition.[32]

In fact, however, neither proposition—the right to revolution, and the right of external intervention—is "self-evident." It might be unpersuasive to deny a right of revolution in all instances, but we also need to realize that violent revolution may produce such deep wounds in the body politic as to ensure that nothing good can possibly come of it. It might be unpersuasive to deny a right or duty of humanitarian intervention in every instance, but we also need to realize how intervention can—and often does—produce yet more dire circumstances (with the evil it inflicts a function in part of the violation of right it entails). Especially do I emphasize the contention that—however persuasive each of these claims may be in certain restricted circumstances, when standing alone—the conjoining of the two doctrines has represented an explosive innovation in the rules of international society, making for war-provoking rather than peace-inducing principles. A retreat from these doctrines, of proven danger when mixed, is imperative.

The issues are illuminated by some key debates in the tradition of reflection on the just war or *jus ad bellum*. The thought of Hugo Grotius, the Dutch jurist and legal scholar, is an especially interesting place to begin. Grotius formulated during the Thirty Year's War, in his *Rights of War and Peace*, what to our ears must seem a surprising doctrine. Grotius made one of the first great statements of the principle of humanitarian intervention, but he simultaneously forbade a population to rebel. The suffering masses had to sit out oppression lest they invite anarchy, it appeared from his curious reasoning, but foreign princes might intervene to succor those self-same masses when found in awful distress. You would think he had this backward, and the weight of subsequent opinion would agree. Eighteenth-century publicists reversed the Grotian resolution—they gave greater latitude to the right of revolution, less to external intervention.

Two things are notable about this history: all the key jurists saw the questions of revolution and intervention as related, and all were wary of justifying both together. The reason, evidently, is that allowing both the right of rebellion and the duty of external intervention would hold peril to domestic and international order. The possibility that each of these doctrines would mutually support each other, producing a free-for-all, could hardly be dismissed. What could possibly be the rule of limitation if everything could suffice for war?[33]

Grotius opened the door to humanitarian intervention, but he denied the popular right of resistance to an oppressive ruler. In an age of religious warfare and widespread slaughter, his reasons had weight. Grotius was not actually as strict on the question of internal rebellion as his hostile critics, like Rousseau, have claimed; he carved out several important exceptions to his seemingly blanket prohibition against rebellion, as when a king breaks a contract with a people, which conveniently, albeit silently, justified the Dutch Revolt against Spain. But Grotius did certainly espy the terror of violent revolution, and he was not alone in fearing it. He was followed by Hobbes, who erected a whole system around the same sentiment. Hersch Lauterpacht, the distinguished jurist and legal scholar, noted:

> This frowning upon rebellion and the favouring of authority were in accordance with what were considered to be the essential needs of the times. The horrors of civil war were foremost in the minds of political thinkers. There was not, in this respect, much difference between Hobbes and Bacon on the one side, and Hooker, Gentillet, and Bodin on the other. They discussed in detail the right of resistance; they all rejected it. So, perhaps with less justification, did Pufendorf. At a time of general uncertainty and of loosening of traditional ties of society, national and international, order was looked upon as the paramount dictate of reason.[34]

That view changed in the eighteenth century. John Locke recognized a right of revolution, as did, of course, the American Founders. Even among philosophers plausibly described as idealists, however, the right of revolution was cabined by restrictions amounting to a sort of absolute necessity, which is how the American revolutionaries of 1776 portrayed their own struggle. They sought not to overthrow the existing order but to preserve their ancient liberties. They sought membership within the society of states, not defiance toward its strictures, declaring themselves in 1776 "as Free and Independent States, [with] full Power to levy War, conclude Peace, contract Alliances, establish Commerce, and to do all other Acts and Things which Independent States may of right do." In an address contemporaneous with Jefferson's Declaration of Independence, Richard Henry Lee emphasized the conservative character of the bid for American independence, stressing its enlightened features: "If so many and distinguished praises have always been lavished upon the generous defenders of Greek and of Roman liberty, what will be said of us who defend a liberty which is founded not upon the capricious will of an unstable multitude, but upon immutable statutes and tutelary laws; not that which was the exclusive privilege of a few patricians, but that which is the property of all; not that which was stained by iniquitous ostracisms, or the horrible decimation of armies, but that which is pure, temperate and gentle, and conformed to the civilization of the present age."[35]

While Grotius' restrictions on the right of rebellion were considerably loosened in the eighteenth century, his allowance of humanitarian intervention was considerably tightened, if not altogether abolished. Pufendorf's objections were memorably restated by Vattel in his 1758 work synthesizing the law of nations:

> It is strange to hear the learned and judicious Grotius assert, that a sovereign may justly take up arms to chastise nations which are guilty of enormous transgressions of the law of nature, which treat their parents with inhumanity like the Sogdians, which eat human flesh as the ancient Gauls, &c. [citing Grotius, *De Jure Belli et Pacis*, book 2, chap. 20, §11]. What led him into this error, was his attributing to every independent man, and of course to every sovereign, an odd kind of right to punish faults which involve an enormous violation of the laws of nature, though they do not affect either his rights or his safety. But we have shewn (Book I. §169) that men derive the right of punishment solely from their right to provide for their own safety; and consequently they cannot claim it except against those by whom they have been injured. Could it escape Grotius, that, notwithstanding all the precautions added by him in the following paragraphs, his opinion opens a door to all the ravages of enthusiasm and fanaticism, and furnishes ambition with numberless pretexts? Mahomet and his successors have desolated and subdued Asia, to avenge the indignity done to the unity of the Godhead; all whom they termed associators or idolaters fell victims to their devout fury.[36]

Vattel's view of permissible intervention was more slippery than this passage by itself would suggest,[37] but undoubtedly a more restrictive view emerges among the publicists after Grotius and the religious wars. Notes Richard Tuck: "Scarred by what their continent had done to itself in the name of humanitarian intervention—for we must remember that this was how the Wars of Religion and the Thirty Years War appeared to their participants—Pufendorf and his successors, especially in Germany, turned to a kind of isolationism," becoming much more restrictive in the justifications acceptable for the use of force.[38]

As conceptions of legitimate intervention were changing, so were conceptions of the right of revolution. Here, too, there was not universal agreement on the question. In a commentary on the French Revolution, Edmund Burke noted that "the latest casuists of public law are rather of a republican cast" and not as averse as they should be "to a right in the people . . . to make changes at their pleasure in the fundamental laws of their country."[39] And, of course, the confederation of European monarchs that rose up in reaction to the French Revolution heatedly denied that there could be any such thing as a right of revolution. Even those who might be suspected of being on the other side of the question, like Immanuel Kant, took a surprisingly restrictive view. Though there was much in Kant that might lead a revolutionary spirit forward, Kant himself drew back. Closely identified with the French Revolution, his denial of a right of revolution made him "anti-revolutionary" in the German political context of the 1790s.[40] The French historian Albert Sorel wrote that Kant "led his disciples up to the giddy heights where his critique held sway, so that they could better admire the scaffolding of balustrades, parapets and guard rails he had so carefully erected to keep them from the abyss." Not that anyone paid attention: the wars unleashed by the French Revolution consumed Europe for another 20 years after the publication of Kant's *Perpetual Peace* in 1795.[41]

Throughout the great struggle between revolution and counterrevolution from 1792 to 1815, questions regarding intervention were of commanding importance. James Madison would remark in 1823 that the British government considered a war of two decades fully justified as a counterstroke to France's policy, announced in 1792 (but subsequently withdrawn) that it could make revolution all across Europe, whenever the people wished to recover their liberties against monarchical or aristocratic oppressors.[42] After the war, Britain broke from the Holy Alliance on the same question, after the "cominform of kings" assumed the right to repress revolutionary disturbances whenever they posed a threat to social repose. British Foreign Minister Castlereagh expressed the characteristic British reservation, later to be given a more emphatic rejection by his successor George Canning. The idea of an "Alliance Solidaire" binding states to support established government, wrote Castlereagh, could only be justified if the powers were also willing to enforce upon all kings and nations the observance of justice and peace within their realms. In the absence of such a system, which Castlereagh doubtless considered impossible to erect, "nothing would be more immoral or more prejudicial to the character of Government generally, than the idea that their force was collectively to be prostituted to the support of established Power without any consideration of the extent to which it was abused."[43] The rule of the Holy Alliance—reprobating revolution, authorizing intervention—was a reversion to the approach that Grotius had seemed to embrace, but had the paradoxical effect of illuminating brightly the shortcomings of this philosophy.[44]

The American Synthesis

It was in the United States that the pretensions of the Holy Alliance received the most thorough refutation. Daniel Webster's speech on the Greek Revolution noted "that a new era has arisen in the world, that new and dangerous combinations are taking place promulgating doctrines and fraught with consequences wholly subversive in their tendency of the public law of nations and of the general liberties of mankind."[45] The main targets of Webster, then a representative in Congress from Massachusetts, were the "two principles, which the Allied Powers would introduce as a part of the law of the civilized world"—first, that "all popular or constitutional rights are held no otherwise than as grants from the crown"—the old doctrine, in other words, of the divine right of kings; and second, the "still more objectionable principle" avowed by the allied powers of a "right of forcible interference in the affairs of other states."

Webster acknowledged that the principle of non-intervention was not absolute: "A right to interfere in extreme cases, in the case of contiguous states, and where imminent danger is threatened to one by what is occurring in another, is not without precedent"; it might "perhaps be defended upon principles of necessity and self defence." The declaration of the Holy Alliance at Troppau in 1820—"that the powers have an undoubted right to take a hostile attitude in regard to those states in which the overthrow of the government may operate as an example"—went far beyond this narrowly drawn exception to the principle of non-intervention. It "established a sort of double, or treble, or quadruple allegiance. An offence against one king is to be an offence against all kings, and the power of all is to be put forth for the punishment of the offender." But this "asserted right of forcible intervention in the affairs of other nations" could not be admitted; it was "in open violation of the public law of the world." By proposing to divide society "horizontally," by insisting, in short, that there are "no longer to be nations," the Holy Alliance departed from the central principle that had lain at the heart of the law of nations. On the basis of the independence of nations, there had been "reared the beautiful fabric of international law. On the principle of this independence, Europe has seen a family of nations flourishing within its limits, the small among the large, protected not always by power, but by a principle above power, by a sense of propriety and justice."[46]

The attitude that Webster entertained in 1824 was also adopted by Abraham Lincoln and William Seward in the 1850s, in response to the Hungarian Revolution and Russia's repression thereof. In a paper prepared with some like-minded fellows, Lincoln affirmed in ringing tones the right of revolution but also insisted that "it is the duty of our government neither to foment, nor assist, such revolutions in other governments." Toward the actions of the Russian government in Hungary, in their brutal suppression of that nation's bid for independence from Austria, Lincoln and his co-adjutors took the view later adopted by John Stuart Mill: Russian actions were illegitimate and gave rise to a right (but not a duty) of counter-intervention.[47]

Lincoln declined a departure from America's traditional policy in the immediate circumstance, but pointed to the logic that would subsequently be adopted when the non-interventionist disposition was ultimately overturned in the twentieth century. Basically, that was to justify military force on the basis of a fundamental threat to the legal order and to posit the necessity of counter-intervention if the legal order was to be restored and reformed. But Lincoln's thinking on this question also displayed a conservative bias to order. He conceded to the Southern states, for example, the natural right of revolution under unbearable oppression, but also denied that secession from the government could be a legal remedy under the Constitution.

William Seward, later to become Lincoln's secretary of state, developed a very similar view. Seward believed that the "philosophy of the American constitution" and the "supreme law" of the creation are "necessarily based on the equality of nations of races and of men." Countering the divine right of kings, Seward asked: "If all are not equal and free, then who is entitled to be free, and what evidence of his superiority can he bring from nature or revelation?" But the same philosophy that conferred the right of revolution also sharply restricted the right of external intervention, and Seward was merciless toward those who would yield to intervention, holding that to do so "would seem to render all sovereignty and independence, and even all international peace and amity, uncertain and fallacious." "The practice of this government, from the beginning," he wrote in 1866, "is a guarantee to all nations of the respect of the American people for the free sovereignty of the people in every other state." Critical to the maintenance of peace, Seward believed, was mankind learning "the simple truth, that however birth or language or climate may have made them differ—however mountains, deserts, rivers, and seas, may divide states—the nations of the earth are nevertheless one family, and all mankind are brethren, practically equal in endowments, equal in national and political rights, and equal in the favor of the common Creator."[48]

In the long nineteenth century, there was a consensus—reiterated in presidential messages and in other state papers—that non-intervention in the internal affairs of other states was not only a basic principle of the law of nations but also a fundamental doctrine of U.S. foreign policy. Though united by commerce, as Webster put it, "The great communities of the world are regarded as wholly independent, each entitled to maintain its own system of law, and government, while all, in their mutual intercourse, are understood to submit to the established rules and principles governing such intercourse. And the perfecting of this system of communication among Nations, requires the strictest application of the doctrine of non-intervention of any with the domestic concerns of others."[49] This was not just a Whig conceit; Democrats shared it, too. Ridiculing the idea that Americans should adopt a single standard of political legitimacy, proclaiming themselves the "knights errant of liberty" and seeking to advance with the sword the doctrines of republicanism, John Tyler compared it to Islam's practice, as Vattel had done, and saw an unhappy end in this beginning: "The gonfalon of Mahometism would be our banner; *there is but one form of govt. upon earth which we will tolerate and that is a republic.*"[50]

The nineteenth-century assessment of the relationship between liberty and nationality is key to understanding this question. American sensibilities gave precedence to "external self-determination" over "internal self-determination."[51] The fundamental right was independence: every people had the right to devise their own institutions rather than to be ruled by foreigners. The very act of so devising—whether it took place through reform or revolution—was thought to conduce toward representative institutions, but if an independent people consented to a monarch or fell into a civil war from which a dictator saved them, that was their own business. In the conception of legitimacy then entertained, the men on the spot had the right, and outsiders none, to decide for themselves, even if this meant fighting it out among themselves.[52] This view was never equated, by its advocates, as reflecting indifference to the cause of liberty. External self-determination (freedom from foreign rule) was a necessary condition of internal self-determination and was itself fundamental to the "liberty and independence" these nineteenth-century Americans prized. Nor did the commitment to "communal liberty" preclude support for "civil liberty." "What the laws of nations do not forbid,"

Seward observed in 1851, "any nation may do for the cause of civil liberty, in any other country."[53] Seward's doctrine, expressive of the views of Lincoln and the Republican consensus, created a wide berth for the progress of free institutions, but did not challenge the fundamentals of the society of states. These understandings of the role of liberty and law, so central to America's early conception of its purpose, and so different from those prevailing today, reveal the chasm between the present and the past on the wisdom and legalities of today's interventionist consensus.

It has been a feature of the American outlook for the last generation, brought to an apotheosis under the administration of George W. Bush, that America's foremost purpose in the world is to "end tyranny." No country was more closely identified with this doctrine than the United States, and no country did more to put it into practice, however unsatisfactory the actual results. Bush was wont to argue, as have most of his Democratic rivals, that these aspirations represent a set of universal truths that Americans have uttered "from the day of our Founding." It's in our DNA, opined former Vice President Joe Biden, justifying the Obama policy championing human rights against China.[54] Historical research will show, however, that the universal truths American leaders have embraced today are not the universal truths propounded by the Founders. The objective of "ending tyranny" through external military intervention stands athwart the classic American doctrine holding such an ambition to be "repugnant to the rights of nations, to the true principles of liberty, [and] to the freedom of opinion of mankind."[55] The self-evident truths of the Declaration of Independence—that all men are created equal and are endowed by the Creator with natural rights to life, liberty, and the pursuit of happiness—did not justify, for the author of the Declaration, the proposition that foreign states had any right to revolutionize another political order, even a tyrannical one. Jefferson also regarded it as a self-evident truth that all nations had the right to determine for themselves the form of government they would adopt. Wishing success to the possibility that the new states in South America would find their way to free government, Jefferson nevertheless insisted that "they have the right, and we none, to choose for themselves."[56]

For the Founders, the belief that the principles underlying the American experiment might have universal applicability existed happily alongside the idea that the United States had neither a right nor a duty to bring others to an appreciation of these truths through force. Rather than being contradictory, these ideas originated in the same school of thought. Like religious intolerance, the denial of legitimacy to other forms of government was seen to cause perpetual war, and such a condition made for an international environment hostile to the preservation and spread of free institutions. For all their arguments over the French Revolution, Hamilton and Jefferson understood that very well; both subscribed to Hamilton's derisory observation in the *Federalist* that "in politics, as in religion, it is equally absurd to aim at making proselytes by fire and sword. Heresies in either can rarely be cured by persecution."[57]

Pluralism and Liberal Internationalism

How and why the United States came to adopt such a revolutionary outlook in its approach to foreign policy is a difficult and indeed convoluted question. One might find precedents reaching back to the War of 1898, which began as a humanitarian intervention against Spanish depredations in Cuba but ended by wresting the Philippines away from Spain, which in turn led to a war against Filipino nationalists made indignant by the U.S. occupation. The U.S. record in Central America and the Caribbean, where it intervened often in the three decades after 1898, is also something of a precedent, though the motives for those interventions were seldom, if ever, revolutionary overthrow to install democracy. In the main, the Marines served as a "high class muscleman for Big Business," as the dissident Marine general Smedley Butler put it, or as a shield to enforce the Monroe Doctrine, preserving the Caribbean as an American lake in which the powers of Europe were not to tread. In the no-holds-barred competition with Communism during the Cold War, the United States intervened often, though usually covertly, for the purpose of overthrowing governments. It did so in Guatemala in 1954. It would not accept the results of the Cuban Revolution, and continued on with attempts to assassinate Fidel Castro after its failed Bay of Pigs intervention in 1961. It sent the Marines to the Dominican Republic in 1965 to prevent a "second Cuba"; it conspired against the government of Salvador Allende in Chile in the early 1970s; it organized the Contras against the Sandinistas in the 1980s. Given the profusion of justifications that have attended U.S. interventions over the last century, perhaps the most straightforward explanation is that the United States got into the habit of intervention and could always find some sort of reason to justify it, though there were also periods where a noninterventionist ethic held sway. After the Cold War ended and motives for restraint became much less compelling, the way was clear for a multitude of new doctrines making intervention seem necessary and just. What had previously been seen as episodic and uncharacteristic became common and pervasive.[58]

Despite a long though intermittent U.S. record of forcible regime change, it is worth contemplating how difficult it is to square the recent U.S. penchant for revolutionary overthrow with the ideals that previously animated liberal internationalism. Much of what the United States has done recently is alien to the outlook of the two great early figures of American internationalism in the twentieth century, Woodrow Wilson and Franklin Roosevelt.[59] Wilson and Roosevelt brought the United States into the two great world wars of the first half of the twentieth century; they overturned the long-standing American policy looking toward the separation of the United States from the center of the international system, which then lay in Europe. They wanted the United States, in the aftermath of these wars, to build a peaceful federative system that looked to the defeat of aggression as its first principle. The commitment to do so represented a fundamental change, but theirs was also a conservative vision with regard to the preservation of core principles of the society of states. It was to preserve those principles that collective action was called forth; neither Wilson nor Roosevelt can plausibly be identified as a democratic liberationist or humanitarian interventionist. To their conception of world order, they brought rather the new and exciting discovery America applied to the life of the individual—that free autonomous development for the world's states and peoples, within the framework of law, would best achieve security and prosperity for nations.[60]

Wilson, admittedly, is the most ambiguous case. In 1913, he abandoned the de facto recognition policy of the United States and took up the cudgels of "constitutional government" in Mexico, seeking to overturn the usurper Huerta. He occupied the Dominican Republic and Haiti in subsequent years. The latter two interventions, however, cannot be properly styled as interventions for democracy. As Theodore Roosevelt remarked at the time, "We have with armed force invaded, made war upon, and conquered the two small republics, have upset their governments, have denied them the right of self-determination, and have made democracy within their limits not merely unsafe but non-existent."[61] Even in the clearest case, Mexico, Wilson drew back from his initial enthusiasm for teaching the Latin Americans "to elect good men," and emerged as a stout opponent of military intervention there that would upset its government: "We shall have no right at any time to intervene in Mexico to determine the way in which the Mexicans are to settle their own affairs," he declared in 1914. There were "no conceivable circumstances which would make it right for us to direct by force or by threat of force the internal processes of what is a profound revolution, a revolution as profound as that which occurred in France."[62] He applied the same ideas to the Russian

Revolution. "My policy regarding Russia is very similar to my Mexican policy. I believe in letting them work out their own salvation, even though they wallow in anarchy for a while." [63] American diplomats and military officers resident in Russia did not share these views and gave significant support to forces fighting the Bolsheviks, but Wilson's idea of what he was doing is important and reveals a vital component of his international thought. In principle, you were supposed to stay out of other peoples' civil wars and domestic revolutions.

Wilson did make Germany's armistice conditional on the abdication of Kaiser Wilhelm, an insistence on democracy that had the grim though unforeseen consequence of saddling Weimar's rulers with responsibility for the "Diktat of Versailles." And Wilson did introduce into American hearts a millenarian and crusading purpose in his war to end all wars, associating it forever with the advance of democracy. But he also believed devoutly in the classic understanding affirming the right of each nation to find its own way to freedom. He insisted, in his war address, "The world must be made safe for democracy. Its peace must be planted upon the tested foundations of political liberty." This was not a program, however, for the forcible implantation of democracy everywhere, but of the need for concert among the democracies in the here and now. "I am not fighting for democracy except for the peoples that want democracy," Wilson observed in 1918. "If they don't want it, that is none of my business." [64]

Franklin Roosevelt is even less to be identified with the policy of "ending tyranny" through armed intervention. Instead, Roosevelt followed Herbert Hoover in adopting a policy of the Good Neighbor, one strictly founded on the principles of sovereignty and non-intervention. The American government under Hoover and Roosevelt had abandoned the policy introduced by Wilson and followed by Harding and Coolidge of refusing recognition to governments brought to power by extra-constitutional means. In the new era of the Good Neighbor policy, the Roosevelt administration instead embraced the "Estrada Doctrine," propounded by the Mexican minister for foreign affairs in 1934, that would accord recognition automatically to any government as it comes into power, recurring to the "de facto" standard that prevailed in the nineteenth century. [65] Roosevelt and his close assistant Sumner Welles opposed the view, proposed by some liberals, that the American government had been "gravely derelict" because it had not "pursued in the Western Hemisphere . . . a policy of 'revolutionary democracy.'" They rejected the idea that the United States "should have assisted in the overthrow of the established governments of the other American Republics in every case where they did not meet the requirements" of liberal opinion in the United States.[66]

The Western Hemisphere community that Roosevelt idealized could not accurately be described as a "democratic peace." Its foundation was not a common commitment to democracy but a common commitment to certain basic principles of international law. Though Latin America retained enough of the old Spanish liberalism to be recognizably of the West, its democratic institutions had faltered by the end of the 1930s, with a dozen states ruled by dictators. Those undemocratic tendencies, though discouraging, were not for Roosevelt an insuperable obstacle. "Peace reigns among us today because we have agreed, as neighbors should, to mind our own business. We have renounced, each and all of us, any right to interfere in each other's domestic affairs, recognizing that free and independent nations must shape their own destinies and find their own ways of life." In 1940, the Roosevelt administration identified five essential principles of the hemispheric order: "1. Respect for the integrity and importance of other States. 2. Self-restraint and acceptance of the equal rights of neighbors. 3. Non-intervention in the domestic affairs of neighboring States. 4. Settlement of disputes by friendly negotiation in accordance with justice and equity, rather than by force. 5. Provision for access to materials and opportunities necessary to a rising standard of living for all American peoples."[67] These principles of liberal pluralism remained the key to Roosevelt's outlook. Less than a year later, in his 1941 State of the Union Address, Roosevelt did give expression to the idea that there were universal human rights that should be enjoyed "everywhere in the world"—freedom of speech and worship, freedom from want and fear—but he did not include democracy among the universals, nor did he tie the growing recognition of such rights to U.S. sanctions.[68]

In the international legal order birthed by victory in the Second World War and the creation of the United Nations, the principles of the inter-American system were consecrated and universalized. Doing so meant that the right of external intervention had been sharply restricted; preventive war, in any normal definition of the term, was made illegal under the UN Charter. A right of humanitarian intervention might be inferred by the vast discretion given to the Security Council by the Charter, but few thought of inferring that until many years had passed. It contradicted the dominant emphasis in the Charter on state sovereignty and the rights and protections that followed from this principle. The right of self-determination in the Charter put the colonial powers on notice that their rule over peoples of color was coming to an end, but states were not deemed to have forfeited their right to put down internal revolts. When circumstances subsequently arose that in today's world would cry out for humanitarian intervention—as with Bangladesh, Cambodia, and Uganda—the intervening states (India, Vietnam, and Tanzania) appealed to their right of national self-defense, not humanity, in justifying their military movements across borders. That was because they believed the humanitarian claim would not cut it in the international community, not because they had poor legal advice.[69]

The constitution of the society of states emerged in Western civilization in the seventeenth and eighteenth centuries. The rules of sovereignty and non-intervention it prescribed for those within the community differed widely from those outside the charmed circle. The older Christian society of states allowed for the conquest and colonization of so-called non-civilized peoples; in effect, it created a gigantic exception to the rules of comity and fair play mandatory within the society of states.[70] The imperial presumption was challenged by a variety of Enlightenment thinkers, including Adam Smith, but to little effect on the policy of Europe's maritime powers.[71] The Europeans, convinced they were in the van of history, found no merit in the observation—advanced by the anti-imperialist Goldwin Smith in 1902—that "the uncivilized or half-civilized races now being crushed by predatory powers in different parts of the world" might "have in them the germs of something which, spontaneously developed, would be as noble and worth as much to humanity as any of the powers themselves."[72]

This historic injustice, under U.S. prodding, was at last rectified in the second half of the twentieth century, a very considerable accomplishment of the legal system bequeathed by the UN Charter and postwar decolonization.[73] But it would be a mistake to say that this system of law and the core notion of the society of states embodied within it represented an alien imposition by the West upon the Rest, as colonization and conquest had previously done. In fact, the Rest accepted international society on the condition that they could join it, from the 1950s on. They embraced the "reformed Westphalianism" of the UN Charter. Dissatisfied with their position as "drawers of water and hewers of wood" within the international economic order, they wanted a redistribution of resources to aid their economic development, demands encapsulated in the "New International Economic Order" projected by the Global South, without consequence, in the 1970s. But they warmed, as weaker states have traditionally done, to the principles of international law privileging state sovereignty and non-intervention. They became especially emphatic about this just about the time, in the 1980s and 1990s, when the West was sloughing off the old rules as increasingly irrelevant to new challenges.

During the Cold War, the basic challenge to Charter principles came not from small states but from the superpowers. The Soviet Union crushed movements for national independence in Hungary (1956) and Czechoslovakia (1968). It also lent its support, in 1960, to armed revolution in support of national liberation—a doctrine the United States then regarded as deeply threatening to international order, so much so that it massively intervened in Vietnam to resist it. In theory, the United States was as committed as ever to international law; in practice, not so much. In his 1953 Inaugural Address, Dwight Eisenhower said: "Honoring the identity and the special heritage of each nation in the world, we shall never use our strength to try to impress upon another people our own cherished political and economic institutions." In the sequel, Eisenhower gave the CIA carte blanche to overturn governments or foster rebellion in Iran, Guatemala, Iraq, Indonesia, and China. The spirit of these enterprises was well conveyed in the report on the CIA prepared by General Jimmy Doolittle, delivered to Eisenhower on October 19, 1954. The United States, Doolittle believed, faced "an implacable enemy whose avowed objective is world domination by whatever means and whatever cost. There are no rules in such a game. Hitherto acceptable norms of human conduct do not apply. If the United States is to survive, long-standing American concepts of 'fair play' must be reconsidered."[74] That these interventions were conducted in secret attests to the hold that Charter principles still exercised in the public imagination, but undoubtedly, the violations subtly undermined these older conceptions of legitimacy.

By the 1980s, Ronald Reagan had come to embrace support for armed groups seeking to overthrow communist governments (in Afghanistan, Nicaragua, Angola, and Cambodia), a departure from international law but one that could in some of these cases be justified as interventions to counter the illegal interventions of others. But Reagan was not really concerned with these legalistic niceties; he wanted to impose costs on the Soviet Union and to win the Cold War. His administration refused to participate in the lawsuit brought by Nicaragua in the International Court of Justice and ignored the subsequent verdict of that tribunal, declaring illegal the covert U.S. mining of Nicaraguan harbors. In other fields of life, violations of norms have the effect of reinforcing the importance of the norms—an increase in the murder rate, for example, does not usually yield the conclusion that murder is suddenly okay, but rather the reverse. In statecraft, however, the bad more easily drives out the good—"Foreign affairs," as Wilson sagely put it, "certainly cause a man to be profane."[75]

The U.S. interventions in the Cold War era, even if usually rationalized as counter-interventions, helped prepare the ground, after the end of the Cold War and the emergence of unipolarity, for a new interventionist creed. What followed was not a single doctrine authorizing intervention but a multitude of new doctrines. One held that the "sole superpower" must respond, if necessary by military force, to acts or prospective acts that shocked humanitarian sensibilities (Bosnia in 1995, Kosovo in 1999); another was the legitimacy of using force to restore democracy (Haiti in 1994). Though the fullest and most militarized expression of extending democracy through force had to await Bush's second inaugural in 2005, the groundwork was laid in the 1980s and 1990s. A bundle of other justifications—seizing drug kingpins (Panama in 1989), averting famine (Somalia in 1992), preventing nuclear proliferation (Iraq in 1991 and 2003)—accompanied these transformations. The traditional prohibition against intervention that was consecrated in 1919 and reaffirmed in 1945 was thus greatly relaxed, and then virtually abandoned. A whole host of interventions were pursued or proposed in the 25 years after 1989 that took, amid the plenitude of justifications offered, the most convenient route to the sea.

Realism, Liberalism, and the Legal Order

The rationale of democratic liberation that the Bush administration offered for the invasion of Iraq was a real and not "made up" reason for the war. It was not discovered ex post facto, after finding no WMD, but was present from the outset as a key justification and motivation for many people both inside and outside the administration. Attention was heightened toward the liberationist rationale after the security rationale collapsed, but it was there from the beginning. It looked toward a vast political reconstruction of the region that would leave the United States, in its victorious aftermath, with the power to coerce others.[76] Though it greatly appealed to American neoconservatives and liberal hawks, however, democratic liberationism is not at all accepted outside the West. Even inside the West, it has faced a skeptical public opinion.

More widely accepted in the world as a rationale for intervention today is military action that is conducted for humanitarian purposes—that is, to relieve ongoing acts of brutality that rise to war crimes and that the international community must punish and stop. Beginning with the commission sponsored by the Canadian government that articulated the conception of the responsibility to protect, R2P received modified acceptance from the United Nations in 2005, though, in fact, sharp divisions exist in the international community over its true scope. The political influence of these doctrines is pronounced: ideas of humanitarian responsibility drove the intervention in Libya and were of critical importance in framing the Obama administration's approach to the Syrian civil war.[77]

At the root of this debate are conflicting perspectives on the maintenance of world order. One view stresses state sovereignty and the traditional law of nations safeguarding independence and the autonomy of domestic actions; the other entails the championing of a single standard of political legitimacy rooted in democracy and universal human rights. One side accords an essential protection to the self-determination of nations, leaving responsibility for their internal affairs in their hands. The other holds that "brutal regimes must not be allowed to hide behind the principles of state sovereignty and non-intervention," and justifies external intervention in response to war crimes.[78]

The form this controversy has assumed in the present age has its own peculiar features, but the argument itself has a long and distinguished lineage. It might also be termed a dispute pitting particularism against universalism, "pluralism" against "solidarism," "polycentricity" against "unipolarity," nationalism against globalism, or independence against empire, but international history displays many variations on the theme. Four centuries ago, Paulo Sarpi, the Venetian friar, articulated in his contest with the Pope a defense of particularism and the liberty of states that the contemporary pluralist easily recognizes.[79] American leaders in the century after 1776 confronted very similar issues and resolved them, as we have seen, in a decidedly pluralist vein. But each side in the contemporary debate, if it wishes, can find plenty of precedents. The defense of humanitarian intervention by Grotius and Gladstone shows that past authority may be found on the other side of the debate as well.

The debate is oddly miscast in the United States today. Realists insist that intervention is bad because it is contrary to self-interest. Though it may indeed be such—I think so, too—the more important objection is that it violates basic principles of international order. But realists, offensive and defensive, seldom put the objection in those terms. They have difficulty speaking in a pluralist vein. Defensive realists stress, persuasively, the disutility of military force, the power of indigenous resistance, the danger of lighting fires that the incendiaries don't know how to put out, the folly of preventive wars, the gap between professed intent and actual result. They do not appreciate, however, that the very points they raise against the project of intervention were embedded within the traditional law on the subject. Instead of casting aspersions against it, they should realize they have an ally in traditional international law, not an enemy. Its rules against intervention and preventive war are their rules. They should embrace it and defend it against the new interlopers, not spurn it.[80]

Whereas traditional international law has been either ignored or demeaned by those who ought to be its friends, it has been transformed beyond all recognition by its supposed champions, the liberal internationalists. Liberal internationalists have made a law (or made up a law) at fundamental cross purposes with the law of the UN Charter, with its emphasis on non-intervention and state sovereignty. They have imposed, often by fiat, new rules for international law that amount to a fundamental overthrow of what were once its basic presuppositions. Under this new dispensation, a key assumption of traditional international law—which accorded to each state the right to defend itself—has been totally vitiated in practice. In effect, the new rules dictate that an autocratic regime threatened by armed rebellion has no right to prolong its miserable existence, that its duty is to expire, and that failure to do so constitutes a breach of the law, justifying external intervention or aid to armed insurgents. This is the law the liberal interventionists sought to impose on Assad, even at the outset of the civil war, when there were comparatively few casualties. It is the law the Western powers did impose on Qaddafi, *in anticipation of* horrendous cruelties. We are a far cry from the traditional legal view that privileged the sovereignty of the state and made it a bulwark of internal and international order. The anarchy that has ensued as the old policy has been overthrown is a testament to the values and theorems embedded in the traditional rule—it is far from representing the "barren," "arid," and "legalistic" formula so often caricatured. Its advocates had always stared long and hard into the pit of anarchy.[81]

The classic rules prescribed by international law toward civil wars presumed that these were best resolved by the locals themselves, without outside intervention. That was a normative judgment rooted in the importance of self-determination, not simply a practical one, though it was certainly reinforced by a wide variety of prudential considerations. Though the larger posture of the law was neutrality in the face of conflicts that outsiders invariably had trouble understanding, its bias was toward the preservation of existing authority, not revolution. It permitted military aid to an existing state but looked with great skepticism on aid to rebels. The displacement of that older law has meant that civil wars, once outside the ambit of legitimate external intervention, have been annexed to the logic of collective security, creating a presumptive duty to intervene whenever there are atrocities in civil wars, or even fears of such atrocities, as there always are. That America is never impartial in its approach to these wars, adopting instead a highly biased view according to sentiment or interest, does nothing seemingly to lessen the appeal of the idea that its right and duty is to intervene in the affairs of others, and even to encourage and precipitate revolution. According to the traditional law, such conduct was emphatically a breach of its obligations.[82]

It is widely accepted as a criticism of a pluralistic international order that it must rest on the fragile, if not entirely disreputable, ground of moral relativism, whereby it is impossible to make a moral judgment save as an assertion of will and not reason. This objection entirely misapprehends the foundations of a pluralistic legal order, which rests on the priority of peace and cooperation among groupings that invariably maintain conflicting visions of justice. Pluralism, notes international legal scholar Brad Roth, "far from being based on any notion of moral relativism or skepticism, is based on a claim for the objective moral significance of the (equally objective) existence and (potentially ruinous) consequences of moral disagreement." The real issue in regard to the rules of sovereign equality and nonintervention, as Roth notes, "is not abstention from moral judgment or even political pressure, but rather presumptive abstention from a limited set of unilateral coercive measures amounting to dictatorial interference in the internal affairs of a foreign political community."[83] A pluralist view does not dictate indifference to human rights; it allows states to afford shelter to dissidents throughout the world and to take in refugees from oppression to their heart's delight. What it does not allow is coercive intervention in a foreign country to secure these rights.

Advocates for humanitarian intervention have made a bid to establish it as a widely accepted norm, but their efforts have met with indifferent success. It is true that a watered down version of R2P was included in the "Outcomes Document" of the UN General Assembly session in 2005, attesting to the idea that the international community cannot be indifferent to genocide and other war crimes. Beyond the expression of moral concern, however, the UN fell well short of adopting the recommendations of the international commission recommending R2P, especially its suggestion that a regional organization like NATO might legitimately authorize such interventions. In the document ultimately agreed upon, as Rajan Menon has noted, "Security Council approval was made a prerequisite for the implementation of any R2P measures. The international community was required only to 'encourage and advise' states to discharge their responsibility to protect, and no obligations were placed upon UN member states. No wiggle room was provided for unilateral intervention. No explicit reference was made to the use of military means for enforcement."[84]

In truth, the putative "global consensus" for humanitarian military intervention does not exist outside the West; even within the West, support for it is thin. Russia, China, India, Brazil, and South Africa, along with much of Global South, reject the notions of legitimate intervention widely prevalent in the West's chancelleries, universities, and think tanks. There is no reason to believe that the attitudes of their people differ essentially from those of their governments on this question (though that is often assumed by those who wish to trifle with the sentiments of so large a portion of the human race). Non-Western opinion is keenly aware "that the world today suffers the painful consequences of interventions that have aggravated existing conflicts, allowed terrorism to penetrate into places where it previously did not exist, given rise to new cycles of violence and increased the vulnerability of civilian populations," as Brazil noted in a November 2011 letter to the United Nations ("Responsibility While Protecting").[85] The precarious legal standing of Western powers on these issues, however, is not widely appreciated. The media repeats without comment the devotionals of U.S. officials to international law and the rule-based order; for violations, one has to search the blogosphere. Entirely obscured from view is the contest between an old international law, still valid but pressed now mostly by America's adversaries, and a new, aspirational international law that breaks down the barriers the old law had erected.

Though the sentiments that have underpinned the movement for humanitarian intervention are admirable—genocide, crimes against humanity, intentional targeting of civilians are indeed atrocious things—we have now accumulated a very impressive record, not available to enthusiasts in the 1990s, that shows the grave difficulties and unanticipated consequences flowing from the attempt to reconstruct foreign societies by force, whatever the motive. Serial interventions in Afghanistan, Iraq, Libya, and Syria have led to the overthrow (or near overthrow) of hostile regimes, but have nowhere succeeded in re-establishing the bases of domestic order. All these countries are in conditions of civil war, for which no resolution seems anywhere in sight. The interventions had various motives, of which "humanitarianism" had top billing only in Libya and Syria, but in all cases the central purpose of the U.S. effort was said to be service to the cause of democracy and human rights. In the name of giving them the best, the United States has helped deliver unto the people of these countries the very worst—the anarchy, sedition, and general mayhem of civil war.[86]

That humanitarian intervention can go badly awry is shown by the consequences of the 2011 intervention in Libya. Though the initial steps were approved by the UN Security Council (with Russia, China, Germany, India, and Brazil abstaining), the Western intervention soon morphed into a six-month campaign to topple Qaddafi (going far beyond the initial authorization, and leaving the skeptical powers feeling used and deceived). "We came, we saw, he died," in Hillary Clinton's aptly Caesarist formulation. The Libyan intervention was a project, especially, of the three most important women on Obama's national security team—Secretary of State Clinton, UN Ambassador Susan Rice, and NSC staffer Samantha Power. They persuaded Obama over the objections of the civilian and military leadership at the Pentagon. For the R2P brigade, the Libyan intervention was all about preventing another Rwanda. Their evidence that Qaddafi intended anything of the kind, however, consisted simply of their accusations and statements of Qaddafi ripped from their cultural context. The interventionists, inside the government and out, women and men, were utterly heedless of the consequences of destroying central state institutions, preferring a fairy-tale version of the Libyan scene to the reality of the splintered-up anarchy the Western intervention brought about. When Pandora's box was opened, it turned out to contain a great many weapons. Their distribution from Qaddafi's arsenals dramatically worsened the terrorist threat in Africa, both north and south of the Sahara. The results from the Libyan intervention have been little short of catastrophic, with the country subsequently given over to civil war and with ISIS for a time establishing a strong foothold amid the ruins. The intervention, with all its terrible consequences for regional stability and Libya itself, was a crime, with the only exculpation being that the advocates had no idea what they were doing and the consequences it would have.[87]

In Syria, the United States also pursued the strategy of overthrow in the name of humanitarianism. By August 2011, it made Assad's removal the keystone of its policy. Ambassador Susan Rice made a furious denunciation at the United Nations in October, accusing Russia of criminal neglect for refusing to support the enterprise. U.S. Ambassador to Syria Robert Ford spread promises of U.S. diplomatic support among those who demanded Assad's overthrow, venturing into the crowds to show solidarity. But beneath the veneer of humanitarian concern lay strategic calculation. Wrote Hillary Clinton in April 2012: "The best way to help Israel deal with Iran's growing nuclear capability is to help the people of Syria overthrow the regime of Bashar Assad." Checkmate against Iran, and a regime friendly to Israel in Damascus, were among the expected benefits. From early 2012, the American government helped facilitate arms shipments to the resistance, paid for by the Saudis and their affiliates. The U.S. was opposed to the transfer of arms to groups it deemed terrorists, including ISIS (a.k.a. ISIL, subsequently the Islamic State) and the Nusra Front, but it was not opposed to the transfer of arms as such; it tried to direct the flow of supplies to so-called moderates, but much of the arms ended up in the hands of Nusra and ISIS. Despite the presence from the outset of radical Sunni jihadists doing their best to kill Assad's forces—not all the demonstrators were peaceful—the United States and its mainstream media blamed Assad for all the violence, including all the killings visited on his own forces, nearly half the total number of casualties. Advocates for this policy widely entertained the false notion that Assad would be quickly deposed, underestimating his considerable domestic support, even among Sunnis, and making the initial steps favoring overthrow easy to take, but guaranteeing a protracted civil war once Assad received outside support from Russia, Iran, and Hezbollah (as he was entitled to do under international law). Obama gravely disappointed the national security complex by not going in much deeper—the brilliant plan of the security establishment was to do to Damascus what was previously done to Belgrade in 1999 and Baghdad in 1991—but the American role, even in the absence of this dire escalation, was hardly negligible. In addition to what it did directly, the United States gave crucial diplomat cover for all the efforts, from so many different sources, to overthrow Assad. Perhaps more inadvertently than otherwise, but with real effect, it raised up strong hopes among many Syrians that the United States would "do a Libya," thus encouraging the rebellion (and producing, among those to whom support was pledged, feelings of deep betrayal).[88]

Ironically, most of the objections that may be entertained against humanitarian intervention were stated in the report seeking to establish "the responsibility to protect" as a global norm. So far as military intervention is concerned, "right authority, just cause, right intention, last resort, proportional means, and reasonable prospects" were all invoked as relevant barriers to the decision to intervene. The Commission conceded that all members of the United Nations have an interest in maintaining a stable international order, and that this interest, save in exceptional circumstances, is best satisfied by abstaining from military intervention. Justifying a cautious approach were requirements that force be disinterested and restricted to the humanitarian aim; that its use be proportional in weighing the consequences of intervention; that it should be employed only in the last resort and use means that discriminate between the guilty and the innocent; that multilateral support is a vital factor in legitimating such enterprises and seeing them through. Despite these sonorous words, no intervention of the past two decades has satisfied all these conditions; they have proved a virtually meaningless impediment to intervention.[89]

Two things the report missed: one is that holding out the prospect of external intervention can itself be a spur to domestic rebellion. Instead of discouraging violent revolts, it encourages them. In addition, any outside intervention will objectively favor one of the parties to the fight, nullifying any prospect of an apolitical intervention restricted to humanitarian aims.[90]

Virtually the sole success in 25 years of humanitarian intervention—entailing "peace enforcement" as opposed to "peace-keeping"—was the Bosnian settlement achieved at Dayton, Ohio, in 1995. The Bosnian intervention worked in 1995 because the military instrument was combined with a more or less realistic diplomacy recognizing the principle of self-determination as a mode of settling civil wars. Richard Holbrooke played his hand skillfully in producing a settlement, his performance having been memorialized by several observers, including himself. The trouble with Holbrooke's approach is that he didn't go far enough, allowing the Republika Srpska to merge with Serbia, the Croatian parts with Croatia. No offense to the late Ambassador Holbrooke, in whose hands this decision did not really rest, but the insistence on making the old borders of Yugoslavia's federation the new borders of independent states—seizing on territorial integrity as the be-all-and-end-all, after it had already utterly broken down—was an injustice and a blunder. It denied the right of self-determination for no good reason, increasing the burden on outside occupiers—the EU is still there ruling the place—and keeping up rather than settling the issues arising from the war. Nor should deserved praise for Holbrooke's effort disguise the censure due to U.S. diplomacy in the preceding years. The United States seized hold of Western diplomacy over Bosnia early on, but it took three years for it to adopt a sensible political stance. From April 1992, when the Bush administration pushed the European diplomats aside with the snide declaration that the Europeans couldn't organize a three-car caravan if their lives depended on it, until 1995, when policy shifted, the official U.S. stance was that a unitary, sovereign state would be created in Bosnia, with hardly any acknowledgment of a principle of decentralization. When U.S. officials figured out that they had to acknowledge at least some Serbian rights to self-rule, even when kicking the Serbs, the war was brought to an end.[91]

In the abstract, it seems impossible to wholly forbid humanitarian intervention in every instance. Never say never, as someone once said. But it is imperative that Western publics acknowledge the evil in a state of things in which it is always a great question whether to start bombing and to support insurgencies, in the event terrible things happen abroad, and whether we do or not depends on some sensational shocker, featured on CNN or in the *New York Times*, that disarms the skeptics, after which we have no choice but to see it through, with ignorant airforces bombing by night and with the establishment of civil order given over to chance. The worst part of it is the dynamic whereby the promise of external aid becomes itself a motive for rebellion, a dynamic that strongly figured in both Libya and Syria.

One of the lessons the international community should have learned over the last fifteen years—something that was at least contestable in the 1990s—is that the institutional capacity to undertake such interventions is totally lacking. That does not mean that the U.S. could throw resources at the problem and get it up to snuff, but that there are inherently limits to ordering the region through U.S. military power. Even the national security establishment sees the problem. In the well-known summary of Phillip Gordon, former National Security Council (NSC) staffer: "In Iraq, the U.S. intervened and occupied, and the result was a costly disaster. In Libya, the U.S. intervened and did not occupy, and the result was a costly disaster. In Syria, the U.S. neither intervened nor occupied, and the result is a costly disaster."[92] Given the U.S. calls for the removal of Assad and the green light it gave to its Sunni allies to funnel arms to the resistance, it is rather absurd to call the U.S. record in Syria one of non-intervention, as Gordon does, but the record of failure, as he insists, is apparent. What all these interventions had in common in prospect was the belief that state overthrow would yield a more humanitarian and more just outcome. What they show in retrospect is that the traditional rules of international law offer a superior guide for defusing conflict in foreign lands and that both international order and American security would have been better secured by observing those rules, rather than flouting them.

Despite this grim record, liberal interventionists cling to the idea that there must, in principle, be circumstances in which humanitarian intervention is fully justified. In effect, the analytical community has adopted a sort of "act utilitarianism," with no conception about how to actually bring about any good at all, and very little contrition over the disasters for which its vaunted humanitarianism is directly responsible. Oddly, such disasters seem not to prejudice the case for intervention, in principle. All right-thinking people remain committed to it, in principle. A different conclusion would be to recognize that investing such discretion in governments, especially the American government, is an experiment that has been tried and failed, and that what we need now is a barrier against coercive intervention that removes discretion from governments and binds them down from mischief by the chains of an inviolable rule.[93]

IT WOULD BE misleading to leave the impression that American policy in the Greater Middle East, in the main, has been guided by humanitarian concerns or that it has looked to international law for sustenance in fashioning an approach. In fact, the initial response to the 9/11 attacks by the Bush administration betrayed a strong desire to cast legal and humanitarian considerations to the four winds. Bush—together with a coalition of neoconservatives, assertive nationalists, and "new sovereigntists"—stressed the irrelevance of these restraints in the name of national safety. Theirs was the ancient plea of necessity, and of the right of the United States to take whatever measures it deemed necessary to ensure its security. As Carl Schmitt once emphasized, the real holder of sovereignty gets to decide the exception, and in doing so frees the executive from any legal restraints. The Bush-Cheney view proposed that the United States could itself declare a state of exception (or state of emergency) for international society as a whole, with its president perfectly free to intervene at will. Even among Bush supporters, there were those who rejected this approach and insisted on conformity with standards of international law—making for a lively legal debate within the administration—but even those wanting adherence to law accepted as axiomatic that the old prohibition against intervention was irrelevant to the new circumstances. Their dissent concerned mostly the means, the realm of *jus in bello*, not the ends of *jus ad bellum*. They objected especially to the Bush administration's allowance of torture. They did not dispute the license given to state overthrow.

These rival critiques of the old international law, from the humanitarian interventionists to the neo-imperialists, are very different in key respects: one elevates the law, the other denigrates it. Both, however, supported the interventionist disposition and put their combined weight behind the strategy of overthrow. In theory, it is easy to separate the plea of necessity from the plea of humanitarianism; in practice, they have been hopelessly intermingled in America's long string of interventions in the Greater Middle East, sometimes in support of the strategy of overthrow, at other times for more limited aims. Both appeals lit up the road that led from the great triumph of 1991 to Somalia, Bosnia, Kosovo, Afghanistan, Iraq (again), and then on to Pakistan, Libya, Syria, Yemen, Iraq (again), and northern Africa. In nearly all of these, some appeal to American security was on the table; some appeal to transcendent moral standards was as well. Together, those made an irresistible force.

Whether undertaken to serve ourselves or to serve humanity, there remains the dismal record: complete failure to achieve the objects announced at the beginning of these wars. The wars against terrorism in Afghanistan and Iraq have fared no better than the humanitarian interventions. America's war in Afghanistan has been an especially grim illustration of the disutility of military force, all the more so because it was almost universally approved at home as a justified response to the attacks of September 11, 2001. Obama in his 2008 election campaign treated it as the good war, in contrast to the bad Iraqi one, and pledged to win it. But it has not been won, with the Taliban at the end of Obama's presidency in a stronger position than at any time since 2002. Osama bin Laden had set in motion the 9/11 attacks from his camps in Afghanistan, so *a war* was eminently justifiable, but *the war* actually undertaken sought not simply retaliation for the offense but the entire reconstruction of Afghani government and society in accordance with U.S. conceptions of human rights, especially democratic elections and the treatment of women. One political culture, in effect, was to be grafted on to another, with force the indispensable bearer of the gift and the Taliban entirely uprooted. Instead of making a separation between the Taliban and Al-Qaeda the purpose of U.S. strategy, the U.S. government treated the Taliban as having co-equal responsibility, though the Taliban had plenty of grievances against bin Laden and might have given him up. Even if Taliban leader Mullah Omar's offer to hand bin Laden over to another Islamic country for trial was insincere, the separation between the two groups was a plausible alternative that could have avoided a prolonged occupation, but one in which the Bush administration officials displayed utterly no interest. Instead, they wanted a big demonstration of the utility of U.S. force.[94]

Once at war, the U.S. ignored the willingness of many Taliban forces to come in and acquiesce to a new regime in Kabul. The U.S. war machine was uninterested in trying to communicate with the Taliban and explore possibilities of a political settlement with them; its purpose from the outset was simply to extirpate them.[95] Since the Taliban find their support in the some 40 million Pashtuns who inhabit Afghanistan and Pakistan, they had a potentially immense base to call upon for volunteers (and a covert governmental apparatus in Pakistan—the notorious Inter-Services Intelligence or ISI—to look after them.) Much of the commentary on U.S. operations has assumed that there was, in principle, a military strategy that would defeat the Taliban, but the deeper truth is that any strategy from outside occupation forces, accustomed to bestow firepower liberally, would have had grave difficulty in "winning" in this graveyard of empires, given the strategic depth of the adversary and the intense resentment that U.S. firepower induced. The Taliban's obvious strategy was to "not lose" and wait for America to tire of seeking to achieve the unrealizable.

The sheer incapacity of force to achieve objectives of "nation-building" after "regime change" was also on display in Iraq. When the war turned ugly, the Bush administration received a drumbeat of criticism over various failures in military planning—that an insufficient number of U.S. forces were used, that it was a mistake to disband the Iraqi army, that the persecution of the Baathists was pushed way too far. Supporters of the war who were disgusted by the mounting carnage understandably wanted to blame George Bush, Donald Rumsfeld, and Paul Bremer for mistakes in execution, but the larger truth is that the U.S. occupier would have likely faced anarchy, rebellion, and civil war whatever choices it made. If it did not persecute the Baathists, it would alienate the Shia. If it gave the Shia the power that their demographic weight dictated, it would alienate the Sunni. In the event, it managed to alienate both. The emergence of three de facto mini-states—of Kurdistan, Shiastan, and Sunnistan—occurred immediately after the fall of the regime, and corresponded to the logic of self-protection the breakage of the state had induced. In fighting the war, U.S. forces could never hope to overcome the antagonism between the occupiers and the occupied arising from the imperatives of "force protection"—which inevitably creates in the locals the sense that their lives aren't worth a damn to the occupiers. Such occupying forces also face the contradiction of relying on force for everything they do, yet preaching peace and reconciliation when attempting to build democratic institutions. The locals notice that, too—that is, what really counts for the occupier. Having observed and implemented the rule of the gun, America's liberal professions fell on deaf ears in Iraq; instead, its aggressive military occupation gave strength to extremist forces who took up guns and bombs in response.[96]

It was often alleged after 9/11 that the old rules of the society of states were relegated to a quaint though dangerous anachronism by the emergence of mass terrorism, and so did officialdom believe. The old rules dictating the inviolability of territorial integrity and the right of every state to defend itself were cast overboard, rendered an insignificant obstacle to the use of force. Wherever the terrorists were—some said they were entrenched in as many as 60 countries—we'd track them down and kill them. The results of these methods have been poor indeed. The two occupations in Afghanistan and Iraq, followed by the great upsurge in drone strikes under Obama, have seeded the growth of terrorist groups rather than extinguished them, playing directly into the strategy—eliminate the grey line—embraced by Al-Qaeda and ISIS. The appeal reaches to the West's own citizens, inviting a cycle of repression and alienation (and such attacks as Fort Hood, Boston, San Bernardino,

Paris, Nice, and Orlando). It is not obvious how to escape the dialectic of hatred and revenge gravely accelerated by America's long-standing wars in the Greater Middle East, but caution in the use of force has to be part of the answer. Also imperative is a policy that avoids the demonization of Islam, an idea that Bush and Obama always found obvious but that was cynically discarded by Trump during his 2016 campaign.[97]

Advocates of drone strikes point to their incredible precision and contrast it with the massive destruction of cities that occurred in World War II, touting technological innovation as a great symbol of moral progress. But the expectation that technological wizardry permits a cleaner and more just way of conducting war, so often highlighted by the advocates of force, has not survived contact with the enemy. In the prelude to the wars in Afghanistan and Iraq, the public was assured that the United States would conduct its military operations with unprecedented discrimination, avoiding civilian casualties; in the sequel, civilian casualties in Iraq and Afghanistan numbered in the hundreds of thousands, outpaced in number only by a tidal wave of refugees. The expectation that a new way of war had been discovered played a key role in easing the consciences of those advocating force. A stricter view of *jus in bello*, perfumed by technological advance, allowed a more expansive view of *jus ad bellum*, with tragic results.[98]

In their actual use, the differences between precise but more powerful explosives and crude but less powerful explosives—between smart bombs and barrel bombs—are often insignificant. The wasteland made in Kobani, Fallujah, Ramadi, or Mosul by smart bombs is not appreciably different from the wasteland made in Homs or Aleppo by barrel bombs. The result mainly depends on the enemy and how he chooses to fight. Destructive though city-taking uses of force are, they are at least designed to take territory, making reconstruction theoretically possible. Drones strikes in Yemen or Pakistan or other lawless frontiers, by contrast, effect no change in who controls the territory attacked, and produce much sympathy among aggrieved bystanders. Almost by definition, they hold out the prospect of endless war; there will always be more targets (and more martyrs to avenge). Strategically, the likelihood that drone strikes add to enemy sympathizers, as U.S. officials military officers have conceded that these terrifying attacks often do, makes them counterproductive. Often based on limited intelligence and guesswork—witness the numerous wedding parties blown up over the last fifteen years—precise aerial attacks inevitably entail random death to civilians, sparking local outrage. They seem to be driven more by a need to show that American leaders are tough enough to use force than by the prospective achievement of a concrete political object. In the main, America's drone wars appear to have put aside the central rule of *jus ad bellum*: that the purpose of war is peace.[99]

The terrorism of Al-Qaeda and ISIS is indeed horrific, making them enemies of the human race, *hostis humani generis*, as the old category in the law of nations put it. Even the principled non-interventionist must feel a need to cooperate in the war against these groups, while mourning the inadvertent role America played in their birth and sustenance. But the idea of terrorism has been debased by its indiscriminate use. It now refers to a wide range of states and peoples who are no more terroristic than America's friends, nor even of the United States itself.[100] The propagandistic use of the "terrorist" label has made the term fundamentally useless as a geopolitical category, though U.S. policy, prodded by Israel, elevated it into the most important one. Most insidiously, the charge of terrorism has been used obnoxiously as a moral sledgehammer to dehumanize others. Instead of real political movements composed of national communities, each with their own grievances and aspirations—such as Palestinians, Lebanese, Syrians, or Iranians—we have substituted a slur intended to deprive these entities of any legitimacy, and against which force and fraud may, in principle, be employed to the maximum. As against this tendency, one must appeal to the equality in national and political rights once willingly bestowed by liberalism. All too often, the United States becomes, in effect, just another ethnic group in the conduct of its foreign policy, latching on to the enmities of "allies" as if they were holy writ, and seeking to deprive enemy nations of the rights bestowed by nature, of which the right to self-preservation is foremost. In making the case against these groups, Americans are happy to pluck incidents from 40 years of history to demonstrate some essential evil in the other side, passing over in silence the injuries done to them, all for the purpose of making any dialogue with the adversary appear alternately pointless or craven. This mode of proceeding is deeply illiberal.

Ironically, recognition that areas of anarchy, or of "failed states," were dangerous to international security was a key justification for relaxing rules against intervention in the 1990s; then, in the new millennium, the United States set about inadvertently creating a lot more of them. The role that functioning states play in the suppression of terrorism was ignored; blowing them away was something that neo-Machiavellians and neo-Kantians could agree on. In the event, we learned again that the only thing worse than a bad state is no state at all, and that effective statehood must be an essential building block of international order. Violating that long-standing precept, and incapable of creating something decent in the aftermath, the United States exacerbated the threat of terrorism in the name of squashing it.

AMERICA'S WARS TO save humanity and to fight terror have left its relation to the international legal order deeply troubled. Projects to revolutionize it have come from the left; projects to abandon it have come from the right. The nation and the world would be better served by rejecting both nostrums and returning to the pluralist prescriptions of the UN Charter.

Apart from humanitarian intervention or R2P, the most important institutional transformation in the post-Cold War era was the institution of the International Criminal Court (ICC). The Bill Clinton presidency began the charge for this reformation, though the United States balked in the end and refused U.S. participation. The trouble with the ICC is two-fold. That it has become, in practice, the African Criminal Court points to one key problem: its fundamental lack of reciprocity. In effect, its remit is reserved for the least powerful, as the more powerful can secure effective immunity from its jurisdiction. It violates thereby a fundamental principle of law. The more consequential flaw stems from the possibility that a looming prosecution may obstruct the devices often necessary in a political settlement. The offer to a terrible dictator—go away and live out your life in an obscure village—cannot be persuasively offered, as it may be trumped by an ICC prosecution. If mediators can only say that he's a dead man either way, he will probably prefer to die in his boots than expire in a pin-striped suit at The Hague. The practical necessities of settling conflict through negotiation will usually require a mutual waiving of certain injuries, not resting on forgetfulness as such but on the necessity, if peace is to be had, of not pursuing justice to the ends of the earth and the end of time.[101]

The failures of the right are equally notable. Here, we find an impatience with the very idea of international law. In these precincts, it is more the object of humor than anything else. But that dictatorial states have served as chairs of the UN Commission on Human Rights does not invalidate the wise precepts of the UN Charter, which had their inspiration more in American ideas than in those of any other nation. The new sovereigntists, with their extravagant conceptions of an America unbound by legal restraint, set forth an unpersuasive vision of the international legal order and America's role in it, one that prizes both executive overreach and legislative recalcitrance. They have asserted a sort of boundless prerogative in the use of force and in the process have quite confounded the legal issue. In law, the consent of the Security

Council is *not* required for defensive uses of force; nothing in the Charter for-bids the inherent right of states to self-defense. Such consent *is* required for uses of force otherwise illegal (humanitarian intervention, preventive war). In recent times, however, no U.S. presidents have been willing to constrain themselves on that score, an attitude seconded by neoconservatives and new sovereigntists alike.[102]

The scare that the new sovereigntists have raised of UN-sponsored interna-tional treaties is also unpersuasive. Such treaties as are submitted by presidents wither on the vine, since the two-thirds supermajority required to ratify trea-ties has been in virtually all cases unobtainable. The U.S. Senate—or at least its stubborn bloc of Republican nay-sayers—has wished, in effect, to affirm no common values with the rest of the world, for the declarations of rights entailed by these scorned treaties usually do not entail serious constraints that encroach on America's effective freedom of action in legislative acts or judicial decision. Those that do, such as UN Convention on the Law of the Sea, entail reciprocal restraints that the country should willingly accept. Yet UNCLOS remains unratified by the U.S. Senate after all these years.

In ratifying human rights treaties (such as those governing the rights of the child, or of women, or of people with disabilities), states have the option of restricting their reach in domestic law through various reserva-tions, understandings, and clarifications, as the Senate did in 1992 in ratify-ing the International Covenant on Civil and Political Rights. Rather than a cudgel to force states to conform, such treaties represent, in practice, a conversation among nation-states about how to state norms of conduct to which all can consent but that have, in domestic legal systems, no binding effect unless the ratifying state provides for such. The most cogent objec-tion to making certain kinds of international treaties binding in domestic courts is that it projects judicial rather than legislative settlement of con-troverted questions of public policy. It is proper to object to some of these transnational enterprises as fundamentally in tension with the principle of democratic self-rule—Brexit should teach a lesson in that regard. It may also be proper to reserve jurisdiction according to the principle of subsidiarity. But the attitude of contemptuous defiance toward the whole lot of such treaties bespeaks an imperious refusal of consort with "the international community."[103]

These tendencies—the unbounded prerogative of the U.S. executive, the contemptuous attitude toward international treaties in the Senate—seem deeply opposed, with one pushing outward, the other pulling inward. What they have had in common is the unwillingness of the American government to subject itself to rules, a posture very difficult to justify for the state that has so often invoked its leadership role in the rule-based order.

It is pertinent to add that the essential circumstance accompanying these transmogrifications was the emergence of the United States as the "sole superpower" whose writ was to prevail in the world. The experience serves to confirm the teaching of the publicists of the law of nations that the system of international law rested on the balance—that is, the avoidance of a situation in which one power could give the law to the others. From a condition of gross imbalance, they warned, you could only expect the transgression of law, with exaggerated ambitions leading, as ever, to exaggerated ruin. A state that could bear such prosperity without abusing its position, as Fénelon put it, would be the ornament of history, and a prodigy not to be looked for again.

The Golden Rule

It will seem a jarring proposition to many, perhaps even a flight of fancy, but I contend that the philosopher from whom we have most to learn about the ways of peace is Thomas Hobbes, the seventeenth-century Englishman. Hobbes is almost invariably identified as a hard realist who rejects even the possibility of international society, and he is uniformly associated with Mars, not Venus.[104] Pursue Hobbes further, however, and we may find in him things of great value for the pursuit of peace. These insights are to be found not in Hobbes' dubious explorations of the absolute supremacy that needed to be vested in the state; here, as Benjamin Constant showed, Hobbes made a mistaken deduction. "The word absolute distorts the whole question," as Constant noted; "nothing could be more false" than the conclusions Hobbes drew with regard to absolutism. "The sovereign has indeed the right to punish, but only in the case of guilty actions. He has the right to make war, but only when society is attacked. He has the right to make laws, but only when these laws are necessary and when they are in accord with justice. Consequently, nothing is absolute or arbitrary in these attributions."[105] Where Hobbes made his most vital contribution was not in his theory of the state, but in his elaboration of the laws of nature, which he identified squarely with the law of nations. These laws—"justice, gratitude, modesty, equity, mercy, and the rest"—Hobbes identified as "means to peace." Here, we find a liberal Hobbes much different from the bellicose representations usually prevailing.

Hobbes, in various passages, does intimate that these laws of nature are inapplicable to the relations among states. In the absence of a coercive power, he asserts flatly, there can be no such thing as justice or injustice, and commonwealths therefore retain the primitive (and unlimited) rights of self-preservation that individuals have in the state of nature. There is, by the same token, no hint in his writings of a world state that would give the law to its constituent members. But there is also much in Hobbes that pushes against these bleak conclusions, especially his insistence that the law of nations is nothing other than the law of nature. He called these laws of nature "theorems concerning what conduceth to the conservation and defence of themselves." He identified them with justice and held they were in conscience obligatory. The science of them he considered "the true and only moral philosophy." By identifying them with the law of nations, he, in effect, drew up articles of peace for the world's peoples. These laws are elaborated in his masterpiece *Leviathan*, published in 1651. Hobbes' list of the laws of nature contained nineteen separate rules, of which the Golden Rule summarized them all: *"Do not that to another, which thou wouldest not have done to thyself."* In setting them forth, Hobbes put the maxims in individualistic terms, referring to what "men" should do, but since he identified these with the law of nature and of nations, we can without fear of misrepresentation identify them also with the rules of peace-seeking for states. Roughly translated and abridged, they are as follows:

- Every state ought to seek peace as far as it can obtain it; it may go to war only when other states will not live peaceably with it.
- A state should be willing, when others are too, to lay down its right to all things and be content with as much liberty against other states as it would allow other states against itself.
- States should keep their agreements.
- States should show gratitude and try to accommodate themselves to others.
- States should pardon those who repent sincerely of their crimes and should look to the good to follow, not the evil of the past, when taking revenge.
- A state should not declare hatred or contempt of others.
- In entering into peace agreements, no state should reserve to itself any right which it will not allow to others, but should rather acknowledge others as having rights equivalent to its own.
- States should submit their disputes to arbitration, should deal equally with others, and should admit that they are not fit arbitrators in their own cause.

- Simply expressed, in terms that the plainest person can understand, states should not do to another, what they would not have done to themselves.[106]

Hobbes was understandably, albeit myopically, focused on the establishment of a *civitas* or commonwealth, and his discussions of international relations are taken up in passing, brought into the discussion to demonstrate his main argument—that is, to show why individuals must divest themselves of the absolute freedom conferred by nature and institute a sovereign power to settle their disputes (and, later, why an absolute power of war had to be vested in the sovereign). Despite these limitations, the ideas he identified with the law of nature provide an outstanding guide to the sort of human conduct necessary for the achievement of peace. Learning these rules required only that an individual, "when weighing the actions of other men with his own, they seem too heavy, to put them into the other part of the balance, and his own into their place, that his own passions, and self-love, may add nothing to the weight." If he does that, Hobbes remarked, none of these laws would appear unreasonable.[107]

The fundamental law of nature, Hobbes insisted, is to seek peace so far as it is attainable. He immediately adds that you are released from your obligation if others will not be peaceable toward you. He does not provide much guidance in assessing how to make that determination, but that need not be an obstacle to a less-than-paranoid consideration of it. Nor does it diminish the value of Hobbes' theorems, which are usefully understood as a simple explication of the posture that states should take toward other states, if peace is their objective. Hobbes' writings provide an ample avenue toward war if that is what states desire, but if peace is their purpose, they can learn even more from his prescriptions. That peace was *his* objective is suggested by the preface to *On the Citizen* in 1642, where he acknowledged that in relations among states man had indeed been a wolf to man, but nevertheless held out the prospect of a universal peace if human beings could learn from moral philosophy.[108]

During the 2012 presidential debates, Ron Paul commended the Golden Rule as a basis for American foreign policy, a proposition met with jeers from the Republican audience. President Obama later weighed in to say that the Golden Rule was a good one, but neglected to explain why it was that the United States consistently sought exemption from its strictures. In the very nature of things, it is undoubtedly hard for a leading power with a sense of mission, as also of exceptionalism, to observe the Golden Rule. Its habits of leadership and its exalted sense of righteousness inculcate a sort of superiority complex. But Hobbes was right. If peace is your plan, the Golden Rule is the rule for you. That it receives expressions and commendations in every civilization makes it yet more eligible as a fundamental rule of the intercourse of peoples, its victories "no less renowned than war."

The idea of the Golden Rule, Hobbes believed, was available to "the meanest capacity." But despite being accessible to ordinary people all over the world, the Golden Rule—this most important rule of all the liberal rules—seems inaccessible to the sophisticated minds of Washington, D.C. America's imperial projectors pay the Golden Rule no mind. Such remoteness may easily be inferred from the compelling historical reconstruction of Stephen Sestanovich, who touts "maximalism" as a long-crucial element in U.S. foreign policy.[109] Maximalism stands, by its very nature, in opposition to the Golden Rule. It is a doctrine of the main chance, of trying every door in the house and entering all those not locked, of pushing advantage for the purpose of victory. Its big victory was in the winding down of the Cold War, when Gorbachev, defying most expectations, kept on making concessions. Even Sestanovich admits that doing the big, bold, over-the-top thing, in defiance of prudence, does not always work out—the wars in Vietnam and Iraq were both products of this kind of thinking.

Hobbes' nine rules of peace-seeking suggest that the "national interest" cannot function as a single lodestar in foreign policy. Insofar as realists embrace the idea that it can—some do, some don't—they have taken a wrong turn. All nations have a right in law to pursue their interests (and a duty to their people to do so), but they must pursue this path within the larger constraints of justice and good faith. That formulation, by Alexander Hamilton, is the ground on which realists proposed their reconciliation with liberals, and liberalism made court with realism, producing the schools of "liberal realism," "ethical realism," and "constitutional realism."[110]

Each of these expressions points to the real doctrine of American realism, as opposed to the cardboard versions extant (often found in textbooks) holding that states aggrandize their power without reference to norms and ought to do so. All the key postwar American realists—Morgenthau, Niebuhr, Kennan, Lippmann—were also liberals in key respects. So, too, they also recognized basic ethical obligations in the pursuit of power and interest, making "ethical realism" also a reasonable descriptor. But "constitutional realism" is an especially useful moniker because it signifies adherence to the traditional rules of the society of states—in other words, the pluralistic or "Westphalian" approach recognizing non-intervention and the balance of power as key norms in the constitution of international society. This quest to assimilate realism to pluralism, alas, is directly contrary to the dominant tendency within the academic discipline of international relations (IR) in the United States, which has taken the pluralism out of realism on behalf of ethically neutral social science. This is a mistake when considering the rights of war and peace, that is, what Grotius called, following Cicero, "the master science."[111]

Largely compatible with Hobbes' prescription, but in advance in the positive duties foreseen, is Montesquieu's determination that the law of nations is founded "by nature" on the principle "that the various nations should do to one another in times of peace the most good possible, and in times of war the least ill possible, without harming their true interests."[112] Going further in the direction of benevolence are the Christian doctrines of loving thine enemies and of turning the other cheek, which in the Sermon on the Mount were attended with no such qualifications as Montesquieu introduced. Montesquieu made the duty of benevolence compatible with the pursuit of interest; Jesus did not. It is striking that Christianity in the United States today has almost no public identification with the observance of such an ethic in practical statecraft. The political influence of evangelical Christianity in the United States seems positively hostile to any such notion as applied to America's putative enemies. A few leaders, like Jimmy Carter, have spoken in this vein, but most U.S. political leaders professing the Christian religion do not. Instead, they visit contempt on the spirit of the gospel as applied to foreign affairs.

It was not always so. John Adams—writing in 1777 that for the Romans nothing was too good for a friend or too bad for an enemy, with the latter on the receiving end of the most vengeful acts imaginable—went on to say, "Our Saviour taught the immorality of revenge, and the moral duty of forgiving Injuries, and even the duty of loving enemies. Nothing can shew the amiable, the moral, and divine excellency of these Christian doctrines in a stronger point of light, than the characters and conduct of Marius and Sylla, Caesar, Pompey, Anthony and Augustus, among innumerable others." Even then, Adams allowed that retaliation would sometimes be necessary to bring the enemy to an observance of the laws of war, but he was yet more cautious after his experience as a diplomat in Europe, having fully experienced "the conduct of governments and people, nations and courts." He then confessed, in 1783, that "gratitude, friendship, unsuspecting confidence, and all the most amiable passions in human nature, are the most dangerous guides in politics."[113] That cautionary note, the product of his own experience, brings us back to Montesquieu's rule, and perhaps even to the austere doctrine of Hobbes. We are concerned not with building the Heavenly Kingdom on earth—there is too much crooked timber around for that—but with the maintenance of peace. This requires not rocket science but what Hobbes called moral science, access to which is available to all. As John F. Kennedy observed in 1963, "World peace, like community peace, does not require that each man love his neighbor—it requires only that they live together in mutual tolerance, submitting their disputes to a just and peaceful settlement."[114]

3

Public Bads in the Illiberal World Order

ONE OF THE most puzzling features of recent American foreign policy and grand strategy stems from the role the United States has played in the promotion of a liberal world trading and financial system. From one vantage point, there is no question that this has been a vital objective for the United States for a long time, getting seriously underway in the 1990s after the fall of Communism. After Donald Trump's election, no one can be sure what will become of it, as Trump has threatened to tear up its signature bargains. That represents a revolutionary departure, at least in stated intent, as the U.S. executive has been the driving force behind freer trade (both in the U.S. domestic political system and in the world) since the 1960s. It is very doubtful that Trump has a well-considered strategy for addressing these challenges, but that does not mean all was well with the neoliberal consensus that, in some of his moments, he repudiated.

The American commitment to an "open system," one that protects the freedom of navigation and promotes free trade and an open field for American capital, has deep roots in American history. After American independence, Jefferson spoke of "throwing open all the doors of commerce & knocking off its shackles" as the dominant wish of his fellow citizens, and even when the United States adopted the protective system (from roughly the 1820s to the 1930s), its sea captains and traders ventured throughout the world.[1] As historians of the "Open Door" have stressed, the conviction that the American economy needed outlets for markets and capital, together with assured access to raw materials, finds expression in American officials throughout the twentieth century. Similar views find expression today. America's domestic prosperity, notes Robert Hormats, "requires a stable world, a well-functioning global economy, and expanding economic opportunities for American products and businesses abroad." Those objectives, as Hormats explicated the hitherto dominant consensus, cannot be achieved by economic means alone: "Enhanced market opportunities, trade agreements, and global financial stability are difficult to achieve without peace and stability, which in turn depend on a wide range of alliances and partnerships."[2] Without the U.S. role, certain basic public goods could not be provided for, imperiling the system; without the U.S. role, the open world would again become closed. This is an often-expressed characterization (and justification) of the U.S. world role. Alliances bring peace; peace brings profit.

Despite these rhetorical pleas for an open trading system, there has been much in U.S. actions, especially since 2002, that belie these commitments. With its bevy of sanctions and its now inveterate tendency to subordinate commercial interests to strategic calculation, the United States has frequently acted to undermine, rather than uphold, the liberal order. Even when the rhetorical commitment to openness remained prominent, it often happened that the national security state closed doors that financial, energy, and manufacturing interests wanted kept open. The injury that the NSA has done to high-tech companies, deeply compromising their integrity, conforms to the same pattern.

These are perhaps the most obvious areas where the imperatives of "national security" have run up against the commitment to an open world, but there are others that are less obvious but no less important, especially the U.S. commitment to "freedom of navigation." This seems to mean the right of commercial vessels to transit the seas without molestation, but what it really signifies is something much more ambitious. In the East and South China Seas, for example, the claim to vindicate the freedom of the seas is paired with a strategy to maintain and extend U.S. military supremacy over China in its home waters, a posture that increases the risks of a military confrontation with China and that as a consequence threatens, rather than supports, freedom of navigation and "openness." There is also much more than meets the eye in the U.S. position in the Persian Gulf and the Greater Middle East, where the disruption and evisceration of hostile regimes have been the leitmotif of policy far more than the "public goods" to which America is ostensibly committed (ensuring egress of Persian Gulf oil through the Straits of Hormuz and providing energy security).

I advance the view that the vaunted U.S. contributions to public goods have in key instances been illusory, and that a retrenchment of U.S. military ambitions is in no wise incompatible with maintaining an open world economy. On the contrary, this advanced strategic posture poses a serious threat to openness. U.S. foreign policy has been driven much more by the outlook and supposed necessities of the national security state than by the imperatives of "openness" touted in the 1990s. Policy has responded much more to the imperative of making the world dangerous for our enemies than either making it safe for American businesses or ensuring public goods. "Public bads" rather than public goods were frequently the consequence.

Freedom of Navigation and East Asia

Among the public goods that the United States has provided to the global trading system, freedom of navigation has invariably been highlighted as critical. Freedom of the seas is a central principle of the liberal vision of world order and part of the larger outlook embodied in the Open Door. Both world order and an open world, it is held, would be gravely imperiled if the United States were to reconsider its globalist role. There are, in turn, two areas where Washington sees freedom of navigation as most threatened: one is the East and South China Seas, the other the Persian Gulf. Freedom of navigation thus ties into two of the most difficult problems for U.S. grand strategy: dealing with a rising China and ensuring energy security. Endlessly repeated is the claim that the United States supplies these public goods in abundance; I seek to refute that account and to argue that "freedom of navigation" is subordinate and in some instances even antagonistic to the forces that really drive U.S. policy.

It is a neat trick by the security establishment to conflate various claims—some minimalist, others maximalist—into one great justification for maintaining the "liberal world order" and the national security state. But invariably the maximalist claims render less secure the minimalist ones. An excellent example is the standoff in the East and South China Sea in which the United States has strongly condemned China's various attempts to assert claims to islands in those domains. The U.S. government contends that "freedom of navigation" is at risk, but this minimalist claim obscures what is really at stake. China has an interest no less vital than the United States in ensuring freedom of navigation for commercial vessels. Its economy is inextricably dependent on the use of the seas for importing goods, especially oil and other raw materials, and for selling exports. It also clearly perceives that this fundamental objective is most threatened by the United States, which alone has the military capability to deny China the use of the seas.

Instead of "freedom of navigation," the United States is really contending with China over two related but analytically separate issues: one is the conflicting claims between China and other powers—including South Korea, Japan, the Philippines, Taiwan, and Vietnam—over the control of rock formations within these contested zones, a control that, in turn, impinges on the claims that each state can make to an exclusive economic zone, which would give it rights to exploit the fisheries and undersea energy and mineral resources. A second dispute, often obscured but probably more important than the economic claims, is the right of U.S. naval vessels to navigate close to China's coastal waters. This, in turn, is closely related to U.S. military plans to deal with a rising China, reflected in the AirSea Battle concept.[3]

The Pentagon has been coy in advertising the AirSea Battle plan as directed against China, but military analysts are uniform in assuming that China is the principal power against which it is directed. And what it calls for cannot but appear as deeply threatening from a Chinese point of view. In a war with China, America would deploy "networked, integrated forces capable of attack-in-depth to disrupt, destroy, and defeat adversary forces." After withstanding an attack and seizing the initiative, "U.S. forces would then sustain the momentum across all domains, rapidly identifying targets and breaking down the adversary's defenses promptly and in depth—targeting the adversary's reserves, fire support, logistics, and command and control. . . . U.S. retaliation could destroy critical portions of China's command-and-control network, along with missile storage, manufacturing and launch sites. Further salvoes might also damage ports, airfields, logistical hubs and perhaps parts of the domestic security apparatus, including facilities associated with the security services and the People's Armed Police Force."[4]

This highly offensive strategy is deeply disturbing. The damage the United States and China could do to one another simply in cyberwarfare is dangerous enough, nor is it obvious why such an all-out conventional war would stop short of the use of nuclear weapons. There is an escalatory feature built into these war plans that recalls the "war by timetable" that brought the world to ruin in 1914. This is particularly worrisome insofar as it arises in a context in which the relative "vitality of interest" favors China as against the United States. Over time, this conjunction between U.S. supremacism and Chinese particularism holds forth clear dangers.[5]

None of this is to deny that China's claim in the South China Sea, centered on the "nine-dash-line," offends against a principle of common equity. It is perfectly understandable that the Philippines, Vietnam, and other littoral states should take objection to being excluded from its fisheries or undersea resources. (China has a better case in the dispute with Japan over the Senkaku/Diayou islands.) At the same time, the concrete interests of the

United States in the ultimate disposition of these territorial claims are quite minimal. Few Americans would believe that they would be worth a major war. And yet there exists a military posture—based on the theory that if you give them an inch, they'll take a mile—that could quite readily produce a war, with multiple potential "tripwires." The official posture of the United States has been to take no position on the merits of these various island disputes, but in the case of the U.S.-Japan relationship, it has made clear that the islands do fall within the terms of the defense treaty. For the other territorial issues in dispute, its formal reticence to take a position has been accompanied by sharp protests against China for the position it has taken, and by probes against Chinese claims by taking the U.S. Navy wherever it chooses to go in international waters. Secretary of State Rex Tillerson raised the stakes even higher by likening China's actions to the Russian seizure of Crimea and warning, in his congressional confirmation hearings, "We're going to have to send China a clear signal that, first, the island-building stops and, second, your access to those islands also is not going to be allowed."[6] Tillerson subsequently walked back the threat, but the danger of a military clash remains.

The best way of mitigating these dangers would be for the United States to stop contesting China's military superiority within its home waters (within the first island chain) and to concede that China has primary responsibility for maintaining freedom of navigation in that domain. Analysts often tout the $5 trillion in trade that traverses the South China Sea each year, making it a vital U.S. interest, but they neglect to mention that four-fifths of that figure, or $4 trillion, are sea-borne imports to and exports from China. This commanding interest argues for a predominant role for China in the protection of its commercial shipping. Concomitantly, the United States might adopt a "sea denial" rather than a "sea control" strategy. Instead of preparing for a war with built-in escalatory features requiring massive attacks on the Chinese mainland, it would adopt a strategy in which this escalation was renounced. U.S. strategy would prepare for a war of attrition (or exhaustion) rather than forcible disarmament, allowing the U.S. to threaten China's use of the seas if it denied the use of the seas to others but eschewing the objective of militarily defeating China in its home waters. The change in stance recommended would be far less provocative to China and would be perfectly compatible with maintaining friendly relations with it, as also with the freedom of the seas.[7]

Such a strategy is far more compatible with what in the past was known as a maritime strategy. When Britain enjoyed command of the sea, its objective was to deny such use to an adversary while retaining it for itself. One of the

valuable features of such a strategy is that it enabled Britain to put serious economic pressure on adversaries without itself constituting a threat to the balance of power. America's AirSea Battle plan is nothing like that. It advertises
itself as a maritime strategy because it is so closely tied to naval power, but it
is, in effect, a continental strategy that employs the seas (or "the commons"
more generally) as a platform from which to launch attacks deep into enemy
territory. Its strategy is one of annihilation (forcible disarmament of the enemy's armed forces) rather than attrition (though it is extremely difficult to
see how the first forays of such a war could bring the conflict to a decision).
Before the rise of air power in the twentieth century, any such objective was
far beyond the reach of British warships, whose ability to reach targets on
land was strictly limited. But it is very much part of the U.S. military's current
posture toward adversaries, and especially toward China. Peace through escalation dominance, deeply reliant on offensive strategies, goes to the core of its
concept of operations.[8]

Of course, the likelihood of the U.S. military being attracted to a limited
war strategy is quite small. It would object strongly to a deal with China that
would pair a retrenchment of U.S. military ambitions with Chinese concession to other littoral states of reasonable shares in commercial exploration,
the most promising method to lessen the danger of the dispute. The U.S.
Navy, like the other services, is heavily invested in strategies of "full spectrum
dominance" that require superiority across the board. The military's attraction to such strategies is partly owing to institutional interest—such strategies require far more financial resources than defensive ones. But its mindset
is also a legacy of the Cold War. When that conflict ended, it bequeathed
to the United States an almost effortless superiority across a wide variety of
military domains. The maintenance of that superiority was a key feature of
George W. Bush's national security posture in 2002 (and indeed of his father's
Pentagon planning in 1992), set forth on the spurious premise that U.S. military forces would maintain a posture so dominant that no rival would think
seriously of challenging it. That premise proved mistaken. China does have an
interest, and the will, to challenge that superiority in its home waters.

The point that stands out from this examination is that the ostensible
aim of U.S. strategy in East Asia—ensuring "freedom of navigation"—in
fact covers a range of other aims, including the maintenance of U.S. military
superiority and support for allied claims against China. Insofar as freedom of
navigation is seriously threatened, it would be as a result of a major U.S. war
with China, which these other ambitions make more likely. Consequently, it
would be more accurate to say that, in pursuit of its other ambitions in East

Asia, the United States is willing to sacrifice freedom of navigation, rather than to say that freedom of navigation is the principal objective of U.S. strategy. It is less important than the military control of the commons—that is, the claim "that the United States gets vastly more military use out of the sea, space, and air than do others, that the United States can credibly threaten to deny their use to others, and that others would lose a military contest for the commons if they attempted to deny them to the United States."[9] All those claims are embedded in the U.S. posture toward China and play out in immediate vicinity to the Chinese mainland.

The Obama administration emphasized, to be sure, that its policy in East Asia had nothing to do with the containment of China; its core objective, reinforced by "the Pivot" of 2011, was "to bolster Asia's rules-based 'operating system,'" one based on the "time-tested principles" of "freedom of navigation, greater transparency, the peaceful resolution of disputes, the sanctity of legal contracts, and the promise of free trade." According to Kurt Campbell, former assistant secretary of state for East Asia under Obama, China has not only been included in the system but has been its greatest beneficiary. It is certainly true that China has benefited economically from this "operating system." If so, however, there is little reason to think that a readjustment of the U.S. role would lead China to overturn its leading features. Campbell's account ignores the degree to which the United States has insisted on being the primary military enforcer of the "operating system," and why China should reasonably take alarm at that pretension.[10]

U.S. policy since the early 1990s has been based on the assumption that unquestioned U.S. military primacy would prevent an arms race and, in Michael Mandelbaum's words, avert the "spiral of mistrust and military buildups" that a balance of power system encouraged.[11] "The same plea was made by two neoconservatives, Robert Kagan and William Kristol: "The more Washington is able to make clear that it is futile to compete with American power, either in size of forces or in technological capabilities, the less chance there is that countries like China or Iran will entertain ambitions of upsetting the present world order."[12] That claim was embraced in the national security policy of the Bush II administration, and has not been subsequently repudiated.

From the Chinese perspective, this claim of the beneficent consequences of lopsided U.S. superiority could not but appear as fundamentally threatening, and the great Chinese military buildup of the last fifteen years has been the consequence.[13] So, too, the United States has been attempting to further develop its system of alliances in East Asia; that this system has a pronounced anti-Chinese aspect may be denied by U.S. policymakers and analysts, but is obvious to the Chinese. The same is true of the now defunct TPP, an attempt to ensure that the United States rather than China writes the rulebook of Asia-Pacific trade. There is much value in the "operating system" that Campbell has described for East Asia—China touts its adherence to these principles as well—but the assumption that the United States should be the chief administrator and enforcer of the system is sheer pretense on Washington's part. It all sounds very benign, but disguised within it is an arrogance of power resembling that which led the United States into Vietnam. That war, too, the reader may recall, was all about the application of neutral principles forbidding aggression.[14]

There is a larger irony in the American posture toward China. U.S. policy over the last two decades has consisted of making China the prize destination of American capital and manufacturing prowess. Previously, the Open Door appeared attractive, especially with regard to China, because it would afford a vast field for American exports. A tee-shirt on every Chinese boy, and a skirt on every girl, would make American manufacturers rich. In the 1990s, this century-old concept was overthrown. Manufacturing followed capital in decamping to China, to produce goods for the American market with cheap Chinese labor, a shift entailing serious costs to the U.S. domestic labor force. The conjunction of this policy with the reassertion of U.S. military supremacy, as Michael Lind has argued, is perverse. It combines "military encirclement with economic appeasement."[15] A better strategy would reverse these dictates, with the U.S backing off from its aggressive military deployments on China's maritime frontier while developing an industrial policy that reduces the severe imbalances in U.S.-China trade.

American policy did provide a great good to East Asia by opening U.S. markets over the last half-century. The propensity toward export-based neomercantilist policies among the big Asian states—Japan, South Korea, China, especially—would have hobbled growth for all of them, had they just had to trade among themselves; America's trade policies resolved that contradiction and greatly facilitated Asia's economic development. The benefits, however, were not shared equally; public goods for them have meant public bads for the U.S. labor force and for America's larger productive capacity. China's trade surplus with the United States grew from $34 billion in 1995 to $84 billion in 2000, rising to $259 billion in 2007 and $366 billion in 2015, the largest on record.[16] That development was not predicted when China's admission to the WTO was being considered in the late 1990s (it was formally admitted in 2001); government officials reasoned on the contrary that, with the U.S. market largely open, and China's historically closed, the United States would avoid the emergence of massive imbalances.[17] Those expectations proved mistaken. Confronted with results so contrary to stated intentions, it is legitimate for the United States to take countervailing measures to ensure its own balanced industrial development and to protect its endangered middle class.

China is not alone in accumulating massive trade surpluses with the United States—Germany, Japan, and South Korea have also followed a neomercantilist path, favoring production over consumption. As a consequence of these persistent surpluses, the net international investment position of the United States has deteriorated rapidly over the past decade, the imbalance falling to over minus $8 trillion by the end of 2016. The problem of how to counteract these surpluses is a great question of contemporary political economy. Though any detailed consideration lies beyond the scope of this book, costs do need to be imposed on countries that run chronic trade surpluses, as John Maynard Keynes recommended in 1948. One promising remedy, addressing the dollar's persistent overvaluation, would be the establishment of a market access charge system that would impose a tax on incoming foreign capital when the trade deficit becomes too large, increasing or decreasing the fee in relation to subsequent adjustments in trade flows. The revenues could then fund programs to offset the disruptive effects of trade and encourage research and development. Changes in the U.S. tax structure, which perversely favor imports over exports, should also be considered.[18] Whatever the precise remedy, the current deficit with China is too large. A new approach is needed.

Admittedly, there are dangers associated with a new trade strategy. The occasion of a Chinese financial bust may not be the best time to revisit the foundations of the U.S.-China economic relationship. (Such a bust is likely given China's extreme reliance on debt lacking an income stream to support it, making cascading insolvencies a matter of time.) The inevitable politicization of industrial policy is also cause for serious concern. Most problematic is the wielding of these issues by nationalist demagogues in the United States who may want a broader fight with China. Combining a new trade strategy with a more aggressive approach to Taiwan or the South China Sea, as some of Trump's appointees want to do, would worsen rather than alleviate the incoherence and danger of U.S. policy toward China. Even registering these cautions, however, there has been something profoundly objectionable in the indifference with which political and corporate elites have looked upon the U.S. labor force over the last generation; broad swathes of the labor force (men and women, white and black) were, in effect, sacrificed to the primacy of foreign policy and the imperatives of capital appreciation. One of the unbidden consequences was the vulnerability of a pained electorate to Trump's demagoguery.

A republican political economy, as Lind has long argued, must have at its center recognition of the importance of a thriving middle class. This introduces a vitally important criterion seemingly unknown to the enthusiastic advocates of the unhindered access of capital everywhere in the world.[19] China, of all countries, cannot legitimately complain if the United States were to undertake such a change, nor may others who run great export surpluses, as the overall objective is, after all, to emulate them. Far less legitimate, however, is the U.S. military role against China, which pushes right up against what any government in China would regard as a core interest. Unless the United States backs off these military claims, the American people will find themselves in a hugely expensive and ever deepening conflict, and one that is threatening rather than conducive to international order and to their own security.

More than 150 years ago, even before Commodore Matthew Perry undertook his intimidating 1853-54 embassy to Japan, William Seward's imagination was set to work in thinking about the shape of world commerce in the future: railroads across North America, an isthmian canal, the acquisition of islands in the Pacific, then on to Asia. Contemplating this mighty prospect, and foreseeing in dim outline the tremendous commercial revolution that would later occur, Seward said the great destiny of the United States was to "furnish a political alembic which, receiving the exhausted civilization of Asia and the ripening civilization of western Europe, and commingling them together . . . would disclose the secret of the ultimate regeneration and reunion of human society throughout the world."[20]

Something like that ultimate regeneration—if not exactly a reunion—has been achieved, a great accomplishment of American openness toward Asia in the last generation. Its symbol is globalization, its epicenter the U.S.-China relationship. And yet deep forces within each society push the two nations into conflict. The grim prospect of a relentless struggle for advantage is softened by the inextricability of the commercial and financial relationship, but the specter remains. Already Chinese recalcitrance on the island issues has led to calls for the United States to push for Taiwanese or Tibetan independence, or to encourage rebellions in China proper, or to ratchet pressure on the Chinese regime on several other fronts.[21] Once engaged on this road of mutual provocation, there is never any good place to hop off and wish you hadn't so committed yourself. The situation therefore has its explosive elements. Combine a risen China with the determined U.S. effort to hold on to every position in East Asia, then shake with disparate estimates of vital interest, and one has an excellent formula for sleepwalkers to blunder into conflict. "It is a common mistake in going to war," says a character in Thucydides, "to begin at the wrong end, to act first, and wait for disaster to discuss the matter."[22]

The Greater Good in the Greater Middle East

"Public goods" are also widely held to be provided by American strategy in the Greater Middle East, and especially in the Persian Gulf. According to the advocates of a forward posture, the U.S. presence in the region has been all about ensuring "freedom of navigation" through the Straits of Hormuz and, more broadly, ensuring "energy security." But here, too, the U.S. record shows motives at work that push strongly against its proclaimed ends. With regard to energy security, for instance, one fact seldom toted up is how frequently the United States has sought to disable rather than enable oil production in the region. The oil industries of Iran, Iraq, and Libya have successively found themselves in the cross-hairs of U.S. economic sanctions or, indirectly, of U.S. military power. Iran's production for export fell drastically as a consequence of the draconian U.S. sanctions imposed in 2012 and 2013, a culmination of efforts to hamper the Iranian oil industry that were ongoing for over three decades and that, according to one study, cost U.S. businesses $135 billion.[23] From 1990 to 2003, Iraq's oil industry was under unprecedented UN sanctions, and it was only the U.S. war in 2003 that ended those. The oil patch in Libya has also been deeply disrupted as a consequence of the Western campaign that unseated Qaddafi in 2011.

The motives that led to these wars were various, but their relationship to energy security has been remote. These conflicts were about oil only in the indirect sense that oil production was a key element of national wealth and power; combating the power that oil afforded meant curtailing the export capacity of these states. The dominant U.S. concern was not gaining control over the oil but preventing actors considered malign, especially Iraq and Iran, from themselves making use of oil resources to build powerful states and nuclear weapons. That the motive was preclusive and not acquisitive does not mean that it was not aggressive.

America's commitment to public goods is often attested by pointing to the U.S. assumption of responsibility to keep open the Straits of Hormuz, from which some 17 million barrels of oil a day exit; seldom observed is

how remote a threat to such navigation actually is, barring offensive strategies against Iran. All the principal nations, Iran just as much as the others,
depend on that point of egress. The only scenario in which an attempted
shutdown of the Straits was, or is likely to be, at play is in the context of a war
against Iran's nuclear infrastructure or capacity to export. Iran would have
an interest in seeking to cut it off only if that nation was itself denied access
to the Straits. Historical experience also demonstrates how resilient oil production actually is, even to determined military attack. Despite repeated
Iraqi attacks on Iranian oil-exporting platforms during the Iran-Iraq War of
the 1980s, production survived. Realistically, a threat to freedom of navigation, barring war against Iran by the United States or its regional allies, is
remote.[24]

Another anomalous feature of the U.S. position in the Persian Gulf stems
from the region's historic role in the U.S. alliance system. During the Cold
War, the dependence of Western Europe and Japan on oil supplies from the
Gulf was a key justification for the U.S. presence there. From the 1950s onward,
cheap oil from the Gulf fueled the recoveries of Europe and Japan, and the
U.S. presence in that region was usually justified in relation to these two more
important interests. But that geopolitical factor has undergone fundamental
change. Increasingly, China has displaced these two traditional allies as an
importer of oil. Its imports averaged nearly 8.5 million barrels per day in the
first four months of 2017, continuing their steady rise. Japan's imports, by contrast, have fallen to only 3.2 million barrels per day. The U.S. position under
these new circumstances has also undergone change. It seems, by virtue of its
sea power, simultaneously to provide a public good to China and to hold a
gun to its head, protecting and threatening China at the same time. Given
China's growing imports from the Persian Gulf, far larger than America's own,
it would seem to follow that China should assume a greater role in the protection of its sea-borne imports. The navalists find that proposition intolerable, raising the suspicion that they value more the ability to interdict China's
commerce than the public good they achieve by protecting "the freedom of
the seas."

The broader question of the relationship between U.S. policy and "energy
security" has also undergone a revolution since 2011. The rise of U.S. oil
production, from some 5.5 million barrels a day in 2011 to 9.2 mbd in 2015,
obviously had benefits for the balance of payments and for energy security
more generally, but it did not lead to a reconsideration of U.S. conceptions
of interest in the region. To officialdom, it didn't matter that the U.S. was
less dependent; what mattered was that the world economy continued to be

dependent and that it was the U.S. responsibility to supervise militarily the flow of resources from the region.

How far U.S. production can be sustained in the new environment of low oil prices remains uncertain, but it is undoubtedly the case that a low-oil-price regime inexorably means that the Persian Gulf maintains or increases its salience in world oil production. Were Washington anxious about "energy security," it should be alarmed by this development: the greater the degree of dependence on the Persian Gulf, the greater the anxiety over its potential disruption if the market becomes tight in the future (as it surely will). In fact, however, U.S. officials have considered this development a good thing because it weakens Washington's geopolitical rivals—Russia, Iran, Venezuela. Nor has the price collapse, in official eyes, undermined the case for a stout U.S. military presence in the region. The increased dependence on the Persian Gulf has actually reinforced that case, on the (false but powerful) assumption that energy insecurity must have a military solution.

The price collapse that occurred in 2014 had one great cause: it was engineered by Saudi Arabia. Remarkably, however, Saudi Arabia's open abdication of the role of "central banker for oil" produced no response among Western governments to supply the now glaring defect. On the theory of liberal hegemony, one might suppose that the United States would have attended to this matter, being in the business of providing public goods. But it did not attend to it at all. Saudi Arabia drove down the price by expanding its own production, eliminating much of the spare capacity it formerly held in reserve. If "energy security" were the aim of U.S. policy in the Persian Gulf, a logical response would be to build up ample reserves against the possibility of a disruption (e.g., by doubling the size of the Strategic Petroleum Reserve or SPR) and by acting to support the domestic price (which it could easily do through additional purchases for the SPR and/or a variable oil import tariff—alternatives explored further in Chapter 5). But Washington has displayed no interest in a policy of this sort. Not energy security in the traditional sense, but simply the maintenance of its dominant military position in the Persian Gulf, has been the well-spring of its approach. Allies that provide access to bases and markets for arms are greatly valued by the security establishment; attention to those requirements is far greater in Washington than to broader questions of energy security.

There is hardly any political incentive to consider energy security when the oil market is glutted and the price is low, but such is precisely the time to prepare for a potential reversal of these conditions. Low oil prices, though temporarily beneficial to consumers, are contrary to the interest the United

States has, with other nations, in avoiding too great a dependence on the
Persian Gulf. Low prices, as consumer tastes return to gas-guzzlers, also work
against the goal of encouraging efficiency and reduced oil usage, as part of the
battle against climate change. Though these considerations carry little weight
in Washington, it does not follow that the interests of Western multination-
als and domestic producers drive policy. Apart from lifting in late 2015 the
U.S. export ban on crude (of benefit to some U.S. companies but of no strategic significance), the American government took no steps to protect U.S. oil
producers from the price collapse, though Saudi Arabia's declared ambition
was to injure their prospects and though policymakers previously touted the
importance of greater U.S. independence in energy production. Domestic
production fell less than feared from 2014 to 2016, but the role of federal
policy in that outcome was negligible.

The relative insignificance of "energy security" in determining policy
toward the Gulf is true today and was also true a decade ago. Much as the
2003 Iraq War has been referred to, especially by radical critics, as a "war for
oil," an enterprise of the capitalist state seeking assured control over vital raw
materials, it was much more heavily influenced by the Israeli-centric world-
view that looked to the destruction or systematic weakening of powerful
Muslim states (Arab and Persian) in Israel's vicinity. From the 1990s on, Iraq,
Iran, and Syria were targeted for overthrow by the neoconservative consensus.
As compared with a tremendous record of neoconservative agitation showing
the need to crush the threatening Arab and Persian states in Israel's strategic
perimeter—and this well before 9/11—the oil companies remained silent.
Most of them wanted to lift sanctions before the crisis came with Iraq, not go
to war. Certainly, the U.S. majors had hopes of gaining access to Iraqi reserves
after the invasion took place in 2003. That they were disappointed in this
expectation—with the Iraqi state favoring the non-American majors, especially companies from China and Russia—does not show that this motive
was trivial at the outset, but it also hardly suggests a commanding motivation
over time.[25] Nor were the Saudis in favor of the war. Saudi Arabia dreaded
the U.S. invasion of Iraq and consented to the military action because it had
little practical alternative, but it foresaw the rise of Shia power flowing from
the war. The Saudis were among those warning that the war would open the
gates of hell.[26]

None of this wrangling over which was more important in 2003—oil or
Israel—should overshadow the obvious and commanding responsibility for
the war of George W. Bush and Dick Cheney. The U.S. president and vice
president did have long involvement with the oil industry. Though neither

is Jewish, both were closely aligned with the Israel lobby. For them, however, neither explanation satisfies. They were American militarists bred in the heartland. They are fairly considered as the pawns of nothing but their own illusions—principally, unlimited faith in the transformative promise of military power to bestow freedom and democracy, combined with exaggerated fears of an enemy they demonized. A heady mixture of American militarism and Israeli solicitation best explains the Iraq War, not the machinations of the oil companies.

To these general factors influencing U.S policy in the region, one must add today the increasing importance of the arms lobby, a point underscored by the sharp increases under Obama of arms sales to the region.[27] U.S. support for Saudi Arabia's war against Yemen, launched in 2015, was predicated on not only the need to salve Saudi suspicions over the Iran agreement, but also the desire to demonstrate U.S. reliability as a supplier of arms. The Saudi war—on behalf of restoring a disgraced leader in an internal conflict—clearly violated the strictures against intervention that Americans held as sacred when transgressed by Russians in Ukraine, and produced a grave humanitarian crisis. The interest in selling arms reinforces another commanding motivation, which is to maintain access to the military bases in Turkey, Qatar, Saudi Arabia, and elsewhere that underwrite the U.S. military position in the region. That consideration does not explain the Iraq War, but it does help explain why the United States was so ready to follow the lead of its Sunni allies in Syria and Yemen.[28]

The conclusion seems unavoidable that energy security is the detritus officialdom has attended to after having satisfied its larger ideological and material aims. Much as energy security is appealed to as the justification for the U.S. role in the region, the sum total of the U.S. contributions on that score has been more negative than positive.

The same may largely be said of another public good to which the United States has ostensibly made great contributions—the prevention of further nuclear proliferation. Admittedly, it was a signal diplomatic achievement of the Obama administration to achieve an accord with Iran (the Joint Comprehensive Plan of Action signed on July 15, 2015, by Iran, the EU, and six powers—the U.S., Russia, China, Germany, France, and Britain). To its credit, his administration accepted the imperative of negotiation and diplomacy even while engaging in assorted "dirty tricks" in attacking the Iranian program. Both sides in the debate at home had an interest in portraying the Iranians as thirsty for a bomb—the Democrats to show that they had prevented it, the Republicans to show that the Democrats had failed to do so—though the evidence for that supposed aspiration is distinctly weak. While some powerful Iranians may well want the bomb, majority opinion, led by Iranian President Hassan Rouhani, does not. As Rouhani stated in 2006: "A nuclear weaponized Iran destabilizes the region, prompts a regional arms race, and wastes the scarce resources in the region. And taking account of U.S. nuclear arsenal and its policy of ensuring a strategic edge for Israel, an Iranian bomb will accord Iran no security dividends." He added that "there are also some Islamic and developmental reasons why Iran as an Islamic and developing state must not develop and use weapons of mass destruction."[29] Driving Iranian policy was not the mad rush for a bomb but the conviction that a denial of Iran's rights under the NPT would be an unconscionable symbol of discriminatory treatment. On this point there was a national consensus in Iran that reached even those—the Green Party—ruthlessly repressed in 2009 after protesting their loss in a disputed presidential election. The harsh and unprecedented sanctions embraced by the Obama administration did impose a huge cost on Iran and are largely credited with the agreement, but what obstructed an agreement for so long was the U.S. insistence that Iran should have no capacity to enrich uranium, a posture at odds with Iran's rights under the NPT. The stiff sanctions gave Iran a compelling incentive to provide reasonable assurances that its program was peaceful, but it was the change in U.S. demands, not the sanctions, that most facilitated an agreement.[30]

Behind the U.S. diplomatic effort was also a long and consistent record of U.S. threats to bomb Iran's nuclear facilities or shut down its electrical grid in the absence of an agreement. Even in the agreement's aftermath, these threats were not taken entirely "off the table" by U.S. officials, though contrary to international law. What ultimately restrained Obama, in all probability, was the sheer incapacity of force to settle the issue, but whether that calculation will sway Trump is unknown. Obama's agreement with Iran averted a war, but it was the threat of U.S. or Israeli actions against Iran's nuclear infrastructure that most brought that specter forward. U.S. threats to undertake a massive bombing campaign against nuclear infrastructure can in no way be considered a key to peace or nonproliferation. Threats to wage preventive war provide no public good of any sort.[31]

A key implication of my position is that Iran should not be attacked even were it to develop nuclear weapons, instead relying on the deterrent strategies adopted during the Cold War. The ability of Israel, with its probable arsenal of 200 nuclear weapons, to deter an Iranian nuclear attack cannot be proven beyond a shadow of a doubt, but there is no good reason to believe otherwise. There are also solid reasons to believe that possession of such weapons by Iran would confer on it no political advantage, but would entail even deeper political and commercial isolation. Advocates of keeping preventive war on the table also lay great stress on the danger of rampant proliferation in the region, especially with Saudi Arabia. Given Saudi Arabia's close financial ties with Pakistan, however, the probability is that "virtual proliferation" has already taken place, that is, that the Saudis could obtain access to such weapons in a pinch. (This might help explain Pakistan's aggressive schedule for the production of bombs.) Egypt or Turkey, were they to pursue such a program, would doubtless confront much of the trouble Iran has faced. None of this means that diplomatic efforts to reach a settlement along the lines that Obama achieved were unimportant. The real danger has always been that an Iranian bomb, or merely the hypothetical capacity to build a bomb, would invite preventive war from Israel or the United States, rather than the idea that nuclear weapons would give any advantage to the Iranians. Warding off this prospect was a compelling reason to achieve an agreement. On the premises of the critics, failure meant war.

The utility of nuclear weapons for deterrence is something invariably put forth when proposals are afoot to replace the U.S. nuclear weapons complex— that massive infrastructure for delivering death on a mega scale whose "modernization" is projected to cost $1 trillion over the next 30 years. It is notable, however, that in the region of the world where mass destruction is most feared, the Greater Middle East, nuclear deterrence is viewed in practice as utterly worthless and incapable of restraining a suicidal regime. That these absurd projections command nearly universal support in Washington is shown by the emphasis placed in the Iran negotiations on the amount of lead time Iran would have in building a single nuclear weapon. That a single nuclear weapon would be of no utility to Iran, giving it no measurable advantage in either deterrence or compellence, but rather heightening its exposure to preemptive attack and deepening its political isolation, was ignored by the Washington consensus. The reason is that the Iranians were generally viewed as existing beyond the plane of human rationality. In the Washington discourse, one had to assume that possibility as the most likely one, in considering the terms of the agreement. The architects of the agreement on the U.S side did not share this view of Iran's rulers, but political realities made it imperative to focus on and make central Iran's "breakout time" for a single nuclear weapon. An objective predicated on Iranian irrationality became, with hardly any adverse comment, the key criterion that policy had to satisfy.

There is a process at work here. To presume irrationality is to throw the Iranians out of the human race; it is to dehumanize them. Dehumanizing them prepares the ground, as nothing else does so well, for war. Iran's agreement with the powers pushed that danger to the background, but U.S. domestic forces, with ample representation in both parties, may yet push it again to the foreground. Trump all but promised to jettison the agreement during his campaign, one of the few foreign policy stances that made him seem agreeable to the Republican establishment. Any agreement that offers advantages to the Iranians—a necessary precondition of their voluntary assent—is seen by a wide swath of Republican opinion, and even many Democrats, as highly suspect and very nearly unconscionable by that very fact. That Obama braved this current was his most impressive diplomatic achievement. That the agreement will survive his departure from office looks very doubtful.

Surveillance State, Sanctioning State, and the New Praetorian Elite

Nowhere has the dominance of the national security state been more prominently on display than in the relation between the NSA and the information technology (IT) industry. There was no more potent symbol of "openness" than the American invention of the Internet. In the late 1990s, it seemed to augur a world ever more closely interlinked in freedom, a fitting symbol and abettor of the larger trends toward an open, globalized world. Few appreciated that what was really being built behind the scenes was a universal panopticon, allowing the NSA to gain a backdoor with which to spy on the entire world, and subordinating the interests of America's IT companies. Since the Snowden revelations, IT companies have staged a rearguard action to demonstrate the integrity of their products, but their defenses have lacked much credibility: their previous assurances are now known to have been serially violated. By 2016, the tech companies, though hardly innocent themselves as respecters of privacy, generally stood in open revolt against the government's stance, symbolized by the widespread industry support of Apple's position privileging security of communication versus the FBI's public demand for a key to unlock encryption in the case of *The U.S. v. Apple*.[32] The Snowden revelations have led to serious efforts by foreign governments to restrict American companies and to build alternatives to the U.S.-dominated Internet architecture (a consequence, it is necessary to add, of the NSA's own unlimited ambitions, not the revelation of them by Snowden).[33] The NSA's attempted takeover and control of the entire apparatus show how thoroughly security has trumped commerce when they have been set at odds in recent times.

These U.S. ambitions set the stage for the advanced stage of cyberwarfare now prevailing between the United States and its two main Great Power rivals, Russia and China. The difficulty of making firm attributions of who did what to whom is very great, with the spy services of each seeking to embarrass or discredit the other while penetrating them as much as they can, all the while shielding their own efforts from public scrutiny and providing nearly uncontested ground for false flags and deception. But the U.S. narrative in the face of these dangers—it is all the fault of Russia and China—is misplaced. Americans were shocked to learn in 2015 that China had gained control of the personal records of over 20 million government employees, but overlooked the point that the United States had attempted, with uncertain success, to penetrate the Chinese government for more than 20 years. Equally shocking allegations of Russia's interference in U.S. elections in 2016—ferreting out compromising materials from the Clinton campaign in order to damage her electoral prospects—suggested that important lines had been crossed, but also raised the question of whether the Russians were just doing unto us as we had done unto them. Each of the major players, with their long memories, has sufficient grounds for retaliation as to make for a highly dangerous field of competition.

Given its historic dominance in these technologies, the United States should have tried to fashion rules of the road to dampen such competition, yet it showed no interest in doing so until very recently. For the global power that has wanted to make its provision of public goods the keystone of its legitimacy, this was an historic failure. In effect, the demands of espionage and surveillance triumphed over the security of communication. By insisting on unlimited "back doors" for itself, the NSA and other government agencies badly compromised the ability of corporations and governments—their own included—to build secure systems.[34] For 40 years, the U.S. government stood against robust encryption, not understanding that allowing ways in for itself would allow other, potentially malign, actors in as well. The result is an Internet ripe for identity theft and malign intrusion, such that the only truly effective way to protect infrastructure is to take it off the Web. Rather than giving order, U.S. policies helped create a proverbial Wild West in cyberspace, with the sheriff at the head of the cattle rustlers. The surveillance apparatus has shown itself in possession of a superficially clever theory of how to secure unilateral advantage in secret, but it has no theory of order provision, which requires a modicum of self-restraint.[35]

What has happened in this arena—with the interests of the IT companies compromised by their role as adjuncts of the surveillance state—suggests the national security state runs the show, not the plutocracy. Instead of using governmental power to support American corporations, the national security state has not been shy about using American corporations for its own purposes. And here, as elsewhere, measures to make the nation more secure have left it less secure.

The primacy of the national security state is also on display in the growth of U.S. financial sanctions to pursue foreign policy objectives. A symbol of this is the $9 billion award extracted in 2014 from the largest of French banks, BNP Paribas, followed by lesser settlements with other European banks. They were charged under legislation first enacted in the 1990s that made it illegal under American law to conduct business with Cuba, Iran, or Sudan. Economic sanctions, to be sure, were part of the panoply of means used against Communist states during the Cold War, but the reach of the new financial sanctions goes far beyond anything contemplated then. European states have protested, rightly, that such secondary sanctions are contrary to international law, but they have little recourse against these edicts. It cannot be denied that these tools are a formidable weapon for U.S. foreign policy; at the same time, it is equally clear that such measures are contrary to the interests of the U.S. financial sector. The employment of such means, and the threat to employ them further, give other states a compelling motive to seek alternatives to a payments system based on the dollar and U.S.-centered banks. The assumption that the U.S. Congress's legislative powers extend to those who use the dollar is quite the claim—all the more remarkable given the simultaneous unwillingness of the Congress to bind the United States to international treaties and agreements. America's use of financial sanctions against allies has been the clearest instance yet of the imperial process wherein associates are reduced to the condition of subjects, but it also seems very short-sighted in satisfying declared U.S. interests. Such attempts to leverage global interdependence and dollar dependency on behalf of security goals, note two specialists, will inevitably lead other states and their courts to "actively resist a U.S.-centered global economy."[36]

The political supremacy of the security caucus is of great significance and bears closely on attempts to theorize American hegemony or American Empire as reflecting a thralldom to the "open door."[37] While "openness" as an objective may well describe the Clinton administration,[38] it does not describe the policy of his successors. The last fifteen years have witnessed serial attempts by the national security state to close doors that financial, energy, and manufacturing interests want kept open. "Sanctions have become the tool for just about everything," one industry executive told the *Financial Times* in 2014.[39]

Given these transformations in policy, we must also suspect that the composition of the social, economic, and ideological elites in charge of American policy has also undergone significant change. Christopher Layne describes "the dominant elites that have formed the core of the U.S. foreign policy establishment since at least the late 1930s" as having roots deep in the "Eastern establishment," including "national media, important foundations, the big Wall Street law firms, and organizations such as the Council on Foreign Relations." Rather than seeing continuity in these elites, however, we must reckon with the possibility that the old establishment is dead and has been displaced by a new establishment. The fact that American elites have favored "strategic internationalism" over the last 60 years does not show that it was the same elites who did so, nor does it show that they did so for the same purposes.[40]

The standing military establishment and national security state that arose after 1945 attests in certain respects to a basic continuity in U.S. ruling circles, but even in that respect, there has been significant change. The U.S. military that arose after the end of conscription in 1973 is markedly different in outlook and sensibility from the military that arose out of World War II. The new military is much more conscious of its distinctness from society than the old, while remaining decidedly invested in the liturgy of threat inflation. Its members are much more intensely theological; once largely Episcopalian, they became increasingly evangelical. The political loyalties of the officer corps overwhelmingly skew toward the Republican Party, whereas previously they were thoroughly nonpartisan.[41]

Civilian elites have also changed. The general movement of political power from North and East to South and West is one indication of that; another is the rise of foreign lobbies. The Israel, Cuban, Taiwanese, and Eastern European lobbies work together on Capitol Hill and in attempts to influence the executive branch. They have pushed an expansionist agenda and have deployed profound influence over foreign policy, often playing a key role in elections. These efforts are complemented by the arms lobby and by the thick growth of think tanks that depend on their largess. Reinforcing all these interests is the profound dependence felt in nearly every state and congressional district on the concrete benefits conferred by military spending. A politically potent multiplier effect really goes to work there.

Within the executive committee of the bourgeoisie, we might say, there are both winners and losers; its composition is not a constant. In certain areas, to be sure, there is an alliance between finance capital and the security complex (between Wall Street and the Pentagon), but the domain of traditional capitalist interests is in areas where they do not challenge the national security state. Yes, corporate lobbyists write the drug laws and the financial services laws, they write the patent laws and the trade treaties, but their writ in grand strategy has been distinctly limited over the last generation, much more limited than it once was. The composition of the committee has changed; it is not the same elite. For 35 years, corporations and capital gained an even stronger position over labor, but alongside this development, and partially obscuring it, was one in which the praetorians prevailed over the plutocrats.

The Open Door and Its Enemies

The primacy given in recent U.S. policy to power over plenty, or to security over commerce, is not especially novel. It is the default option for states in the grip of existential conflict, as in the two world wars. Trade sanctions were employed during the Cold War on numerous occasions. It was long a subject of complaint among Americans upset by Japanese mercantilism that "security" trumped "commerce" in internal debates within the U.S. government—the Pentagon and the State Department urged the primacy of the U.S.-Japan military relationship against any attempt by the Commerce Department to bring economic retaliation against Japan for its discriminatory practices. These and other instances show that the phenomenon is by no means unusual in the epoch after 1945. Trading economic favors for military access was always part of the deal.

This pattern qualifies, but does not undermine, my thesis that there has been significant change over the past fifteen years in the direction of a policy much more aggressive than the 1990s, more aggressive even than that pursued during the Cold War. The extra-territorial or secondary sanctions now so much favored would not have passed muster with European governments throughout the Cold War. It was only in the 1990s that Congress was sufficiently bold to attempt to dictate the economic policy of allied governments, a project that then met with stiff resistance. Now American law pushes outward on a host of fronts. Instead of being an outlier, that tendency is becoming characteristic. Trump and the Republican-controlled Congress, instead of reining it in, may yet push it further. It is also difficult to think of a precedent for what the NSA did to IT companies; surely, that is a highly significant milestone in the annals of the national security state, showing a newfound primacy of power over plenty (or fear over interest). While the U.S. role has supported the global economic system in some respects, it has also restricted it, interfered with it—indeed, sought command over it—in a way that undercuts its original raison d'être and that, to boot, has often been hostile to traditional business interests. Even the TPP and TTIP have a significant security dimension: they are best understood as payoffs to U.S. corporations for exactions otherwise imposed by the security caucus, a way of rounding out the overall benefits and burdens that were intended to limit criticism of the dominant security-driven tendency. The trade deals are now defunct because of populist opposition, but the exactions of the security caucus remain.

When American officials spoke a century ago of the financial and economic interests of the United States, they had in mind the ability of American businesspeople and financiers to gain access, on equitable terms, to the world's commerce. This was the classic Open Door policy, formulated in the diplomatic notes of John Hay with regard to China in 1899 and 1900. There, it meant support for China's territorial integrity and opposition to carving up China into commercial spheres of influence that would deny access to U.S. firms. Secretary of State Hay (with very limited success) opposed those discriminatory arrangements. George Kennan famously denounced the Open Door notes in his lectures on American diplomacy as an example of a sort of idle utopianism in American foreign policy, strangely detached from practical effect, which made U.S. diplomats intervene fruitlessly in foreign quarrels.[42] But the conception proved enduring and was joined with an analysis of perceived weaknesses in the domestic economy. American policymakers came to strongly believe that American prosperity depended on new opportunities to export capital and on access to overseas markets and raw materials. The Republican administrations of the 1920s made the policy one of worldwide application, despite their continuing support of high domestic tariffs. American officials were anxious to deal with regimes that respected the property rights of foreign firms, but the U.S. approach was otherwise apolitical. It did not demand concordance of political regime type in seeking opportunities for trade but approached matters in a businesslike spirit, going where the opportunities were greatest. This vision, embraced by Republican internationalists like Herbert Hoover, was generally a hopeful one. It offered not only a possible solution to America's domestic ills but also, it was thought, a sure guide to prosperity among the nations, likely to incline them away from war.

There was, however, a darker side to this vision, one that emphasized the domestic consequences of an America that was economically isolated from the world. That darker side emerged starkly in 1940, when the United States seemed, really for the first time, to be facing the prospect of a Eurasia ruthlessly dominated by totalitarian powers, all of them hostile to the American political and economic system. That situation suddenly thrust America, wrote Gerald W. Johnson, "into a form of isolation that we had never con-templated and most emphatically did not want."[43] The crisis produced fears of a domestic garrison state that had both a political and economic dimen-sion. Politically, it meant the dystopian prospect of converting the United States into the militarized and mobilized nation that Wilson had feared; economically, it meant "that the United States would have to adopt a regi-mented, state-planned economy, including government-imposed restrictions on imports, exports, and capital flows."[44]

These two factors—the need for access, the fear of closure—were empha-sized by the revisionist historians of the 1960s, led by William Appleman Williams and fellow students of "the Wisconsin school," who believed it pro-vided a fundamental key to the deep purposes of U.S. foreign policy.[45] When the revisionists were breaking into the historiographical scene with their fresh and startling hypotheses, the memory was still strong of the circumstances of the early 1940s, when an America isolated economically from the world did seem a stark danger. In the 1960s, the revisionists took seriously the possibility (as indeed did the U.S. political elite) that revolutionary socialism might win hearts and minds throughout the third world, shutting out the United States.

Today, the prospect of closure seems utterly remote—unless, of course, we impose it ourselves. Nearly all powers, major and minor, have rejected autar-chy. They see the advantages of trade, foreign investment, and a flourishing private sector. That is not to say that everybody has bought into "the gos-pel according to *The Economist*." There are clearly differences among states in their attitude toward the protection of domestic industry, the degree to which they emphasize national production over consumption, the favoritism they give to capital over labor in social and economic policy, or in the latitude they allow for partial state ownership in critical economic sectors (especially energy). At the same time, there is a broad acceptance that "closure" would be bad for them. This was not clear at all in the 1960s.[46]

The main reason for this widespread change in belief is the relative success of the contrary models. The diametrically contrasting experiences during the Cold War of East and West Germany, of mainland China and Taiwan, and of North and South Korea constituted an impressive tutorial for world leaders, all of whose peoples care deeply about a rising standard of living. These lead-ers also learned to contrast the limited growth achieved under import sub-stitution policies in much of the developing world with that achieved under a regime more open to trade and investment.[47] One does not have to accept every jot and tittle of the Washington consensus to see this point. The archi-tects of the Beijing Consensus see it, too. So do social democrats in much of the developing world. The change in outlook is especially symbolized by Vietnam—in the 1960s, the maniacal carrier of a faith in revolutionary communism; lately, the avid supplicant to the TPP, by which it hoped to facilitate inward investment by transnational corporations as a source of domestic jobs and export earnings. Gaining this required Vietnamese acquiescence in a set of U.S.-dictated rules that would have seemed inconceivable to them back in the day.

This general shift of opinion does not constitute a slam-dunk argument for raw, savage capitalism, but the parameters of the argument have clearly shifted over the last half-century: just about all foreign leaders understand that they can develop their economies only if they reject autarchy, just as they accept that the means of production cannot rest mainly in the hands of the state but must include a private sector based on private property and market incentives. By the steady and plainly visible hand of their own interest, they were led to seek the same basic objectives promoted by the pioneers of the Open Door—that is, access to overseas markets and raw materials, opportunities for inward and outward investment. The proportional need for these things differs according to position, but the basic pattern is clear. No significant power aspires to autarchy; all are dependent on trade and access to capital and are in that sense embedded in the world market. When there is a denial of access to the world trading and financial system, the operative cause is likely to be American economic sanctions, not revolutionary expropriations.[48]

It is customary among Open Door historians and analysts to write as if the Open Door had displayed an amazing continuity in U.S. foreign policy[49]; in fact, it has undergone great change. At its inception and for the next two generations, the Open Door promoted commerce and investment without regard to the regime type of trading partners, and in that respect was quite like China's policy today. In neither its first phase (from 1890s to 1930s) nor its second phrase (1950s and 1960s) did the United States promote democracy as part of an Open Door policy. In the Caribbean from the 1890s to the 1930s, the U.S. sought to improve revenue collection above all, with indifferent success, but on the plausible theory that state capacity was an indispensable condition of economic development.[50] In the 1950s and 1960s, it was locked in alliance with a host of eminently undemocratic states. New Left writers in the 1960s were struck by these alliances, associating the Open Door not with democracy promotion but with counterrevolutionary zeal in the service of capital (though in the name of anti-communism). As Carl Oglesby commented in 1967, the "Free World" that American leaders celebrated included more than the Western democracies. "It includes Spain and

Portugal, Mozambique and South Africa, Paraguay and Argentina, Thailand and Formosa" (none of them governed democratically at that time). Given this disjunction, the freedom denoted by the term could "only mean freedom of capital access: The Free World is the world economic area in which the American businessman enjoys greatest freedom of commercial maneuver."[51] Oglesby underestimated the sincerity that officials like Dean Rusk brought to their vision of a world free from aggression, in which all peace-loving states had a stake, but unease with America's far empire of authoritarian despots, to which Oglesby pointed, did have lasting consequences.

The backwash from Vietnam led to a reconsideration of America's alliances with right-wing despots in the mid-1970s, with congressional Democrats urging pressure on allied states that abused human rights, a cause taken up by Jimmy Carter during his presidency. Under Reagan, the focus shifted to support for anti-communist insurgents (Nicaragua, Afghanistan, Angola, and Cambodia) in the name of extending freedom. By the mid-1980s, a convergence between Democrats and Republicans on the importance of human rights and democracy, increasingly applied against allies and enemies alike, produced a new U.S. policy very different from that of the past; only then and in subsequent years did the promotion of democracy, as opposed to the promotion of trade and investment, become the distinguishing feature in America's idea of the Open Door. After that came a steady accretion of steps to the summit, that is, to Bush's second inaugural in 2005, commanding the zealous pursuit of democracy and freedom abroad as the *ultima ratio* of the American regime. Rather than reversing the tendency, Obama fell in with a variant of it by supporting the overthrow of governments in Libya, Syria, and Ukraine. No one associated the Open Door with these objectives in its early days. An earlier generation would have considered such objectives as quite unsound, nullifying the whole point of the Open Door policy and contrary to the law of nations.[52]

Recovering Liberalism

The "liberal world order" is often invoked, but much more rarely defined or investigated. Looked at from afar, "liberal" objectives have been prominently displayed in the armory of U.S. policy; looked at in detail, there has been a lot of confusion and hypocrisy in these claims. One aspect of this, as noted earlier, is how minimalist objectives have been used to justify maximalist purposes, though the minimalist objectives are, in fact, threatened by tying them to far more ambitious aims. Want to guard against piracy from desperate Somali ruffians? Well, then, adopt the AirSea Battle strategy and gird for deep strikes into China. Most implausibly, the national security apparatus styles itself as the great mainstay of American and world commerce, without which it would otherwise collapse. In Thomas Friedman's expression of 1999, "The hidden hand of the market will never work without a hidden fist—McDonald's cannot flourish without McDonnell Douglas, the builder of the F-15. And the hidden fist that keeps the world safe for Silicon Valley's technologies is called the United States Army, Air Force, Navy and Marine Corps."[53] In fact, the market functions perfectly well without a hidden fist; McDonald's prospects have little to do with U.S. bombing capacity and are more hindered than helped by demonstrations thereof. Friedman's example of Silicon Valley was especially ill-chosen, given what the NSA would do after 9/11 behind the scenes. The system of exchanges in the world economy is far too complex, and too deeply rooted in the welfare of the nations, for its existence to depend on whether America gives a thumbs up to another military intervention. Over the past 30 years, the principle of the Open Door won general acceptance, though nations still haggle about the details.

The globalized trading system can thus stand on its own two feet, underpinned not by military force but by a principle greater than force—that is, the intense desire of both developed and underdeveloped nations to join in this system and to partake of the benefits it offers. U.S. naval dominance in all the seven seas is not required to maintain this system of exchanges, as all the world's major navies have the same interest in ensuring freedom of navigation, being themselves greatly dependent on ocean-borne commerce. Especially absurd is the assumption that world commerce would dry up unless the U.S. Navy undertakes "up the gut" naval demonstrations in narrow seas (Baltic Sea, Black Sea, Persian Gulf, Yellow Sea, South China Sea), often bringing the formidable striking power of the carrier battle group close to adversary shores. The maintenance of the world of economic exchange built up over the last generation, identified with globalization, is not dependent on whether the United States maintains military dominance over China in its home waters or has the capacity to launch another big war in Eurasia. This claim is ventured repeatedly by the security caucus, but it depends on non-existent threats (e.g., the revival of a threat to commerce comparable to German submarine warfare in the world wars). A Great Power war with China, unfortunately, is not impossible, but it is the hawkish prescription for dealing with China that alone brings such a threat to the fore.

There are, to be sure, conceivable threats to openness—including a global pandemic, a financial collapse, or a neomercantilist trade war—but these have very little, if anything, to do with the major purposes and commitments of the U.S. armed forces. Indeed, the contribution on that score is negative: expenditures on military preparedness have serious opportunity costs and make it much less feasible to find funds for other types of preparedness. The question of opportunity costs is of signal importance. It is also very diffuse because, in principle, there are many things to which money sunk in weapons could be otherwise devoted. So let us narrow the question to take in what specialists would recognize as serious threats—solar flares that might disable electricity generation, at potentially catastrophic cost, or global pandemics that threaten the prodigious loss of life and that, by their very existence, would have paralyzing effects on commerce.[54] Even before Trump, who has brought a new level of hostility to non-military preparedness, these dangers received in Washington little attention and scarce funding. Unfortunately, they have not come in the form of a recognizable bad actor, against whom weapons could be procured, so they have suffered comparative neglect. One day there will be a big price to pay for this institutional myopia.

The perceived dependence of the global trading system on American military power is part of a larger narrative, deeply entrenched in national mythology, which ascribes every good thing that has happened in the world since 1945 to U.S. military power, and every bad thing to the malign influence of enemies. Call it the George Bailey syndrome, or how the world goes to hell in our absence. Much as it flatters the pride, this narrative is surely not self-evident. Is it really true, for instance, that the maintenance of the Great Power peace between Russia and America from 1945 to 1989 was owing entirely to America, and not at all to Russia? That the Cold War was brought to an end by America alone, and not also by Russia? A similar question might be raised of accounts of Hitler's defeat which star the United States but which ignore Russia's contribution to that end, the founding act of the post-World War II order. The attribution of the "Great Power peace" to U.S. action is so deeply embedded in the national consensus as to be made almost impossible to question, though it neglects the proposition that it takes two to tango. One patiently awaits the encomium by which the rising of the sun in the East is due to our sentinels standing guard over the world.[55]

To question America's contributions to world public goods today is not to deny the existence of great accomplishments in the past. The post–World War II reconstruction of Western Europe and Japan, to which the United States made a vital contribution, was undoubtedly the grandest achievement. Americans, as Harry Truman stressed in his memoirs, could be especially proud of the successful rehabilitation and conversion of America's most formidable enemies in the world war, with Germany especially proving an apt pupil.[56] So, too, in Asia, especially in the years since the end of the Vietnam War, the willingness of the United States to open its market to exports provided a vital public good to them: it resolved what would otherwise have been an impossible contradiction for Japan and the neomercantilist "tigers" who followed in Japan's wake. In both regions, American military power allowed Germany and Japan to marginalize their once dominant military sectors, solving the riddle of the previous generation and conferring vital public goods on them and their neighbors.

While there were positive accomplishments, however, there were also grave drawbacks. The Vietnam War was the most dramatic U.S. failure of the Cold War period, but there were a litany of other interventions scarred by hubris and militarism during that long twilight struggle. That Soviet-style Communism proved a bankrupt system should not cast a rosy glow over every hare-brained scheme in the U.S. wars—cold and hot—prosecuted against it. In fact, the demonstrated weakness and fragility of the Soviet Union show plainly that this aging and ailing system was in no position to launch its putative plan of worldwide conquest, contradicting the depictions of exaggerated threat dominant at the time. That command economies could not successfully deliver the rising living standards craved by the world's peoples also set profound limits to their appeal—a point obvious in retrospect but seldom digested at the time. The Soviet collapse, however, was momentous not only as a grand historical judgment against Communism but also in opening new doors for the United States. This new dispensation created an imbalance of power and, for the United States, a new set of imperial temptations. Since that time, but especially in the last fifteen years, the great order-preserving and public-good-providing character of U.S. policy seems much more difficult to discover.

Especially notable as counterevidence to the sunny portrait of America's liberal purposes—and of its beneficence in bestowing public goods—is U.S. culpability in sowing disorder in the Greater Middle East. There, the American formula for ensuring stability and establishing peace and liberty has proven deeply destructive. Absurdly, this quest was informed by the view that destroying existing state structures was a viable path to the goal of peace, when its manifest tendency was to unleash anarchy throughout the region, giving extremist groups a wide field of maneuver. In seeking the overthrow of so many governments, the United States became deeply complicit in sowing disorder, a far cry from its order-building efforts in Western Europe and East Asia after World War II.

Among both critics and supporters of American foreign policy, there is a strong temptation to identify it with the maintenance of a liberal world order. The customary practice is to accept whatever the United States has done, or whatever rule it has promoted, as "liberal." If the American vision of world order has flaws, it then follows that these flaws must be ascribed to liberalism.[57] In fact, however, the most cogent critique of the U.S. role arises from within the liberal tradition, not outside of it. To show that the United States has played fast and loose with the rules is not to show that an international system regulated by rules is undesirable. On the contrary, it is to suggest that U.S. policies that cannot be squared with the Golden Rule show no real attachment to a rule-based order, but bespeak the very presumption and special treatment they ostensibly displace. Liberal militarism, whether prosecuted under the imprimatur of democratic liberation or humanitarian intervention, shows similar pathologies. There is, as we saw earlier, nothing liberal in the policy of externally sponsored revolution, and the striking thing is that liberalism should now be identified with that policy. Its historic identification is with gradual meliorism, not revolutionary change.[58]

Liberalism's promise was always to find a way around force; the war system was its deadly enemy. The early liberals, like Montesquieu and Smith, saw that it might be possible to bend human beings and make them tractable by appeal to their interest, not brute force. Liberal thinkers, notes political theorist Timothy Fuller, "elaborated the basis for confidence that a more or less spontaneous commercial order, supported by constitutionally limited government and the rule of law, need not depend only on coercive power. What is promised is a more enduring stability than coercion alone could ever provide."[59] The same promise was held out with respect to international trade, the Enlightenment believing that it would be possible to construct an international order founded on mutual interest rather than glory-seeking, the product in the past of so much senseless and unprofitable war. The hope was well expressed by Montesquieu, who noted that though the passions of human beings prompted them to be wicked—and there was no greater wickedness than that which the nations had perpetrated on one another—"they have nevertheless an interest in not being so."[60]

It was Adam Smith, and not some "crazy Marxist" or "radical leftist," who thought it ruinous to go to war for the sake of trade, who denounced the going into debt to fight wars, and who saw that the facility of running up the national debt would be a spur to the propensity to make war. James Madison shared these beliefs. The Father of the Constitution held that republics resting on the people were least prone to war, because they had in them a mechanism whereby "avarice" would be a check upon "ambition." But Madison emphasized that republics would remain vulnerable to imperial temptations, and for the reason Smith identified: their capacity to fund wars through debt would short-circuit the normal process by which sheer gargantuan cost (i.e., avarice) might constitute a restraint on ambition. These liberal themes are very old, but more pertinent than ever. Policies and pretensions the opposite of those recommended by the classic liberal writers and statesmen somehow have earned pride of place in the citadel of liberalism. Such disturbing appropriations injure the good name of this beneficent doctrine.[61]

4

Taps for Republican Liberty

Internationalism's Broken Promises

Among the most dramatic moments in America's rise to world power was the great speaking tour that Woodrow Wilson mounted in 1919 on behalf of American membership in the League of Nations. Wilson would collapse in Pueblo, Colorado, in September 1919, and then suffer a massive stroke that incapacitated him in the great debate over the League. But in a series of prophetic speeches before the end, he "shouted out" the case for American entry and warned of the awful consequences if America rejected the League and "broke the heart of the world." Wilson held that the alternative to the League, and to the general disarmament it would make possible, was a set of institutions in the United States that would prove fatal to liberty: vastly enlarged executive powers, "a great standing army," "secret agencies planted everywhere," "universal conscription," "taxes such as we have never seen," restrictions on the free expression of opinion, a "military class" that would dominate civilian decision-making—all of it "absolutely antidemocratic in its influence" and representing an "absolute reversal of all the ideals of American history."[1]

The United States did not join the League, as Wilson urged, but when it did enter the world stage, it was with the idea that such dire consequences could be avoided, were the very thing the United States was fighting against. The irony of the last 75 years is that, by joining the world and seeking to transform it, America has experienced a great many of the consequences it sought to avoid in that venture. Not every little bit of Wilson's dystopia, to be sure, came true. There are precious few restrictions on the free expression of opinion. Taxes, while much higher than in Wilson's day, are lower than in other states of the free world complex. In other respects, however, Wilson's role as

Cassandra proved prescient. Since the 1940s—with just about every subsequent decade adding new reinforcement—a national security state coupled with a military-industrial complex has arisen that exercises enormous domestic influence. It is not the "garrison state" with universal conscription feared by Wilson and by so many observers in the 1940s, when Roosevelt spoke of an America isolated from trade by the totalitarian powers and forced to mobilize all its resources, but there is no mistaking its great importance. Call it the "Emergency State" or the "Surveillance State," the "National Security State," or the "Deep State"; it has dominated foreign policy and grand strategy over the last generation. The vastly enlarged powers of the presidency, especially with regard to the initiation of war; a standing military establishment that towers over the rest of the world; secret agencies that have put the whole planet under surveillance; and a military class that, if it does not dominate civilian decision-making, has been elevated to godlike status in the organs of public opinion—all these have entrenched themselves in the century since Wilson's dark prophecy.[2] These trends, as Wilson insisted, are uniformly undemocratic in their influence and represent a reversal of precious American ideals. The Founders dreamed of an American world in which the institutions of the national security state would be pushed to the margins of its civic life. That such institutions are now at the center of it should provoke a serious reconsideration of the path the United States has taken.

To understand the process by which this has occurred, and why what has occurred is contrary to both liberal and republican values, we can do worse than consult earlier prophecies as to how it would unfold. War, in this analysis, was the serpent most likely to cause a deformation of republican institutions. James Madison's is the classic statement:

> Of all the enemies to public liberty, war is, perhaps, the most to be dreaded, because it comprises and develops the germ of every other. War is the parent of armies; from these proceed debts and taxes; and armies, and debts, and taxes are the known instruments for bringing the many under the domination of the few. In war, too, the discretionary power of the Executive is extended; its influence in dealing out offices, honors, and emoluments is multiplied; and all the means of seducing the minds are added to those of subduing the force of the people. The same malignant aspect in republicanism may be traced in the inequality of fortunes and the opportunities of fraud growing out of a state of war, and in the degeneracy of manners and of morals engendered by

both. No nation could preserve its freedom in the midst of continual warfare.[3]

A second statement describing the main lines of movement comes from John C. Calhoun's speech against the conquest of Mexico in 1848. Calhoun, a figure understandably disdained in U.S. history because of his defense of slavery and white supremacy, was nevertheless an acute theorist of constitutionalism (and even, paradoxically, of minority rights). "You know the American constitution too well," he told his fellow senators,

> you have looked into history, and are too well acquainted with the fatal effects which large provincial possessions have ever had on the institutions of free states, to need any proof to satisfy you how hostile it would be to the institutions of this country, to hold Mexico as a subject province. There is not an example on record of any free state holding a province of the same extent and population, without disastrous consequences. The nations conquered and held as a province, have, in time, retaliated by destroying the liberty of their conquerors, through the corrupting effect of extended patronage and irresponsible power. The conquest of Mexico would add so vastly to the patronage of this Government, that it would absorb the whole powers of the States; the Union would become an imperial power, and the States reduced to mere subordinate corporations. But the evil would not end there; the process would go on, and the power transferred from the States to the Union, would be transferred from the Legislative Department to the Executive. All the immense patronage which holding it as a province would create,—the maintenance of a large army, to hold it in subjection, and the appointment of a multitude of civil officers necessary to govern it,—would be vested in him. The great influence which it would give the President, would be the means of controlling the Legislative Department, and subjecting it to his dictation.[4]

The institutional movement to the executive that Madison and Calhoun projected as arising from war and conquest subsequently occurred, most dramatically in the twentieth century; at the same time, their analysis seems quaint in foreseeing this as a movement simply from state to national authority and from the legislature to the executive. In the main, to be sure, that occurred, but much more also took place, giving rise to a national security apparatus far larger and more powerful than anything they could have imagined. Generally speaking, however, these passages brilliantly illuminate the path that has been taken. We know something of extended patronage, irresponsible power, the inequality of fortunes, and the seduction of the popular mind as spawns of the war system and the war party.[5]

Sacralizing Militarism

The dimensions of the national security state, the nerve center of American Empire, are not easy to describe. The core of the network is the armed forces of the United States, but it embraces as well its police and regulatory agencies. Included within it are its impressive array of foreign bases, its panoply of external sanctions, its global military commands, its vast spying and surveillance apparatus. Michael Glennon describes a double government—with a secretive cadre of national security experts running the government behind the scenes ("Trumanites"), who have wrested effective power from the elected branches of the government ("Madisonians"). This characterization perhaps understates the degree to which the Madisonians are in on the same game—the "military-industrial complex" was always just a shorthand version of the military-industrial-congressional triangle—but Glennon's account has the merit of drawing attention to a permanent government apparatus with distinct interests and incentives of its own.[6] Nick Turse describes a "geared-up, high-tech Complex" nothing like the "olive-drab" military-industrial complex of Eisenhower's day. What it is—"this new military-industrial-technological-entertainment-academic-scientific-media-intelligence-homeland security-surveillance-national security-corporate complex"—defies normal description. Turse just calls it "the complex" but emphasizes the dependencies cultivated by the national security state in the broader economy and culture.[7] Stretching beyond the military et al. complex are the prison-industrial complex, the homeland security complex, the multifaceted array of U.S. institutions dedicated to the proposition that coercive powers to destroy or incapacitate are indispensable remedies for the maladies of the human condition. They all reflect a movement in American maxims "from liberty to force."[8]

This transformation is sustained and propagated in the incessant public celebration of the nation's soldiers. Service to the armed forces and skill in the application of violence are, according to sportscasters, celebrities, and politicians, at the pinnacle of human striving. Our soldiers, we are repeatedly told, "represent what is best in America." They are "a generation of heroes." Everything they do, it seems, they do for freedom, and our freedom is owing to them and them alone. In public ritual, patriotism has become identified almost exclusively with service to the armed forces, no matter how remote the connection between our imperial wars and the preservation of our liberty—no matter, indeed, that the imperial commitments of the national security state threaten rather than preserve domestic liberty. Perhaps the hyperbolic praise is a function, in part, of the unspoken knowledge that military service often results in awful psychological consequences for those who serve, making this incessant and over-the-top rhetoric a guilty expiation for the dehumanizing sins we ask soldiers to commit in the name of patriotism. Perhaps, too, it stems from the more cynical recognition that the valor of an individual soldier may justify, in the public mind, a reinvigoration of the very ideas that got him killed in the first place. A perfectly reasonable and honorable motive—giving due recognition of the sacrifices made by soldiers—is perverted into an all-purpose justification for the use of force. That this exaltation of soldiers is accompanied by inattention to their health care—witness the scandals afflicting the Department of Veteran Affairs—suggests that its real purpose is to suspend criticism of the motives and results of the wars that America actually fights. Whatever the source of this ubiquitous propaganda, we are well along a road similar to that which Alexander Hamilton described, by which war leads to frequent infringements on the rights of the people, a condition that, in turn, weakens "their sense of those rights" and leads them "to consider the soldiery not only as their protectors, but as their superiors."[9] The people are told this all the time at sporting events. Why should they not come to believe it?

In classical republican thinking, the danger of a large standing military was that it would disorder republican institutions, leading to the usurpation of civilian rule. The step from considering the military as superiors to thinking of them as masters, as Hamilton wrote, was "neither remote nor difficult." President Dwight Eisenhower was thinking in these classical terms when he famously warned of the acquisition of unwarranted influence by "the military-industrial complex" and the "potential for the disastrous rise of misplaced power."[10] America does not have in prospect a Caesar crossing the Rubicon, but it does have an entrenched institutional apparat dedicated to the cultivation of enmity with adversaries. America's world position has also been seen to require a presidency of greatly enlarged power and discretion, with what ultimate consequences no one can say.

The entrenchment of this vast special interest within the national government has many supports. The weapons contractors, the bases, the supporting network of corporations and unions, the role of money in political campaigns, public propaganda touting the apparatus as a global force for good—all this adds up to a formidable domestic interest. These well-organized interests devote keen attention to the issues and make financial support conditional on political compliance. They have attached to them the interests of foreign allies and their domestic sympathizers, who care very deeply about the issues at stake.[11] The military-industrial complex has been far-sighted and judicious in distributing dependencies in all 50 states and nearly every congressional district.[12] In such a situation, neither major party can or will speak against it. Even representatives in Congress skeptical of the national security complex enthusiastically support spending in their own states and districts, because it might make the difference between victory and defeat in the next election. What Robert Dahl once called "the intensity problem" is seen brightly in this example: a distinct minority that feels passionately about its cause is going to carry a lot more whack than a larger but less passionate group.[13] And so we have a situation of "domestic capture," and not of this or that economic sector, but of the government itself.

The great and everlasting irony of this massive security apparatus is that it has done so poorly in providing the good at which it is ostensibly aimed. Rather than providing security, it fosters an air of permanent crisis and permanent insecurity. We cannot live in a world in which aggression triumphs, because aggression triumphing anywhere will ultimately arrive at our doorstep. That was the theory of the Cold War. It was not abandoned, but supplemented, in a subsequent epoch, the post-Cold War, when we learned that we cannot live securely in a world in which tyranny or terror exists, because ultimately our security and the triumph of freedom are inseparable. Above all, we cannot live securely in a world in which our great power rivals gain assurance of their own security, because their efforts to do so threaten us. Conjoined, these theorems have produced American forces strung out through the world as tripwires or as aerial attackers coiled to strike, making it essentially speculative where the next war will be, but holding out the ever-present prospect that the world's superpower will be in the thick of it. The neatest trick has been to summon all the deepest wells of patriotism, and of all we hold dear at home, on behalf of theories of ending aggression, or ending tyranny, or ending terrorism once and for all, which have done none of these things, but have provided ripe opportunities for further spending on armaments and associated activities of the security complex. Benjamin Constant's observation is pertinent: "It is one thing to defend one's fatherland, another to attack people who themselves have a fatherland to defend. The spirit of conquest seeks to confuse these two ideas. Some governments, when they send their armies from one pole to the other, still talk about the defence of their hearths; one would think they call all the places to which they have set fire their hearths."[14]

It was precisely the vast expansion of objectives associated with the use of force that has enforced and made manifest this separation between "why soldiers fight" and "why the elite fights." For the former, certainly for the best class of them, patriotism is the motivating factor, really thought of as the defense of their hearths. For the security elite, however, hearth and home become the universe; the elite entertains objectives that have a remote connection with hearth and home. This was so under the rationale of the collective defense against aggression during the Cold War—witness Vietnam—but it was yet more true of the objectives entertained over the last 25 years, always presented in the uplifting tones of humanitarianism and the pursuit of liberty and justice. This distinction is well conveyed in a discussion by Bolingbroke, where he contrasts a state that keeps its own particular interest in view with those that set up "for the Don Quixotes of the world, and engage to fight the battles of all mankind." A state that does the former, guarding its security and prosperity by careful attention to the national interest,

> has an invariable rule to go by; and this rule will direct and limit all its proceedings in foreign affairs; so that such a state will frequently take no share, and frequently a small share in the disputes of its neighbours, and will never exert its whole strength, but when its whole is at stake. But a state, who neglects to do this, has no rule at all to go by, and must fight to negotiate, and negotiate to fight again, as long as it is a state; because, as long as it is a state, there will be disputes among its neighbours, and some of these will prevail at one time, and some at another, in the perpetual flux and reflux of human affairs.[15]

Bolingbroke's contrast between two enduring approaches expresses a classic critique of intervention, but it also gets to the inner demons of many U.S. combat veterans. These men have choked at disgust over the mismatch between what they thought they were doing and what they ended up doing. Partly, such disgust reflects simply the encounter with war, with all its brutalizing ugliness, festooned by guilt over the killing of the innocent, but the soul is also tortured by having been misled, having undertaken the fight for a certain set of reasons (the nation's security) that bore no relation to the real reasons, whatever those were, invariably paraded under the banner of a battle of all mankind.[16]

The motives that animate most people in the great security complex—whether as soldiers or bureaucrats or spies—are honorable and patriotic. I am far from contending, and do not believe, that the idea they have of the beloved republic is any less sincere or heartfelt than my own. But I do contend that America's world role depends, in order to link it to the patriotism that moves them, on a range of "theories" of world order and American security that are dubious in the extreme; that there is a disjunction between their patriotism and those theories that cannot be bridged by endless assertion and repetition. The U.S. Navy does want to ensure that all Americans learn to believe that the rocks of the South China Sea are equivalent in worth to, and symbolic of, "all we hold dear back home," but they are not, and only a propagandist would say otherwise. American soldiers fought for freedom in our recent Middle Eastern interventions, but they did not secure it; indeed, they damaged its prospects. American theories of world order, as we shall see below, are very problematic, based on a slender array of historical examples inapplicable to contemporary conditions, yet held to obsessively. If one asks the question why?—why the emphasis on exaggerated threats, a long tradition of which does exist in the United States—material advantage and "special interests" do come strongly into play. The need for the security complex to have enemies and to be holding the line all over is crucial. Those who manage this complex, make its weapons, and profit from its largess have thought a lot about its requirements. They are smart enough to know where those lie.[17]

It is also the "special interests" represented by the national security state that help explain the persistence of major U.S. alliances, which would otherwise be deeply vulnerable to corrosion because of their unequal distribution of costs and benefits. As Alexander Hamilton observed, "There is, perhaps, nothing more likely to disturb the tranquility of nations than their being bound to mutual contributions for any common object which does not yield an equal and coincident benefit." This domestic interest also explains the stability of the alliance formation, why it has successfully resisted what Hamilton called "the eccentric tendency" of confederations to split apart when they prove unable to solve the burden-sharing question.[18] For the interested parties, the U.S. security state and foreign governments, it is indeed a quite satisfactory arrangement, and will probably endure for as long as public opinion can be hornswoggled into believing that these partial domestic interests represent the whole.

The Security Theory of Republican Liberalism

In the vast and pervasive weight of the national security complex, a set of consequences have followed that are very similar to those foreseen by earlier writers in the tradition of republican liberty, with their fear of large standing forces. Considered from the standpoint of republican security theory, the deformation is easy to see. The growth of these domestic institutions confirms the old suspicion that a permanent establishment specializing in war would need war and rumors of war to demonstrate the need for its specialties, and that great interests, once created, tend to perpetuate themselves and to grow.[19]

The existence of this phenomenon in the United States should occasion no real surprise. It had been prophesied. The explanation was developed brilliantly in Joseph Schumpeter's "The Sociology of Imperialisms." Drafted in 1918 in dire and tragic circumstances, on the eve of the collapse of his homeland, Austria-Hungary, Schumpeter supposed capitalism to be bereft of the imperialistic urge and treated imperialism as an "atavism" representing precapitalist forces that had survived into the bourgeois epoch. Across the ages, the key phenomenon was that the war machine, "*created by wars that required it*, . . . *now created the wars it required.*" Schumpeter wrote that of ancient Egyptian imperialism, but he applied the insight widely. Schumpeter spoke of the Roman policy

> which pretends to aspire to peace but unerringly generates war, the policy of continual preparation for war, the policy of meddlesome interventionism. There was no corner of the known world where some interest was not alleged to be in danger or under actual attack. If the interests were not Roman, they were those of Rome's allies; and if Rome had no allies, then allies would be invented. When it was utterly impossible to contrive such an interest—why, then it was the national honor that had been insulted. The fight was always invested with the aura of legality. Rome was always being attacked by evil-minded neighbors, always fighting for a breathing space. The whole world was pervaded by a host of enemies.[20]

Schumpeter's thought itself might be characterized as an ideological atavism, a surviving remnant of liberalism in a scene where it had been routed by militarism. Recognition of the phenomenon against which Schumpeter warned in 1918 was by no means new; it had been diagnosed by America's Founders, as by other thinkers in their age. "I have beaten the Romans, send me more troops," as Rousseau related the words of Hannibal. "I have exacted an indemnity from Italy, send me more money."[21] Alexander Hamilton found it "astonishing with how much precipitance and levity nations still rush to arms against each other," given that war had "deluged the world with calamities for so many ages."[22] Never, said Jefferson, had so much false arithmetic been deployed as in the calculation favoring the benefits of war and preparedness. That standing forces played a critical role in perpetuating Europe's war system was widely credited in the early United States, whose thinkers explored the question systematically. A key purpose of the federal constitution is that it would enable America to largely dispense with the engines of despotism— that is, standing armies—that had been the ruin of liberty in the old world. This danger formed the central justification for the union in the early numbers of *The Federalist*. Insight into this security problem was the weighty substratum on which the federal government was built.[23]

The Founders are often thought of as concerned simply with domestic matters, but their thought actually bears witness to Cicero's observation, highlighted by Grotius, that "the master science is the one which deals with alliances, agreements and bargains between peoples, kings, and foreign nations; that is, with all the rights of war and peace."[24] The Founders gave this old insight a new basis of peculiar relevance to republican states, showing that such states could not maintain their institutions intact, or preserve the liberty of their citizens, in the midst of perpetual war. The type of international system that a state inhabited bore mightily on the type of regime that could be established. A war of all against all, it was readily seen, would suffocate liberalism. Insecurity, as Hamilton expressed it, compels "nations the most attached to liberty, to resort for repose and security to institutions which have a tendency to destroy their civil and political rights. To be more safe, they, at length, become willing to run the risk of being less free."[25]

The republican liberalism the Founders embraced was thus well aware of the danger that military establishments, forming distinct interests within the state, would deform republican institutions by acquiring an exaggerated importance. To our bereavement, we cannot avoid the conclusion that what they warned against has, in fact, occurred. The development is not only anti-republican in disordering the working of our political institutions, but also anti-liberal in its attachment to coercive remedies and its readiness to compromise individual rights.[26]

In his famous oration of July 4, 1821, when Secretary of State John Quincy Adams warned against going abroad in search of monsters to destroy, he prophesied that were America to enlist "under other banners than her own . . . the fundamental maxims of her policy would insensibly change from *liberty* to *force*." In Adams's ornate telling of the consequences, "The frontlet upon her brow would no longer beam with the ineffable splendor of freedom and independence; but instead would soon be substituted an imperial diadem, flashing in false and tarnished lustre the murky radiance of dominion and power."[27] This classic understanding of the antagonism between liberty and force suggests, in turn, an understanding of the relationship between liberalism and force. The traditional view of this relationship, in keeping with Adams's own, held the maxims of each to be in collision with the other. In the words of Oswald Garrison Villard, writing in the aftermath of Wilson's crusade to make the world safe for democracy: "For war and liberalism to lie down together anywhere, at any time, with any excuse, means only one thing—disaster to liberalism." Villard had good cause for alarm. Taking note of the gross restrictions on freedom of speech that occurred during Woodrow Wilson's tenure, his contemporary Walter Lippmann found it "forever incredible that an administration announcing the most spacious ideals in our history should have done more to endanger fundamental American liberties than any group of men for a hundred years."[28]

A consciousness of the collision between liberalism and force, felt so acutely by these early-twentieth-century liberals, is no longer characteristic of American sensibilities. It has been displaced by a heroic narrative emphasizing the indispensability of force, even massive force, to achieve the supreme goods, not simply compatible with but a requirement of liberty. These new lessons, which arose out of the Second World War, repudiated the disenchanted outlook of the previous generation and inculcated the idea that liberalism must lie down with force, though in the name of peace and freedom. As a new and better Europe arose from the ashes of World War II, that lesson was validated (then called into question by the experience of Vietnam). America's mobilization of the warfare state also coincided with other remarkable advances in human liberty. It played, for instance, a significant role in the U.S. civil rights movement, as acute embarrassment arose in successive postwar administrations over the impossibility of reconciling America's treatment of its segregated African Americans with its newfound world position. We can acknowledge these accomplishments without forgetting the older lesson, once held with passionate intensity, that liberalism would be in danger of losing its soul if its embrace of force became too close.

There is much in contemporary practice that bears out the historic warning. The logic by which, in order to be more safe, people are willing to be less free continues to exert its historic pull, as shown in the excesses of the war on terror and in the government's avid efforts to create a surveillance state of universal reach and penetration. That the United States has quadrupled its prison population over the last several decades, as it prosecuted its wars on drugs and crime, shows a propensity to solve social ills by coercive means that is fully consonant with the militarization of its foreign policy. These developments are adverse to liberty (and also decidedly averse to the freedom and equality of African Americans, erasing the partial benefits inadvertently bestowed by the warfare state). In both domestic and foreign policy, a set of cultural codes for punishing wrongdoing, combined with the stout destructive and carceral capacities of the modern state, have proved very consequential. May we not see in these various developments a change in maxims from liberty to force?[29]

For a free state, the maximization of power is a fatal objective for foreign policy. Constitutional democracies may be less subject to the abuse of power than other states, but they are hardly exempt from the frailties incident to human nature. The people of America, as Hamilton put it, are "remote from the happy empire of perfect wisdom and perfect virtue."[30] So they remain in the age of Trump. Constitutional democracies, moreover, have reason to fear not only threats from abroad but also overly centralized power at home. In the long history of reflection on the security predicaments of free states, domestic hierarchy or tyranny is as significant a problem as international anarchy or conquest. That crucial theme, though missing from much contemporary academic writing on international politics and missing, too, from the conduct of recent American statecraft, was at the core of the republican security theory to which America's Founding Fathers made such distinguished contributions. That theory is far more sophisticated and relevant than contemporary ideas of domination and superiority because it places the preservation of free institutions and the control of power at the core of its concern.[31]

Even from the perspective of the mundane and ordinary pursuit of interest, the focus on power—who can crow loudest about who has most of it—entirely obscures the more fundamental question, which is whether power serves security, prosperity, and liberty.[32] Kagan observes in *The World America Made* that "foreign policy is like hitting a baseball: if you fail 70 percent of the time, you go to the Hall of Fame." The analogy is flawed. Security, prosperity, and liberty are objectives that should be secured all the time, 365 days in every year; failure should be rare. That Kagan sets the bar so low reflects his recognition that American interventions do not, in fact, have a sterling record of success.[33]

Given the obvious importance and priority of these goods, it is somewhat incredible that the cottage industry asserting or repudiating the idea of America's decline seldom puts these criteria at the forefront of the inquiry. The extended investigation seems predicated on the assumption that whoever has the most power is in the most desirable condition, and that the more any state can make other states do what it wants them to do—whether by means "hard," "soft," or "smart"—the better off it is. Such an inquiry, however, is entirely misdirected from the standpoint of republican security theory. The traditional view judged policy by asking whether it best contributed to security, prosperity, and liberty. This was, as it were, the prime directive. If policymakers attended to that directive—as opposed to always asking whether a state had accumulated the maximum amount of power and professing bewilderment if it was not in the business of acquiring more—they were on the right track. The focus on maximizing power is entirely contrary to the first rule of republican liberalism, nicely stated by Tocqueville: "Unlimited power is in itself a bad and dangerous thing. Human beings are not competent to exercise it with discretion." If the "jealousies and rivalries" arising out of the pursuit of power were the great tableau on which history was writ, "checks and balances were their antidote"—thus did John Adams, always inveterate in applying these strictures to both constitutionalism and diplomacy, summarize his liberal and enlightened philosophy of statecraft.[34]

Liberal internationalism began with the idea of taming power. Woodrow Wilson's project was a less adroit example of institution building than America's Founders had exemplified, but it was in the same spirit. The promise of liberal internationalism was that it would rein in the spirit of militarism—abroad, of course, but especially at home. Having gone into the world to crush the specter of domestic militarism, alas, the consequence of America's global role was to entrench it.

Internationalism is invariably presented as a set of ideas that constitute a restraint on the exercise of the power impulse, but we should not exclude the possibility that it has often functioned over the last 50 years as a mask disguising it. Such would be the less charitable interpretation. More charitable is to see this as a tragic outcome, in which the very attempt to abridge the anarchy of the international system ended by enmeshing the United States within that anarchy, communicating its diseases through prolonged contact. Enemies learn one another's weapons; the battle against evil left its expected residue. What was intended to make America more secure ended by instilling more insecurity, and with it collateral damage to liberty. For early-twentieth-century internationalists, the choice, as Daniel Deudney expresses it, was "either to transform the system or be transformed by it."[35] In the event, the attempt to transform the international system has transformed America, producing a concentration within its own institutions of the very ills it was intended to escape. Ridding the world of militarism meant ingurgitating 50 percent of it ourselves.

Even as the empire has threatened liberal ideals and republican values at home, it has presented an illiberal face to America's adversaries, depriving them of national rights that we would surely claim if in their shoes. Its legitimating doctrines have repudiated central aspects of the pluralist or Westphalian tradition, among them non-intervention, the balance of power, and the idea of concert, all of which suggest the need for limitation and restraint. Its formula of ideological antagonism and regime overthrow has been war-provoking, not peace-inducing. It badly needs a renovation in its basic architecture, one that recurs to first principles about the role of military power in a liberal republican regime. Madison's precept regarding a standing military establishment is one such principle: "On the smallest scale it has its inconveniences. On an extensive scale its consequences may be fatal. On any scale it is an object of laudable circumspection and precaution."[36]

The Old Testament and Its Rivals

The great alternative to America's globalist military posture is the system of the previous century that it displaced, known by its architects and advocates as one of neutrality, non-intervention, and non-entanglement. Though "isolationism" was seldom the term used by advocates to describe this policy—they typically regarded it as a slur—the old policy did seek to isolate the United States from the frequent wars that had disturbed the European system. As alliances were a potential route to war—not at all an implausible conjecture—they were looked upon skeptically as well. In much of the nineteenth century, political independence was complemented by high tariffs—seen by some advocates, like Henry Clay, as contributing to war avoidance—but in many other respects the United States remained virtually borderless, with an open door to European immigration and to capital investment. It combined political detachment from Europe with commercial engagement with the world, all behind a tariff wall intended to protect American wages. By comparison with the European powers, its military expenditures in peacetime were minimal.

The old foreign policy of the United States, with whatever catchphrase we view it, did have a certain grandeur, or came to acquire one. It was coeval with the foundation of the republic, and amazingly endured in its essentials for over a century. It was closely associated with the prestige of the Founding generation, considered as demi-gods by their successors. The historian Walter McDougall calls it the Old Testament in the American bible of foreign affairs, in contrast with the New Testament that grew up after the war with Spain in 1898 and vaulted ever upward after 1945, devoted to various species of global interventionism.[37] The old foreign policy, as Grover Cleveland put in 1885, was "commended by the history, the traditions, and the prosperity of our Republic. It is the policy of independence, favored by our position and defended by our known love of justice and by our power. It is the policy of peace suitable to our interests. It is the policy of neutrality, rejecting any share in foreign broils and ambitions upon other continents and repelling their intrusion here. It is the policy of Monroe and of Washington and Jefferson—'Peace, commerce, and honest friendship with all nations; entangling alliance with none.'" Adherence to the strict commands of neutrality and non-intervention, wrote Secretary of State Martin Van Buren in 1829, were "cardinal traits" of American foreign policy. "The obligatory character of this policy is regarded by its constituents with a degree of reverence and submission but little, if anything, short of that which is entertained for the Constitution itself."[38] A century later, in 1926, Calvin Coolidge attested to the fit between the traditional policy and the "tremendous good fortune" that surrounded America's international position. "We have no traditional enemies," Coolidge said. "We are not embarrassed over any disputed territory. We have no possessions that are coveted by others; they have none that are coveted by us. We fear no one; no one fears us."[39]

If the dominant tendency from the 1790s to the 1930s was to justify policy in relation to the original understanding, the locus classicus of the original understanding was George Washington's Farewell Address in 1796. From the outset of independence, American leaders had seen in principle the desirability of no entangling alliances with the European powers, though necessity had forced the United States into a political alliance with France in 1778. Conscious of the danger that the federal union would founder on the bitter passions unleashed by the French Revolution, Washington encouraged Americans to avoid cultivating excessive antipathies or attachments with foreign nations: "The nation which indulges towards another a habitual hatred or a habitual fondness is in some degree a slave. . . . Sympathy for the favorite nation, facilitating the illusion of an imaginary common interest in cases where no real common interest exists, and infusing into one the enmities of the other, betrays the former into a participation in the quarrels and wars of the latter without adequate inducement or justification." He advised the nation to steer clear of foreign entanglements, holding that America's "great rule of conduct" toward foreign nations was "in extending our commercial relations, to have with them as little political connection as possible." Europe and the world would be engaged in frequent controversies "essentially foreign to our concerns." Washington pledged fidelity to existing engagements and entertained the potential need for temporary alliances in "extraordinary emergencies," but generally advised a course that combined political

detachment with cultivating liberal intercourse with all nations. He identified the latter objective—liberal intercourse—as a policy recommended "by
policy, humanity, and interest." "Observe good faith and justice towards all
nations," Washington urged; "cultivate peace and harmony with all. Religion
and morality enjoin this conduct; and can it be, that good policy does not
equally enjoin it?"[40]

Much of the specific import of these ideas arose from circumstances peculiar to the early United States, and they were closely connected at that time
with the need to maintain the union. (Differing sectional interests, economic
interests, and ideological affiliations and repulsions at home made foreign
war the occasion of a potential split within the union, always a prospect of
fundamental concern to the early generations of American statesmen.) But
it is also important to understand that the doctrine of neutrality was itself
a ground norm of international society, a means by which states proposed
to avoid the calamity of general war, or at least to mitigate its dangers. The
traditional doctrine accepted that wars would occur but attempted to confine
their consequences, so far as was possible, to the belligerents themselves. The
rational arrangement, as Jefferson expressed it, was that "the wrong which two
nations endeavor to inflict on each other, must not infringe on the rights or
conveniences of those remaining at peace." It would be monstrous, he said,
to prefer the alternative conception—"that the rights of nations remaining
quietly in the exercise of moral and social duties, are to give way to the convenience of those who prefer plundering and murdering each other."[41]

The idea of collective effort against aggression—embraced by Wilson, the
two Roosevelts, and the presidents of the post-World War II period—stood
foursquare against the Jeffersonian and nineteenth-century outlook, but both
were conceptions of the society of states. Each reflected the principle that
civilized states should be bound by rules, and they both sought to keep the
dreaded specter of all-out, universal war as a passing nightmare and not as a
living reality; the means they proposed, nevertheless, were 180 degrees opposite. The older conception was that those making war were not, at the same
time, to make a pest of themselves. Neutrality allowed states, by opting out, to
continue their normal errands and preserve an ocean of peace amid islands of
war. The new conception was that war anywhere was everybody's business; all
states had to be prepared to "get in" if the peace were to be maintained.

In the twentieth century, especially after the experience of Hitler and the
low, dishonest decade of the 1930s, neutrality acquired an odious coloration,
signifying detachment in the face of overwhelming evil, and thereby perhaps complicity with it, but in the nineteenth century, it was considered an

idealistic and progressive principle. As James Madison wrote, "The progress of the law of nations, under the influence of science and humanity, is mitigating the evils of war, and diminishing the motives to it, by favoring the rights of those remaining at peace, rather than of those who enter into war." Sixty years later, in the aftermath of the Civil War, the progressive character of neutrality was reaffirmed by Charles Francis Adams, Lincoln's minister in London during the sectional conflict. The "great victory" that had been won in that struggle, Adams argued, was "the right of the United States to remain at peace, no matter what parties may choose the fearful work of mutual destruction." The nation would " 'sway the rest' not by its power, but by its example; not by dictation, but by adhering, in the day of its strength, to the same pure and honorable policy which it proclaimed and defended when relatively weak."[42]

The treasured right to remain at peace turned out to be a lot more complicated when all of Europe was at war. This had occurred in 1812, when neutral America was squeezed on the high seas by rival exactions from Britain and France; it occurred again in the world wars of the twentieth century. Neutrality had prospered in an age of limited war, but it could not survive—at least, it did not survive—the age of total war. The fact that it did prosper in an age of limited war, however, should excite our interest in its potential applicability to our own day.

A key weakness of collective security is its necessarily indiscriminate character, constituting a standing temptation to intervene throughout the globe. Essential distinctions in politics—between the greater and the lesser, the vital and peripheral, the real and the seeming—get washed out in the theory of collective security.[43] One result was the Vietnam War, when a big promissory note, the biggest yet, got called. The principle that aggression must be stopped by counterforce anywhere it occurs assumes that foreign conflicts feature evil aggressors and innocent victims, whereas international and civil conflict more often displays some culpability to each party and a litany of grievances on both sides.[44] Because the principle is universal, accepting it means a yet greater enlargement of the security frontier and the remit of U.S. military power, extending it well beyond formal allies. Its expansive logic is also shown in the readiness with which it has been applied to civil wars.

A key advantage of neutrality is that it does not place upon another people a burden they are often very ill-equipped to shoulder. It goes without saying that the American people, who dispose the fate of millions, are blessedly ignorant with regard to the causes and complications of conflicts in most foreign locales. When they have been forced, in large numbers, to learn about the strange ways of a Vietnam or an Iraq, they have mostly come away from the experience with a feeling of incomprehension, though they invariably learned a tremendous amount along the way (after it was too late to do them any good). But this limitation of knowledge, for a global power with vital interests on every continent, in fact belongs very much to the foreign policy elite as well. For nearly all of them, for example, Libya was an abstraction, and they had no more idea of what made its multiple groups tick than the man in the moon. The imperial temptation is invariably attended with a tremendous amount of "epistemic uncertainty," which then gets filled in by cultural presumption. Collateral damage, the kind not intended, the kind that comes from good intentions, invariably arrives as a result.

The critics of collective security in the 1930s drew attention to how difficult it was, in particular instances, to decide the rights and wrongs of foreign quarrels. They argued that economic sanctions, promoted by the advocates of collective security, were unlikely to be anything other than a road to war, placing the United States in a situation where, if sanctions failed, the choice would be between total war and abject surrender. Ultimately, they believed, the very attempt to abolish war would promote its universalization. Instead of containing conflicts, as the nineteenth-century law of neutrality had done, collective security would broaden them.[45]

The generation of the 1930s was first deeply attracted to this reasoning but then felt compelled to abandon it in the face of Hitler's determined attack on the foundations of international order. The last thing the law of neutrality was made for was the threat that Hitler's Germany posed; here, indeed, no moral equivalence was possible in viewing the contest of the European powers; here, indeed, collective effort in opposition was mandatory. Men and women resolved this question in relation to the evidence laying directly before them—the line of European history that culminated catastrophically in the two world wars. To paraphrase Schumpeter, the U.S. war machine—and America's newfound attachment to collective security—was created by the war that required it.

Experience since that time, however, shows how unique was the juncture that produced Hitler's conquest of continental Europe in the early years of the war, when German forces were sprawled from Brest to Stalingrad, and from Norway to North Africa. For any Great Power to revive such a project today would be an error by a hundred years, totally impracticable given nations as they are. The assumption that other conflicts display the same blinding moral clarity as the struggle against Hitler is also very implausible and an inadequate basis for statecraft in the contemporary world. Yet more implausible is the idea that civil wars have this blinding moral clarity.

In its formative period, ideas of collective defense were closely tied to the maintenance of a balance of power—that is, the prevention of a situation in which a preponderant continental power would consolidate the resources of a major world region. The lesson of the 1930s was that aggressor powers would employ "salami tactics" (taking one slice at a time), which could only be countered successfully by stopping them in the first instance. In effect, this made the principle of opposing aggression anywhere an equivalent to maintaining the balance—that is, preventing an aggressor state from dominating the international system, or at least one of its key regions. Collective defense is thus linked to the balance of power via a domino effect, in which conflicts over a disputed frontier in an obscure region come to symbolize everything vital.

The assumptions on which this analogy is built are seriously flawed. Material conditions have changed deeply. The object or utility of conquest was transformed most obviously by the nuclear revolution, which conferred a surfeit of destructive power on the possessors of "the bomb." Nuclear weapons made redundant the capture of industrial resources such as might in theory come from a physical conquest, the key focus of geopolitical theories in the era of the two world wars.[46] The broader, more prosaic lesson pointing against the utility of conquest is that national wealth is better pursued and secured through internal development. The conquest of vast new peoples would be a hindrance, not a help, to that objective, and carries with it to boot a proven record of shaking authority at home.

The huge difference in strategic setting between the 1940s and today is also borne out by considering the positions of America's two most important rivals in Eurasia, China and Russia. Look all around the rim of China, and there is considerable potential for unrest and conflict, but with fourteen neighbors of its own by land, not counting its neighbors across the narrow seas, China cannot deprive them of the will and capacity for independent action. It can punish them through economic sanctions, but only at the cost of injuring itself. The more it presses upon them, the more it can expect resistance and insubordination. This forms a limit to Chinese expansionism in Asia far more important than the U.S. Navy. Give China free rein in Asia, and it would not seek to incorporate Vietnam within its national territory. That does not preclude a war between these states, as occurred in 1979, but it does preclude a war with the stakes represented by Germany's domination of continental Europe in the 1940s.

The same conclusion is even more apt for Russia, which has to deal with a vast range of more or less hostile governments on its extended periphery. It, too, has fourteen landed neighbors, not counting Japan and the United

States, with whom it has close maritime frontiers. To think in terms of old ideas of Russian "dominance" over Europe—as so many writers and politicians have done—neglects Russia's manifold weaknesses, with 11 percent of the GDP of the European Union and its vulnerability to exclusion from markets it needs and wants. Magnifying Russian power also obscures what is at stake in the Ukraine crisis, which concerns not only Russia's use of force but also the interests of the Russophone people in Ukraine's southeast, who are not divested of their natural rights because they live on the fringe of empire. The Ukrainian revolution and the civil war it provoked have above all been a dispute between competing ethnicities, both of whom entertain reasonable fears of domination from the other. Only with a total absence of historical or geographical perspective can one put Putin in the class of a Stalin, a Hitler, or a Napoleon. The relentless focus on Putin in the U.S. media also conveniently permits an easy demonization that has the intended effect of delegitimizing the reasonable and legitimate interests of Russia itself.

The formidable barriers to dominion faced by even Great Powers show that the world has become "unconquerable," in the phrase of the late Jonathan Schell.[47] Nationalism's extension to the four quarters of the globe, together with technological and organizational catch-up, has made it so. That fact renders irrelevant the hoary specter of a hostile power in control of Eurasia. In the abstract, and gaining in authority by its long historical lineage, the idea makes a certain sense as a focus of strategic planning; concretely, it stipulates a totally implausible threat, of lesser probability than an alien invasion from beyond the solar system. The more plausible danger is that the conditions of domestic order and legitimacy break down in more areas, a worrisome danger to be sure, but one for which external military force has grave difficulty supplying the remedy.[48]

Though the specter against which collective defense against aggression ostensibly guards—the control of Eurasia by a hostile power—is contrary to fundamental realities, action taken in the name of the theory still carries significant dangers. The theory of friends working together, when conjoined with the old theory that aggression anywhere must be nipped in the bud, has produced tripwires just about everywhere, with the United States assuming its now customary role as the indispensable frontline force, committed in principle to the threat of war as a primary diplomatic tool. Under such circumstances, the powers are only one bone-headed move away from a major war. The expectation that condign punishment must everywhere be dispensed by the United States is a key disfigurement of the contemporary world system.

A plural and independent world does not need a centralized enforcer: it is dangerous for the world; it is dangerous for the enforcer.

In essential respects, too, the unbalanced division of responsibility has had a distorting effect on allies, whose conception of interest and burden of responsibility is adversely altered. They become more like subjects of a monarch than independent nations making their own way. The difficulty with this relation goes beyond economistic calculations of burden-sharing, reaching to basic principles of national self-reliance and responsibility in questions of security. It would be good for them to assume more control over their own destinies and to acquire, as a matter of course, primary responsibility for their own defense. Only by exaggerating what those requirements are can such a proposal seem impossible.

The unbalanced division of responsibility, when paired with the claim to military superiority, has also fatally prejudiced the opportunity for arms control agreements, once seen as of vital importance by liberal internationalism, but now relegated to virtual irrelevance as the Great Power competition has resumed its treacherous course. The objective of maintaining military superiority in far-flung regions close to the frontiers of other Great Powers—widely seen as necessary to buttress the credibility of American security guarantees— is at profound cross purposes with arms control. The latter must rest on reciprocity and be a device for the achievement of mutual security; the aspiration to achieve security through intimidation and superiority entirely precludes the prospect of reciprocal limitation.

In history, the most intractable problem for systems of collective defense is the organization of effective systems of cooperation in the absence of a coercive or taxing power for the whole. If each member of a coalition retains the effective right to determine its obligations, and there is no coercive power to overcome its inclinations, the coalition always stands in danger of falling apart. The same fatal weakness that the American Founders attached to past confederations—the subject of a long investigation by James Madison in the *Federalist*—attaches also to systems that seek to bring under a common policy the actions of disparate nations. The Founders were prolific in sketching out this weakness of confederations, applicable also to systems of collective defense. As Hamilton summarized the case, "In every political association which is formed upon the principle of uniting in a common interest a number of lesser sovereignties, there will be found a kind of eccentric tendency in the subordinate or inferior orbs . . . to fly off from the common center."[49] The larger these constructions are, the more cohesion seems to escape them, but even smaller confederations face the fundamental problem of effective coordination and arriving at a reasonable balance of costs and benefits for the coalition members.

The American role, once it manifested itself during and after the Second World War, resolved these classic difficulties by overwhelming them with U.S. abundance. In effect, it pursued the cooperative policies in security, trade, and finance normally associated with federative systems while also acting to arrest the "natural" tendency of confederations to fall apart. As the lender of last resort, the market of first resort, and the ultimate guarantor of allied security, American power and leadership overcame the classic conundrum of confederations, as of systems of collective defense, in providing cohesive power to the coalition. What it did not overcome and shows no prospect of overcoming was the disparate burdens falling on the coalition members. America was always there to take up the slack; doing more than its share was a point of pride to its political leaders, and increasingly became a sort of institutional necessity if the prerogatives of the national security state were to be sustained.

It has been the conceit of the imperial party that the United States emerged as the world's de facto government in the twenty-first century—providing an array of public goods that the nations would have been incapable of securing on their own.[50] As we have seen, the United States has often been deficient in the provision thereof (e.g., energy security, Internet security, war avoidance); its claims on that score are suspect. But the deeper problem arises from the construction of this government. In the tradition of republican liberty, a government needs to be representative in order to be considered just. But there is no equivalent in America's hegemonic rule to popular representation, or indeed to other devices—the separation of powers and judicial review, for example—that the Founders employed to preserve a balanced republican regime in the United States. It goes to the very definition of republican government that it should embody a regime of countervailing powers, but such an arrangement would be looked on with horror by our imperial mandarins.[51]

A world government it may be in certain respects, then, but it is as plain as day that this "government" has been constructed in a way that ignores or violates central precepts informing traditional notions of "free government." Looked at through the lens of the philosophy of constitutional government, it is a grossly deficient thing, overloaded with monarchical principles and oligarchical interests (though keenly supported by an exceptionalist ideology that seeks to disguise its obvious democratic deficits). Since the United States has paid for most of it and on occasion has listened to allied voices, Mandelbaum

cleverly characterized the system as one of "representation without taxation."
Be that as it may—the distribution of burdens within the alliance has indeed
been strange—a government, if it wishes to be considered a liberal government, must pay attention to certain traditional criteria. America's rule over
the international system, in its capacity as "the world's government," has not
done so.

Nor is it any more plausible to accept that America's putative role as the
umpire or referee of the international system confers on it the standard of
legitimacy.[52] It is, of course, true the international system lacks a true umpire;
that is one of its defining features. That it needs an umpire has always been a
perception underlying projects of reform, really from the first moments they
arose in the sixteenth century.[53] The ideological coherence of America's world
position has rested on the proposition that one player—indeed, by far and
away the most powerful player—should also be the referee or umpire of the
world system.

Much as interested parties assuming the role of referees in a great sporting contest would be found obviously unfair by neutral observers (and would
enrage the fans of the disfavored team), the situation is actually worse in foreign affairs, where the relevant "calls" are often hidden behind closed doors
and not exposed to the intense scrutiny of instant replay. What the rules even
are in any particular situation, of course, is subject to far greater latitude in
diplomacy than in a football game. The absence of a true umpire in the international system points toward international institutions, rather than unilateral declarations and assertions, as the keystone of legitimacy. Given that
international society is fractious and prone to conflict, almost never agreeing
on everything, the next best rule is that suggested by James Madison, discuss-
ing the need for a Senate in *Federalist* 63:

> An attention to the judgment of other nations is important to every
> government for two reasons: the one is, that, independently of the
> merits of any particular plan or measure, it is desirable, on various
> accounts, that it should appear to other nations as the offspring of a
> wise and honorable policy; the second is, that in doubtful cases, par-
> ticularly where the national councils may be warped by some strong
> passion or momentary interest, the presumed or known opinion of the
> impartial world may be the best guide that can be followed. What has
> not America lost by her want of character with foreign nations; and
> how many errors and follies would she not have avoided, if the justice
> and propriety of her measures had, in every instance, been previously

tried by the light in which they would probably appear to the unbiased part of mankind?

"Union and Independence" was the motto of the Founders, and it remains a serviceable motto today. Unlike other nationalists, I think that union must be a fundamental symbol of American purposes in the world; unlike conventional internationalists, I believe that the idea of union instantiated in America's system of "liberal hegemony" is not the only one available. Earlier ideas of international comity focused on neutrality rather than collective defense have much to commend them, as does a conception of international order that rejects the notion that one exceptional power should function as the umpire of the international system. That pretension ineluctably results in empire.

5

The Renovation of American Foreign Policy

Isolationism and Globalism

Exasperated by the endless and growing conflict in Vietnam, Walter Lippmann had come in 1967 to the end of his tether. He had watched an administration pour blood and treasure into a fruitless war, on behalf of a hare-brained theory of security. (We must fight them there, or else we will have to fight them in Los Angeles.) Lippmann had made his reservations known to Lyndon Johnson, who all too characteristically tried to charm Lippmann, then needle him, then condemn him to the outer reaches of insanity. The president spread rumors: Lippmann was decrepit; he had lost it; he was an isolationist. Lippmann, however, was fully compos mentis. His reply to the charge of isolationism was to acknowledge its truth: "Neo-isolationism is the direct product of foolish globalism . . . . Compared to people who thought they could run the universe, or at least the globe, I *am* a neo-isolationist and proud of it."[1]

Lippmann, who had an astonishing run as America's most respected voice on foreign affairs for some 50 years, is best known in the foreign policy establishment for his formulation of "the fundamental purpose of a foreign policy." Set forth in his 1943 book *U.S. Foreign Policy: Shield of the Republic*, Lippmann wrote that the fundamental principle required the bringing into balance of commitments and power. "Without the controlling principle that the nation must maintain its objectives and its power in equilibrium, its purposes within its means and its means equal to its purposes, its commitments related to its resources and its resources adequate to its commitments, it is impossible to think at all about foreign affairs." In 1943, he took aim at isolationism, charging that its persistence in the changed circumstances of the twentieth century had left American strategy bankrupt and in default. By

1967, he charged the opposite error on American globalism and was prepared to lift from the dead the specter—isolationism—over the burial of which he had once presided.

The Too Much and the Too Little, intervention and isolation, escalation and withdrawal—such are the perennial terms of the foreign policy debate. Though opposites, they are related, it being a widely repeated maxim that the excesses of intervention produce isolation, that the excesses of isolation produce intervention (with Lippmann himself exemplifying both dynamics at various points in his career). Most Americans, however, probably do not consider themselves as wild-eyed interventionists or head-in-the-sand isolationists. Neither maximalists nor minimalists, they are in-betweeners. Even diehard liberal hawks and on-the-warpath neocons recognize some limits, and complain bitterly of the "caricature" of their position as one of indiscriminate intervention; then, too, most so-called isolationists want engagement, commerce, and a positive message for the world. In fact, "isolationists" have normally rejected the term as applied to themselves, usually calling themselves nationalists or non-interventionists instead.[2] Lippmann's candid admission of neo-isolationism was uncharacteristic of even those disgusted by the excesses of American intervention, as he certainly was in 1967. His close friend J. William Fulbright agreed with Lippmann's outlook but rejected the term, calling instead for a "new internationalism."[3]

At the beginning of the twentieth century, non-interventionists and anti-imperialists disliked the term "isolation" because it ignored the tremendous influence of the United States—so weak in standing military forces, so strong in world influence. Before its imperialist thrust in the 1890s, wrote Goldwin Smith,

> the American Commonwealth had the largest population of freemen in the world, and one which was rapidly growing. Its heritage reached from Arctic regions to regions almost tropical, with a range of production embracing nearly everything needed or desired by man. The world was full of its inventions and its manufactures. It was the tutelary power of this continent. It was in the van of political progress. Its influence was felt more or less in the politics of all nations. If such a state was isolation, it was an isolation the influence of which was as wide as humanity.[4]

No, these so-called isolationists insisted, the policy they recommended was not hermitlike or ostrichlike; no, it did not detract one iota from the benign influence that America should exert upon the world; no, it was not cowardly and pacifistic, but rather cautious, in keeping with the traditional precepts of the American system, about expanding justifications for the use of force. If it was isolation to incorporate into policy such sensible cautions, then they were isolationists. "When the others are all over ears in trouble," asked William Graham Sumner, "who would not be isolated in freedom from care? When the others are crushed under the burden of militarism, who would not be isolated in peace and industry?"[5]

How to resolve the eternal debate between the Too Much and the Too Little is indeed the great question. It is, however, a confusing question, with many different aspects and curiosities beyond that of proper nomenclature. For one thing, the debate has changed greatly over time and is vastly more complicated than the one that took place a century ago, when Mahan espied a straight-up contest between "imperialists" and "isolationists."[6] Three world wars have been won; a formidable military establishment has been built; the security frontier has been expanded with the inclusion of formal and informal allies; the range of objects over which force is seen as legitimate has expanded greatly. Time has given the air of permanence and normality to developments that, in the early days of the debate, were widely seen as impermanent and abnormal.

There is considerable resistance in the public to an imperial role. The percentage of Americans agreeing that the United States "should mind its own business internationally and let other countries get along the best they can on their own" reached in 2013 all-time levels—52 percent. Only 20 percent of Americans thought that way in 1964. The percentage of nay-sayers had risen to a high of 43 percent in 1976, when disenchantment with the Vietnam War took its toll, and had fallen as low as 30 percent in 2002, after the 9/11 attacks, but shot up to majority status as frustration with Iraq and Afghanistan deepened. In Pew's latest survey, in 2016, it fell back again to 41 percent, probably reflecting the rise of ISIS and the renewal of the cold war with Russia, but it is still within the range of post-Vietnam disaffection. By a two to one margin (61 to 32 percent), American voters believe the Iraq War was a mistake. (The veterans of that war feel the same way.) By the same percentage (64 to 32), they believe that the United States "is doing too much around the world and it is time to do less internationally and focus more on domestic problems."[7] The surge in support for destroying ISIS after two Americans were gruesomely executed in the fall of 2014 shows that public opinion is fickle and can move in hawkish directions in response to specific incidents, but the public sensibility remains broadly skeptical of intervention.

The various polls measuring public opinion on foreign policy suggest a fundamental contradiction between the aspirations of the foreign policy elite and the public, pitting the court against the country. Each takes profoundly different views of the primacy of domestic as against foreign policy. A substantial portion of the establishment usually urges more confrontational and hawkish gestures, while the public sits on the sidelines, otherwise preoccupied and not wanting to be bothered by foreign policy, but definitely in a mood to take on no new commitments and major expenses. It is not easy to predict how this conflict between political class and popular sentiment will play out, just as it is not easy for foreigners to predict which side of America will show itself when they come calling and cajoling for U.S. help. It is in the nature of such epic contests that neither side in the argument is ever truly down and out, but the public's caution about intervention has become a serious restraint on the outward thrust of U.S. foreign policy (as it was not in 2003).

Other sources of domestic restraint against interventionism are more difficult to discern. It was once a favored argument that Congress's constitutional mandate to declare war served as a potent form of blockage against imperial adventurism. Protesting Andrew Jackson's incursions into Florida in 1818, Henry Clay noted that the express and exclusive grant to Congress of the war power was intended to prevent such enterprises. The members of the "immortal Convention," Clay observed, saw "that nations are often precipitated into ruinous war, from folly, from pride, from ambition, and from the desire of military fame." By committing the subject to the legislature, the hope was to spare the United States "from the mad wars that have afflicted, and desolated, and ruined other countries."[8] Clay's expression of the old faith imputing to Congress a role standing athwart military adventurism was repeated many times subsequently, but it is contradicted by the behavior of the Congress we have, which has been as fully and completely under the spell of the national security state as any of the other branches of government. Contrary to earlier expectations, Congress has proved a willing abettor of wars of folly, though its preferred mode of conduct has been an aversion to declaring itself one way or the other. As the storm raged above, it has liked to stay below deck, reserving always, of course, the right of the crew to take potshots at the captain.

Ironically enough, a major source of restraint on U.S. interventionism comes from within the national security complex itself, by those who must fight the wars. It is undoubtedly in the interest of the U.S. military to embrace a view of the world that makes its forces necessary, and the military avidly pursues evidence of malign foreign intentions and capabilities to which its forces can supply the remedy (evident in the enthusiasm of its leaders for renewing the cold war with Russia in Europe).[9] The military, however, is also conscious of the costs imposed by the wars of the last fifteen years and wants to avoid resource-sapping new engagements. It gains from conflict and tension, in short, but suffers unduly from war. Had George Bush and Dick Cheney not faced the opposition of the Joint Chiefs of Staff, a war with Iran in 2008 would have been much more probable. In 2011, the Libyan intervention was viewed very skeptically by the brass (as well as by the civilian leadership at the Pentagon under Robert Gates). Institutionally, there is more caution about the use of force within the uniformed military than from the civilian national security apparatus. That may not count for a lot—the military is obliged to follow civilian orders—but it does count for something.[10]

In one vital respect, the maximalists (hawks, globalists, interventionists) have a standing advantage in the eternal argument. When doves win, it is just for a day; when hawks win, it is for something like eternity. NATO expansion to the Baltics and the Balkans is a classic case in point. That was rammed through by the Bush administration in the fevered atmosphere of 2002-03; now it seems unquestionable. The Bush administration won the argument over Afghanistan and Iraq in 2001 and 2002; the United States remains affixed to both places, its original dreams shattered but its (reduced) forces still in place. Henry Kissinger pointed to the logic and power of that viewpoint during the Vietnam War, arguing that the commitment of 500,000 troops to South Vietnam had settled the question of whether Vietnam represented a vital interest of the United States. The efficacy of the plea is to wash away as irrelevant arguments questioning the wisdom of the commitment in the first place, however misguided. Mortification over the loss of pride and position is as old as the nations, but holds with yet greater sway for great empires and for those, like the United States, whose entire position in the world is seen as resting on "credibility."

In any given situation, there is precious little agreement in the commentariat on what signifies maximalism and minimalism, indiscriminate intervention and hidebound isolationism. In his West Point address in 2014, President Obama enumerated the range of reasons for which the United States was prepared to use force, "unilaterally if necessary." These included "when our core interests demand it—when our people are threatened, when our livelihoods are at stake, when the security of our allies is in danger." The inclusion of the security of allies, a notoriously flexible category, made this a list of rather expansive aims, but it was considered as minimalist by the cadre of national security bureaucrats who exercise profound influence on the key decisions. They were furious when Obama did not escalate in Syria. Obama's larger record has been denounced as isolationist (as well as craven) by legions of Obama's critics on the neoconservative and nationalist right, always impatient under signs of restraint.

Perennial complaints over burden-sharing have fueled much of the public discontent with America's world position, but there is further potential for a revolt against militarism in both parties—by Democrats because it threatens social welfare spending; by Republicans because it magnifies the powers of the central state. Though Democratic hawks definitely have some explaining to do to their base on this point—why exactly does the primacy of foreign policy produce domestic welfare?—it is the apostasy of "limited government conservatives" among Republicans that is most remarkable. "Why," asked Carl Oglesby in 1967, "have the traditional opponents of big, militarized, central authoritarian government now joined forces with such a government's boldest advocates?" They should have known better, Oglesby argued: "It is pre-eminently through the ideology of the Foreign Threat, the myth of the tiger at the gates, that frontier and global imperialism and domestic authoritarianism have always rationalized themselves."[11] But they did not know better. It is anomalous that the party of social welfare should so prize guns, and yet more anomalous that the party of federalism should rush headlong into centralization, but there it is. Substantial elements of the bases in both parties are aware of the disjunction and shake their heads at it, but with limited effect.

In crucial respects, the "national mood" is something of a fiction. It often stands in contradiction with itself and cannot generate anything approaching a consensus. The nation does not want war, but it recoils at the thought of accommodation to rival centers of power. The public readily imbibes the ideology of the national security state, even as it bridles at the costs. The public does not in the main approve the elite's understanding of internationalism— "the belief that, to be secure, the United States must exert the full panoply of its power—military, economic, and ideological—on the international system in order to shape its external environment"[12]—but the public has proven willing to back up the state if it is challenged in this quest by other powers, throwing the fuel of Jacksonian nationalism on the fires lit up by America's strategic ambitions.[13] Fear of U.S. casualties, combined with plenty of *thumos*, makes for reliance on airpower—the ability to blow things up, now with great precision, across vast distances. The military tool chosen from obeisance to domestic constraints is not necessarily the one capable of achieving a strategic aim, but it has faced little public backlash thus far. Amidst this welter of opposing and rival interests, diffusing their power in antagonism, empire holds the balance and is well-placed to decide for the public good.

Though interventionism is associated with "engagement" and isolationism with "withdrawal," there are certain respects in which the actual positions of these camps are quite the reverse. Hawkish internationalists say that American military power and its system of guarantees are the linchpin of the system, and that to question those guarantees is to counsel withdrawal and isolationism. In greater measure, however, what passes for "internationalism" today is just a chauvinistic projection of American aspirations onto the international scene, a thing originally made possible only under circumstances of the most unbalanced power, but which is often blind to the ideals previously understood to animate internationalism. Old ideals of the equality of peoples—of the equal right of the world's peoples to autonomously determine their own destiny—were swallowed up in new imperial ventures, concerned to ensure right conduct everywhere. Arms control went by the board. It is the interventionists with their vast sanctioning projects against "hostile states" who seek to cut off American businesses from external interaction. It is the globalists who insidiously sought to convert the new American invention of the Internet into a universal panopticon, reflecting an institutional paranoia in the security state that extended even to close allies.[14]

This reversal of position is also characteristic of the debate on the non-military dimensions of foreign policy. The historic debate over foreign policy between interventionists and isolationists was always fundamentally informed by the prospect of war and the status of military alliances. But, of course, there is a vast other set of considerations that raise critical problems, have a global character, and ought to be a key part of the agenda for American foreign policy. Among these are the specter of relentlessly increasing temperatures, making for extreme climate change, rising sea levels, and food insecurity; the danger of widespread pandemics, imperiling world commerce and public health; the alarming state of the world's oceans, facing an increasingly hazardous future (for them and for us).[15] These challenges require both national exertion and international cooperation if they are to be addressed. They raise acute problems in which all the world's nations are vitally interested, but which none can successfully address singly. And yet among Republicans, especially, those most avid for U.S. security commitments across the globe are loath to commit the United States to international treaties or collaborations that address these issues. "Internationalist" or "interventionist" in one sphere, they are "isolationist" in the other.

A New Internationalism

Despite the curiosities in the debate between maximalists and minimalists, there is a real sense in which those polar opposites do inescapably structure the debate at hand. In nearly every strategic setting, there is a choice between U.S. escalation and restraint. Most participants on either side, however, have instinctively recoiled from the charge of extremism. A long tradition supports this aversion to extreme solutions. In Aristotle's immortal words, "One may go wrong in many different ways . . . , but right only in one; and so the former is easy, the latter difficult; easy to miss the mark, but hard to hit it; and for these reasons, therefore, both the excess and defect belong to Vice, and the mean state to Virtue."[16]

The reconciliation I endorse, to be unfolded in the following pages, also positions itself between the Too Little and the Too Much, though it is not a theme-less pudding midway between extremes. America should not withdraw from the world but reframe the terms of its engagement with it. It needs a new internationalism, not a generalized withdrawal into itself. The retrenchment in the U.S. military position I recommend will, of course, be denounced as isolationist by critics, and I do not deny that it squints toward isolationism in certain respects. If our only choice regarding U.S. military commitments is between indiscriminate globalism and hidebound isolationism, I would with little hesitation make the latter choice, like Lippmann in 1967. But even with respect to military policy, the policy recommended here falls well short of isolationism and "no entangling alliances."

The needed renovation of American foreign policy in crucial respects flows directly from the diagnosis already set forth. I have sought to show that the United States does not and cannot function as the legitimate umpire of the international system; that its ostensibly liberal ends have concealed highly illiberal means; that its universalistic and revolutionary doctrines, holding the world's states to one standard in their domestic configurations, have been destabilizing to international order; that its military policy and posture have been overly aggressive, deeply reliant on offensive strategies that aim at the annihilation of the enemy's armed forces; and that the very people who most loudly praise the "liberal world order" have lost touch with critical elements of the liberal tradition.

If these ills are properly diagnosed, the remedy follows directly. Rather than the revolutionary tradition that justifies state overthrow, the United States should return to its tradition of liberal pluralism, rejecting madcap ventures to overthrow the government of states. Rather than claiming a superior role as judge, jury, and executioner, it must share power in accordance with the Golden Rule. It should reconsider its belief in the efficacy of the use and threat of force, and undertake the gentle remedies that liberalism once encouraged. It must adopt a more defensive military posture, emphasizing attrition rather than annihilation, and rekindle its interest in arms control and limitation. It must reconnect with central elements in the liberal heritage, making the preservation of domestic liberty the first rule of its conduct and reintroducing ideas of counterpoise and balance in the conduct of foreign relations. It needs restraint rather than braggadocio, acceptance of its role as a nation among nations rather than arrogant pretensions extolling its exceptional virtue and superior wisdom. I call it a renovation because, in conceiving of an alternative to America's globalist posture, it does so by reverting to first principles and reconnecting with America's tradition of republican liberty.

This new strategy is non-interventionist with respect to the conflicts that have embroiled the U.S. in the Middle East and the Global South, emphasizing the advantages of the traditional law of neutrality over aid to insurrectionaries. It is not a pallid call for "selective internationalism" that would retain "permanent forward operating bases" in East and Southeast Asia, Europe, the Persian Gulf, and Central Asia. Such attempts to follow the policy of the trimmer, sometimes identified with realist prescriptions, in fact trim nothing: "empire on the cheap" is still a formula for endless expense and unexpected war.[17] I also call for a redefinition of responsibility within America's major alliances in Europe and East Asia, with local forces assuming primary responsibility for their own defense. Unlike all globalists (but also unlike many non-interventionists), I propose measures of reconciliation with Russia, China, and Iran, sure to roil conventional opinion in this country. Within these constraints, however, I argue for maintaining the North Atlantic Treaty and its pledges of mutual aid and support, and also the security treaties with Japan and South Korea. Nor do I think the United States should renounce the nuclear guarantee to NATO, Japan, and South Korea—a guarantee, however, which should have as its sole purpose the deterrence of the first use of nuclear weapons by a hostile power.

The United States needs to maintain the great friendships it has formed in Europe and Asia over the last 70 years, in short, but it also needs to "reach across the aisle" and work out rules of the road with putative adversaries. The internationalism projected here is focused on the United Nations system, both in its requirement of concert among the Great Powers as institutionalized in the Security Council, and in the profound restatement and revision of pluralist norms in its Charter. The ethical foundations of this system—instantiated

in what I have called the old international law—stand opposed to the globalist and revolutionary aspirations the United States developed over the
last 25 years. Critics will call it isolationism, but it is, in fact, a form of internationalism superior to America's hegemonic version. Such a reorientation
would reduce the prospect of war with the other Great Powers, the overriding
responsibility of these nations. It would help refocus America, Russia, and
China on what remains one of their most important responsibilities: seeking to defuse the dangers posed by the massive nuclear arsenals built during
the Cold War (together with the new dangers posed by their antagonism in
cyberspace). It would also facilitate their cooperation in working to compose
the raging conflicts in the Middle East.

A new internationalism should be founded on the old internationalism
of the UN Charter, but it must also respond to new circumstances, especially
the grave challenges threatening the global ecosystem. Building on a pluralist
foundation, it would seek cooperation into matters like climate change and
global public health, of urgent import to humanity. The dangers raised by
rising temperatures, increasingly acidic oceans, and global pandemics actually
constitute a far greater threat to American well-being, even to the physical
security of Americans, than dangers from terrorism or hostile states. If one
considers current trends in the climate and oceans, especially, we are looking
at a very grim future prospect that could have gigantic implications for coast-
line communities, for food supply, for habitability of the globe, for the generation of refugees. Considering the actual distribution of resources and effort,
it is apparent that our fixation on the military dimension of things has meant
the relative neglect of these other critical challenges. America's military-based
form of internationalism is often touted as fully consistent with and indeed an
indispensable foundation with the other internationalisms required, but in a
critical respect it is deeply at odds with them. Competing for the slender share
of discretionary funds in the federal budget, the security sector has feasted
while others were left famished. One sort of engagement with the world, led
by the spear, has flourished; another sort of engagement, addressing urgent
questions of climate and disease, has floundered. Trump seems set to heighten
this contradiction even further.[18]

A new approach is also required in American political economy. There
can be no prospect of withdrawing from the increasingly globalized economy.
The international financial system is a fragile thing, deeply interdependent;
no nation can maintain its prosperity separately, and the management of the
world economy requires international negotiation and treaties if it is to avoid
hard times. But we should be leery of extrapolating from this condition of

embedded interdependence to the claim that the maintenance of the world trading system requires strict fidelity to the neoliberal gospel, an outlook that permits no deviation from a world privileging the free movement of goods and capital. Were U.S. trade policy to move toward the prescriptions of the "national school," as I think it should, it would again have an industrial policy and a labor policy, something already enjoyed by its principal economic competitors (China, Germany, Japan, South Korea, especially). It would aim for greater balance in production and consumption, exports and imports. These limited and sensible aims would rechannel but not overturn the entrenched pattern of global trade and financial interdependence. That there are dangers of a trade war in such an approach is true. But a reasonable policy also needs to address the excessive deficits in trade and the economic and social havoc wreaked by exclusive fidelity to neoliberal prescriptions.

It is a dour reflection on the state of things that, on the commanding issues of war and peace, the political division in the country over intervention and alliances can hardly get coherently registered in the political arena. Fifty percent of Americans may consider themselves as non-interventionists but, in the home of representative democracy, their voices have been nearly inaudible in legislative debate, the mainstream media, and the think tanks. When a challenge does emerge to the globalist consensus, as with Trump, it takes an illiberal and norm-traducing character that is emphatically not about making America more modest again, when this is precisely what is required. Rather than the militarized globalism to which we have become accustomed, and the belligerent nationalism that offers itself as a false alternative, the United States needs a new internationalism, as Fulbright aptly called it. Such an approach would look for a fundamental change in U.S. doctrine regarding the use of military power, not simply a marginal adjustment in America's world position or a reshuffling of burdens with America still at the lead. A new internationalism asks how U.S. security, prosperity, and liberty can be satisfied with a national security apparatus cut by a third or more. There is a legitimate argument over where to draw the line of retrenchment; the non-interventionists themselves are not agreed on the point. But we need a fundamental overhaul, a choice, not an echo.

The new internationalism I propose is radically different from what the military-centered internationalism of today has come to mean, but still authentically in line with the vision of previous internationalisms, based on concert more than collective defense, and insisting on the Golden Rule, as opposed to neoliberal or neoconservative rules decreed by the hegemon. But I do not wish to disguise my attraction, shared with other non-interventionists, to the isolationist principle of repelling the contagion of war from these shores. That is indeed a key purpose of the reorientation of U.S. policy proposed here.

Return of the Lippmann Gap

General principles never translate without difficulty into concrete circumstances. Irving Kristol once remarked that intellectuals are particularly ill-suited to really understand the world of foreign policy, being too far removed from the levers of power and concrete questions faced by policymakers. The world of intellectuals and academics is beset by galloping abstractions, essentially irrelevant to the cares of seasoned and "in the know" practitioners. Kristol certainly had a point; the contrast between practitioner and outside critic is real. At the same time, it is useful to remember that, at the time of Kristol's writing, in 1967, academic specialists were warning that the rivalry of Vietnam and China was far too deeply entrenched to make credible Washington's image of a Red Tide sweeping Southeast Asia under centralized control. In retrospect, we can clearly see the academics right and the policy-makers wrong. Nationalism trumped ideology. Obscure scribblers had it right over the insiders.[19]

The failure in Vietnam shook the Cold War consensus, without destroying it; the failures in Iraq and Afghanistan shook the public consensus even further, though paradoxically had the effect on the elite of confirming the main axioms of policy. Despite the 2011 congressional sequestration, total military spending under Obama's eight years exceeded the amounts under Bush, when two high-tempo wars were underway. The security complex is supported by a vast array of powerful interests, institutions, and ideologies, rendering it very powerful indeed. But it is not invulnerable to challenge; in fact, it is beset by numerous dysfunctions that sap at its underlying strength. Of these, two seem especially important. One is the sheer gargantuan cost of the U.S. security apparatus. A second is the growing gap between commitments and resources, that is, the re-emergence of the Lippmann Gap.[20] Both point to an endemic crisis.

Despite the seeming permanence of the establishment consensus, the clash between "defense" and "the general welfare" looks inexorable. An aging population, with its appetite for expected benefits, will drive federal expenditures relentlessly higher over the coming years. Public appetite for taxation, by contrast, seems altogether unlikely to keep pace. Deficits, having fallen from well over $1 trillion at the outset of the 2008-09 financial crisis to a low of $438 billion in 2015, are now on the rise again. Current forecasts put the 2016 budget deficit at $590 billion, rising to $1.2 trillion by 2026. The ten-year cumulative deficit estimate is $8.6 trillion, with debt held by the public (excluding the Social Security Trust Fund) rising from $14.1 trillion to $23.1 trillion, or 76.6 percent to 85.5 percent of GDP. This is the so-called baseline budget, assuming no major new expenditures (like a war), no major financial crisis, and no tax cuts.[21] Some items are almost certainly underestimated: long deferred spending on infrastructure cannot be deferred much longer, and won't be, once bridges start collapsing. Within the interstices of these iron constraints, national security expenditures look vulnerable if they cannot meet a standard of necessity. For the young, especially—they who see restricted job opportunities, inherited debts, growing expenditures on the elderly, and precious little investment in themselves—the insatiable consumption of limited resources by the national security complex looks to most of them like a threat to their welfare.

Anxiety about the budget deficit and the relentless accumulation of debt has been a feature of national politics for generations, assuming its modern form with the Reagan tax cuts and defense buildup of the 1980s. In the past, it was always assumed that the credit markets would penalize with higher interest rates a government that demonstrated profligacy in its fiscal accounts, but a sluggish economy and the miracles of modern central banking rendered that restraint almost nonexistent in recent years. Interest rates fell even as budgetary discipline relaxed. After the financial crisis of 2008, America could borrow as much as it liked. I noted earlier the observation of Adam Smith and James Madison that the capacity to borrow would be an invitation to war, because debt disguised the ultimate costs. Over the last generation, the United States has run a massive social science experiment confirming the veracity of the observation. Will this peculiar and unexpected situation—an essential absence of fiscal restraint—last forever? That seems highly unlikely.

A second contradiction in U.S. policy is the gap between resources and commitments. The big expansion in the scope of American commitments undertaken at the end of the Cold War occurred in a strategic context much less threatening than today's. With the end of the Cold War, America's dominant position in the international system seemed to make the Lippmann Gap irrelevant; there was no longer a gap between power and commitments, but a surfeit of power in relation to existing commitments. Over the next 25 years, prompted partly by the absence of effective opposition, commitments continued to expand, and the Lippmann Gap returned.

The re-emergence of the gap was not predicted by those responsible for its re-emergence. Fifteen years ago, the idea prevailing among neoconservatives and assertive nationalists was that everybody would be cowed into submission and indolence by a U.S. military superiority that was impossible to calculate or overcome. The possibility of Great Power conflict, given Russian and Chinese weakness and dependency in the 1990s, looked utterly remote. The commitments were undertaken on the assumption of an easy maintenance of U.S. military superiority, in the age of unipolarity; they must be maintained in a world in which the diffusion of power and technique has been a persistent trend.

One dimension of the changing balance is the invigoration of Chinese and Russian military power since 2000. Russia has doubled its expenditures; China has quadrupled hers. The big increases in U.S. military spending of the previous decade were used up in fruitless contests and did not cover anything like the modernization requests of the armed services; the wars were paid for, in part, by delaying modernization and, of course, by running big deficits. A big wave of ever more expensive modernization requests lies in wait as a pressing need if U.S. commitments are sustained. If America means to be the world's dominant military power, capable of projecting prodigious amounts of firepower abroad, it must pay for the privilege. Despite the gargantuan annual expense, it did not do that in the Obama years.

Given its hostility to Iran, Russia, and China, together with half a dozen possible flare-ups in which American credibility would be challenged by lesser states or groups, the United States needs something like a three and a half war standard, not the "one war" or "one and a half war" standard to which relative budgetary stringency (in relation to its modernization program, especially) has consigned it. For much of the post-Cold War period, Russia and China were essentially out of the picture as enemies with whom war was conceivable. This is no longer the case. The United States has local military inferiority in the Baltics, for instance, and can only cover that with "escalation dominance." It has local military inferiority in the South China Sea, and can only cover that with "escalation dominance." This once looked easy; it has now become hard. Anxiety about the permanence of conventional superiority in distant theaters is a key reason behind the establishment's refusal to countenance a "no first use" of nuclear weapons pledge (and a further key source of American insecurity under the present strategy). In antiquity, the Romans resolved their strategic predicament by fighting one war at a time, but if the RICs have the evil and conspiratorial tendencies so often ascribed to them, would it not be in their interest to block that stratagem? The anxiety prompted by that question generates requirements for U.S. military forces well beyond Trump's expensive requests.

Were big increases in the military budget to materialize, to be sure, it would not bring security; on the contrary, a further military buildup would greatly increase the risk of conflict, as compared with an alternative course that undertook a retrenchment in those objects for which the United States would be prepared to fight. Trillions of dollars in additional defense expenditures, paired with the forward deployment and strategy of U.S. forces, would not fundamentally alter the capacity of Russia or China to do grievous harm to the United States if war commenced between America and its two Great Power rivals. The United States could quadruple the number of drone strikes in Pakistan, Afghanistan, Iraq, Syria, Yemen, Libya, and Somalia, while adding Iran and others to the list, and would be no closer to stabilizing the area or mitigating the threat of terrorism.

The means by which the U.S. security complex proposes to close the Lippmann Gap, then, are illusory. It ought to do so by adopting constructive approaches to political settlement rather than by ratcheting up its military efforts. Unfortunately, such a course faces profound obstacles. America's alliance commitments are considered in Washington as "unbreakable" and "indissoluble," and the remedy, with little dissent, has been seen in terms of a forward military presence that must possess escalation dominance over adversaries. But it is also true that this strategy is very expensive and, given likely domestic constraints, fundamentally unaffordable. From Washington's interior perspective—imagining what it must do to close the gap, giving up on the prospect of political reconciliation with adversaries—it has a serious problem in generating resources sufficient to cover its commitments. It not only has a Lippmann Gap, but also no obvious remedy by which it may be closed.

The Nixon Precedent

In the post-World War II period, the most spectacular precedent for reconciling with enemies as a way of closing the Lippmann Gap came in the presidency of Richard Nixon. It had been the revolutionary fervor of "Red China" in the 1960s that most alarmed Washington and made it critical to avoid defeat in Southeast Asia, prompting the commitment of over 500,000 troops to South Vietnam. By 1972, Nixon was in China meeting with Mao Tse-Tung, the widely feared and reviled Chinese leader. His trip to Beijing was followed by a visit to Moscow, there to sign two nuclear arms accords governing offensive and defensive weapons. That these visits coincided with North Vietnam's massive spring offensive and the ferocious U.S. countermeasures, including the bombing of Hanoi and the mining of Haiphong harbor, made it all the more remarkable. By 1972, the American relationship with both communist powers had been transformed.

At his second inaugural in January 1973, after having defeated George McGovern by a wide margin in the 1972 presidential contest, Nixon summarized the principles that should guide American foreign policy. Nixon's leitmotif was the recognition of limits, standing in sharp contrast with John Kennedy's 1961 call to bear any burden and pay any price in defense of liberty. Nixon reaffirmed the old consensus—unless America works for peace, there will be no peace; unless she works for freedom, there will be no freedom. But the burden of his remarks was as much the responsibility of others as of America's. Affirming that the United States would stand by its treaty commitments and support vigorously the principle (ostensibly at stake in Vietnam) "that no country has the right to impose its will or rule on another by force," Nixon also struck several other notes of conciliation, restraint, burden-sharing, and national responsibility:

- We shall continue, in this era of negotiation, to work for the limitation of nuclear arms, and to reduce the danger of confrontation between the great powers.
- We shall do our share in defending peace and freedom in the world. But we shall expect others to do their share.
- The time has passed when America will make every other nation's conflict our own, or make every other nation's future our responsibility, or presume to tell the people of other nations how to manage their own affairs.
- Just as we respect the right of each nation to determine its own future, we also recognize the responsibility of each nation to secure its own future.
- Just as America's role is indispensable in preserving the world's peace, so is each nation's role indispensable in preserving its own peace.
- Together with the rest of the world, let us resolve to move forward from the beginnings we have made. Let us continue to bring down the walls of hostility which have divided the world for too long, and to build in their place bridges of understanding—so that despite profound differences between systems of government, the people of the world can be friends.
- Let us build a structure of peace in the world in which the weak are as safe as the strong—in which each respects the right of the other to live by a different system—in which those who would influence others will do so by the strength of their ideas, and not by the force of their arms.[22]

Nothing could be more contrary to Nixon's avowed pluralism than George W. Bush's declaration in 2005, when he pled, "The survival of liberty in our land increasingly depends on the success of liberty in other lands. The best hope for peace in our world is the expansion of freedom in all the world." Nixon's stated vision of order, in contrast with Bush's, was emphatically pluralistic in rejecting a single standard of political legitimacy. In this he followed John Kennedy's call for a world made safe for diversity, as Kennedy had followed Eisenhower's belief that "only in respecting the hopes and cultures of others will we practice the equality of all nations," and as Eisenhower had followed Truman in fixing on the prevention of aggression, not the reconstruction of the world's polities, as the key to international peace. I discussed previously the process wherein these maxims achieved a sort of inversion during the Cold War, but their violation then is no good argument for their non-observance now.[23]

Nixon and Kissinger brought Russia and China into the society of nations and sought to have good relations with both; that, too, is an important precedent that a new internationalism should honor. To have better relations with each than either had with the other gave flexibility and a margin of safety to U.S. policy—it was partly a calculation of realpolitik for Nixon and Kissinger—but the vital requirement for the policy's success was an understanding that both Russia and China were Great Powers, with the keen sense of national honor and interest. To contain them, you also had to reassure them. A similar bargain with Russia was pursued in the negotiations that ended the Cold War, but the Nixon-Kissinger precedent is more interesting, as it was carried out in more difficult circumstances, with adversaries unwilling to hand the U.S. victory on a platter, as Gorbachev in effect did. The United States does not face today the same strategic circumstance it confronted in the late 1980s; today's circumstance is much more similar to the 1970s in presenting multiple points of international tension. Perhaps the most remarkable feature of Washington's security consensus is its seemingly determined attempt to drive Russia and China into one another's arms (and then into Iran's). Only in the world of the national security state, nourished by deep ideological rancor and selfish interest, can such a policy seem rational from a geopolitical standpoint. The power of the constellation in Washington that has pushed toward this outcome, however, cannot be gainsaid.

It is not my intention to idealize the Nixon and Kissinger policy, though in its great pronouncements (like the second inaugural address), it does offer a useful corrective model for what has ailed U.S. foreign policy in the last generation. Its great weakness was not the offer of détente with the communist powers—though that was what killed it in domestic opinion—but that a key purpose of that détente was to better pursue its militarized policies elsewhere. It gave up as unprofitable and dangerous the pursuit of ideological antagonism with the Great Powers, but then pursued the Cold War crusade with a vengeance against smaller powers.

In searching for the principles of a renovation, the Nixon precedent is thus undoubtedly imperfect. Nixon and Kissinger's conduct ultimately showed a continuing attraction to force: "peace through strength" rather than "peace through reconciliation" better expresses their true outlook. Their efforts at reconciliation with the Soviet Union ultimately proved abortive, suggesting the hazard, domestically, of attempting conciliation with historic rivals. Extending the principles of an accommodation to Iran, for which I advocate below, would undoubtedly be found by Kissinger as exceedingly naive. These qualifications notwithstanding, there was considerable wisdom in Nixon and Kissinger's prescriptions for building "a new structure of peace." They wanted to defuse the prospect of confrontation between the United States and its two historic rivals, and their path shows some of the essential steps required for that enterprise.[24]

Toward a New Détente

The structure of peace that Nixon and Kissinger wanted in the 1970s was drowned out by renewed Cold War. Its consummation flickered again brightly in the late 1980s and early 1990s as a real possibility, only again to succumb to a powerful hawkish countertrend. In the 1990s, Russia and China were too weak and dependent to seem to Washington the objects of a concert. Though this word was sometimes uttered by policymakers, it was increasingly belied by the conduct of the United States toward its historic antagonists. Instead of ensuring them a status commensurate with their dignity and interest, the United States sought to extend its military superiority over them. The less they threatened American safety, the more we undertook a full court press against them, insisting on a big presence in their own geopolitical space and devising war plans that aimed at the obliteration of their armed forces on their own territory. The idea was to make American military supremacy so supreme that "hostile nations" could never challenge it, but all this succeeded in doing—a great capstone to 20 years of effort—was giving them an incentive to fear us and a motive to reinvigorate their own military efforts. Most injuriously, external pressure also gave power and justification to the security complexes within both Russia and China, strengthening them against their more liberal opponents at home. For a liberal sensibility, this is a grim and predictable outcome; for neoconservatives, it simply confirms their world-view. That is the beauty of the neoconservative ideology and one of the great keys to its persistence, a fact of which they may be dimly aware: it is guaranteed to produce antagonism, after which they can say: "See, we told you so."

Despite all the bad blood that has been created by this policy, as the nations entered the well-known spiral into antagonism, such a reconciliation of aims is still available were the United States to pursue it. Russia and China are not opponents of a pluralistic conception of international order. They are eminently tractable adversaries, dogged in the pursuit of their interests but open to negotiation and compromise. Such a policy would base relations with Russia and China on the recognition of their vital interests. It would surrender and condemn the idea that it was the U.S. intention to overthrow them or to interfere in their internal affairs. It would treat them as possessing the rights that all nations have to self-protection. It would restore an older conception of diplomacy based on the resolution of disputes for the version now so much favored (and so much influenced by ugly practices of the twentieth century) that sees communication with foreign governments as the occasion for propaganda and the issuing of threats. It would base policy on the Golden Rule, seeking to understand their national and political rights as having equal weight—in the eyes of God and of the law of nations—with our own.

Is it so unreasonable to take the concerns of historic rivals seriously? Not if you are looking for the rule of equity, as opposed to selfish advantage. Recall that justice, as Hobbes showed, requires doing just that. Put yourself in the shoes of the other; set your own passions and self-love aside; do unto others as you would be done.

The crucial issue, almost never discussed in the Western press or acknowledged by the American government, arises from the pretensions of the U.S. military and allied states directly on the borders of these two giants. No Great Power would submit without protest to such demonstrations on its frontier. The assumption that these forward deployments are necessary for deterrence, and that in their absence either power would mount a gigantic land grab against their neighbors, is fundamentally implausible. These forward deployments are war-provoking, rather than peace-inducing, seriously raising the danger of "war by accident." Instead of ensuring that Chinese and Russian arms are kept holstered, these "in your face" deployments force both powers into countermoves that raise the danger of war.

To recognize the rights and vital interests of these two great adversary nations is not to render apology for the domestic actions of their leaders; it is not to be an apologist for Vladimir Putin or Xi Jinping. It is, however, to be an apologist for the basic rights and importance of Russia and China as nations among nations, and it is to object to the convenient trick by which exclusive attention to the calculations and presumed evil propensities of enemy leaders serves to obfuscate the legitimate interests of their peoples. That concession is normally associated with realism, with the precept that it is imprudent to interfere in the zones of vital interest of other states, especially great states; but liberalism, with its insistence on natural right, has something to teach in that regard as well. If we would not accept the buildup of hostile forces from an external superpower on our borders, why should they? The domestic popularity of their countermoves against the U.S. superpower—whether in annexing Crimea or building artificial islands in the South China Sea—is something that should count, given the great likelihood that governments of a perfectly democratic complexion would have pursued the same policies.

To stop treating Russia and China as enemies would inevitably affect the U.S. relationship with its friends. Enmity with Russia is greatly sought (not quite demanded) by Poland and other Eastern European countries. Enmity with China is courteously requested, but requested nevertheless, by Japan and other allies in East Asia. They all want to say: if you really love us, you will join us in hating them. A new internationalism would mean the abandonment of this antagonism and a return to the wisdom of Washington's Farewell Address, with its warning of the invidious consequences of habitual hatred and the infusion of the enmities of friends into U.S. policy. Or as Richard Nixon put it to a NATO summit in 1969, "Those who think simply in terms of 'good' nations and 'bad' nations—of a world of staunch allies and sworn enemies—live in a world of their own. Imprisoned by stereotypes, they do not live in the real world."[25]

In both theaters, such an adjustment would doubtless cause palpitations in allied leaders, but the change should not entail a formal renunciation of our principal alliances in Europe or East Asia. At a minimum, it would mean a restriction of the American strategic frontier vis-à-vis Russia and China—placing areas within their sphere emphatically outside of our own. It would mean also a military posture essentially different from the "front-line" policies so long established, one whose purposes align with the classic ideas of maritime strategy. The U.S. should be the reserve force, not the front-line force; the force to be called on in unexpected adversity, not the first responder, the backup plan when all else fails, not the world policeman. Allies would undoubtedly prefer an America that carried its disproportionate burden from the past into the future, but it is hardly obvious why they should think it prudent to reject a more modest U.S. role, if such were America's resolution.

If it were serious about a retrenchment, the United States should want, in retreating, to help establish a new diplomatic constellation, not throw everybody into a panic. Ideally, it would be negotiated with both allies and enemies, the objective being to reach an understanding about permissible action. If the U.S. were willing to make reasonable concessions to their point of view, Russia and China could again be partners.

The best argument *for* this course is that a contrary act of determined withdrawal from these treaty commitments, in a spirit of defiant nationalism, might indeed be destabilizing; the best argument *against* is that it wouldn't actually change anything, allowing the expansionists back in the saddle. A priori, it should not be thought inconceivable that both of these worries could be reasonably addressed in a negotiated settlement. It would be the point of the negotiation to do so. To those who would say, however, that the United States should prepare to fight in Russia's near abroad, or for tiny islands in the South China Sea, the answer must be, with Warren G. Harding: "I do not want to clarify these obligations. I want to turn my back on them."[26]

Reconstituting the European Alliance

Much as the indispensability of the U.S. role in Europe is treated as a sort of first axiom by the security establishment—in Washington, Brussels, and Berlin—there are substantial reasons to doubt it. There is a threat of Russian domination only in the overheated imaginations of the security caucus, who cannot tell the difference between a boundary dispute and Napoleonic ambitions. The Russians want decent treatment of the rights and interests of "their people" in their near abroad, in whom they have a justifiable interest, and they object strenuously to aggressive Western military demonstrations on their borders, but otherwise they are attracted to multilateralism and quite conservative about the use of force. The Ukraine crisis hardly disproves this, given the culpable role of the West in sponsoring the February 2014 revolution in Kiev. With or without Ukraine, Russia's vaunted Eurasian project was just a customs union, a defensive barrier for a vast region of weak industries. Russia knows that its increasingly decrepit nuclear weapons are good for nothing save deterrence, and that to employ them as an instrument of intimidation would make Russia a pariah and be grossly self-defeating. The Russian elite is conscious of Russia's deep societal and demographic weaknesses and, all things considered, would prefer a good relationship with the West to a better relationship with China. A coalition of Germany, Sweden, France, and Britain alone—to say nothing of the larger EU—is easily a match for Russia in Europe, but the more basic point is that Russian foreign policy cannot be about the "domination" of Europe. That would be an absurd objective for them, and they know it. In relation to the other European powers, Russia is less powerful today than at most periods from 1713 to 1913, yet on none of those earlier occasions was it able to dominate the continent. Russia came closest in the decades after 1815, an era often described today as an episode in Britain's "liberal hegemony."

For most of the post-Cold War period, Germany continued to want an American presence in NATO not so much because of the danger from Russia but because of skepticism over finding an acceptable formula, in the absence of the Americans, for a European security structure. The U.S. insertion into Europe via NATO took security questions off the table for the European communities and, later, the EU; Germans doubt that any kind of consensus could be achieved on a new blueprint, and have long felt existential dread over the possibility that they should be the ones to provide it. It would, they fear, put more stress on the EU than it could handle, encouraging division.

"NATO exists for three reasons," held Lord Ismay in a classic expression: "to keep the Russians out, the Americans in and the Germans down."[27] But this 1949 statement of NATO's first secretary-general, endlessly repeated because it was clever, did not quite foretell the future: the Germans were not kept down but raised up, as they have gratefully acknowledged; they accepted, and even wanted, the political and military restraints that defined their position in NATO and on the Central Front (e.g., the deployment of NATO forces that kept German forces separated and incapable of independent action). In the post-Cold War era, as in the Cold War, the function of the United States in Europe has not been to keep the Germans down, but to avoid—for Germans and other Europeans—the delicate question of the military role that Germany would play in a European order shorn of American power. The Europeans have never had a ready answer to that question since 1945, and they do not have one now. For want of anything better, the U.S. role looks rather good.

It is understandable that Europe should prefer the known advantages of its alliance with America over a separation, but this conservative preference does not show that the European balance would be seriously threatened, or that the EU could not find an acceptable substitute, if the United States were to exit. The point will be controversial, but I think it expresses a basic truth: if she had no other alternative, Angela Merkel could close her eyes, tap her slippers three times, and reconstitute the old European concert in short order, with nary an American soldier or airman or spy in sight. The Germans have never wanted to do this, as the alliance with the United States has long been considered in Bonn and Berlin as the rock of their salvation. But Merkel or a future German chancellor could do it if they needed to. A U.S. posture that proceeds on the assumption that "old Europe" has no alternative to the American connection would read the tea leaves incorrectly. As Merkel observed, responding to Trump's bluster: "We Europeans have our fate in our own hands."[28]

The renewal of cold war with Russia in Europe was the most lamentable, and perhaps even most inexplicable, blunder of the Obama presidency. Victoria Nuland marched into Kiev with as much élan as any neoconservative could muster, successfully encouraging the February revolution, but the grim and predictable result was a stark deterioration of U.S.-Russian relations and the breakdown of the post-Cold War peace. Given Obama's larger philosophical commitments, his acquiescence to this revolutionary policy is very difficult to understand. The episode certainly suggests the power of the institutional apparat against the musings of the incumbent president, though Obama showed no public signs of resistance to the policy.

The best argument against NATO is what its avowed proponents have done to it, essentially transforming it from a defensive alliance into an expansionist engine—from something quite estimable and constructive to something quite objectionable and destabilizing. NATO has had two great purposes over the last 25 years: one was to project U.S. military power into the Greater Middle East; the other to march baldly into Russia's geopolitical space. The NATO of the Cold War did neither of these things; widespread evocations of NATO's "seventy-year record" of peacekeeping in Europe neglect the doubling in size and expansion in scope it underwent in the last two decades. Both enterprises have come a cropper, yielding less rather than more security and bringing the utility of the alliance in its new configuration into grave question. If the choice is between what NATO has become and a complete break, the latter is the better choice.

But those stark choices do not represent the only alternative. The United States might instead retain its commitment to the North Atlantic Treaty but step back from the kind of military role it has projected for itself. Under such a change, a European general would become the SACEUR (Supreme Allied Commander, Europe). The United States would recommit to the arms control pledges it made as part of the post-Cold War settlement, withdrawing its forces from Eastern Europe and dismantling the antiballistic missile systems it is stationing in Poland and Romania, giving up its suspect claim that these are directed against Iran, not Russia. It would retract its now invigorated program of naval exercises on Russia's northern flank and its provocative notion of establishing a U.S. naval presence in the Black Sea. It would seek a political rather than military solution to the problem of European order, leaving primary responsibility for military strength in the hands of the Europeans themselves. At the same time, it would retain its nuclear guarantee, pledged to meet fire with fire against any power that used nuclear weapons first in a European conflict. It would abandon its doctrine of preparing further states on Russia's western and southern perimeter (e.g., Ukraine and Georgia) for future NATO membership.

The first step would be a settlement of the issues over Ukraine. The narrative by which that crisis is entirely Russia's fault and a clear case of Russian aggression is not persuasive. The key wrong done by the United States in the crisis was to support the overthrow of a democratically elected government, outside of democratic procedures. This guaranteed an extreme outcome. The February 2014 revolution meant the transfer of the armed power of the state from one group to another, done not peacefully, but under threat of force. This act created a state of nature, that is, a situation in which the right of one group to take up arms (those Russophones in the East) followed inexorably from the prior resort to forcible means by another (the Westerners). If the Easterners had that right, which on these ancient principles they surely did have, they also had a right to seek foreign assistance from Russia, and for Russia to give it on grounds once urged by Daniel Webster, narrowly approving "a right to interfere in extreme cases, in the case of contiguous states, and where imminent danger is threatened to one by what is occurring in another."[29] Of course, Putin did not exactly follow this course, disguising Russia's role in southeastern Ukraine supporting the rebels. His lies over Russia's role did her no good. Russia encouraged the revolts, but then was totally surprised by the determination and ability of the Ukrainian nationalists to stage a ruthless counterattack, putting at risk the very people the Russian government was supposed to be looking after (forcing the more blatant though still disavowed Russian intervention in August 2014). There is plenty of blame to go around for this man-made disaster, especially bad for the intended beneficiaries of the U.S. role. It is a profound tragedy for the Ukrainians that they should have sought entry into the West by imitating, not Poland in the 1990s, but Poland in the 1930s. The war, which the Ukrainian demonstrators at Maidan brought very much upon themselves by treating contemptuously basic constitutional principles about the transfer of power, has set the country back a generation. The subsequent rift with Russia has also been bad for Europe and the West generally, hindering European economic recovery and making cooperation more difficult on other global issues.

Though the EU bears some responsibility for the Ukraine crisis, airily refusing the Russian offer of negotiations before the crisis broke, the United States was clearly of critical importance in offering the Ukrainians the promise of support and encouragement for the overthrow of Yanukovych by the Maidan. (That these expectations were severely disappointed after the event does not show that they were insignificant before the event.) Had the American government made clear that it did not approve of street demonstrations as a means of changing governments, and urged the demonstrators to work for their favored candidates in the scheduled presidential elections, most of them would doubtless have returned home. Instead, the United States and other Western governments embraced a method of change that they would be horrified to adopt in their homelands. The peaceful transfer of power after elections is a sacred rite in American politics, the most important emblem of the democratic faith, but America's liberal press expressed no concern—on the contrary, they celebrated it as a great triumph of democracy—when Ukrainian nationalists chose street protests over ballots to effect the transfer of power there.

A settlement of Ukrainian crisis should acquiesce in Crimea's incorporation within Russia, lift the economic sanctions, and give the inhabitants of the Donbass a choice, via an internationally supervised plebiscite, between incorporation in Ukraine and Russia. Probably, they would choose incorporation into Russia.[30] The advantage of that outcome is that Russia would then bear responsibility for the reconstruction of the region, now in a state of near total devastation. Even staunch advocates of Ukrainian independence have recognized that Ukraine's obsession over wresting these provinces from Russian control is an obstruction to its economic development and political reform.[31] Crimea was historically part of the Russian homeland and has a predominantly Russian population today; its transfer to Ukraine in 1954, under Khrushchev's drunken orders, was an historical accident. Russia was content with an arrangement, previously negotiated with Ukraine, in which its naval base at Sevastopol remained under Russian control in return for substantial Russian rents paid to the Ukrainian treasury. These should be resumed under the settlement projected here, with both countries also given an equal share of the revenues to be gained by the exploitation of the Black Sea's undersea resources. In return for this accommodating stance, Russia would be expected to give—and would give—guarantees of nonaggression against Ukraine, the Baltic states, and Poland.

The viability of these new arrangements for European security ultimately rests on the analysis of Russia intentions. These have, in my view, a fundamentally defensive character, deriving from the legitimate Russian objection over the West's military encirclement, frustration over Western meddling in Russia's internal affairs, and justified anxiety over the treatment of Russophones in its near abroad. The United States has never taken an interest in the latter question, especially pronounced in Ukraine and the Baltics, a fact that highlights the real motives of the security establishment. Outrage over alleged Russian machinations in the 2016 U.S. election, too, could stand some introspection about the extent of American machinations in Russian affairs. If such introspection were to occur—don't count on it—the needed return to mutual non-intervention, rather than escalating sanctions, would be on the table.

Since the foundation of the North Atlantic Treaty in 1949, Americans have repeatedly complained about the disparate share of burdens between the United States and its allies. Those complaints have some justification, but it is seldom noted that most of these disparate burdens are entirely a consequence of U.S. policy, especially in the post-Cold War period. The United States was the driving force behind NATO expansion in the 1990s and 2000s; it could have easily pursued a different policy without substantial objection from its traditional allies. The Europeans, too, were not responsible for the even greater disparity in burdens, as measured by spending on defense budgets, which arose from America's hugely expensive wars in the Greater Middle East over the last fifteen years. The preponderance of European opinion was decidedly opposed to the war in Iraq, and even those governments that did support the war (e.g., Britain and Spain) did so over the objections of majority opinion within their own countries. The burden-sharing problem is largely of American making, reflecting not the deficiency of the European contribution, but the excesses of the U.S. one. Rather than approaching them as deadbeats—or worse, seeking to undermine the EU—it would be better to act on the assumption that they have the capacity and the will to take primary responsibility for their own conventional defense. If they wished to fortify their conventional defenses in response to an American decision to constitute the reserve force of the alliance, as opposed to its front-line force, they would have the opportunity to do so, and a reasonable U.S. initiative would give them time to accomplish that.

For Europe, what is needed is a return to demilitarization in the contested space between Russia and the West, a much safer environment than what the current trajectory of move and countermove will produce (more expense and the greatly heightened danger of incidents leading to war). In the 1990s, the mantra was that NATO should go out of area or out of business; the new mantra should be the elaboration of a new structure that reconstitutes the agreements that ended the Cold War and that no longer sees the alliance as an interventionist arm "out of area."

East Asian Retrenchment

A similar reorientation of policy is advisable in Asia, founded on the retrenchment of U.S. military aspirations against China. As I suggested in Chapter 3, the Chinese have had very solid reasons to resent, and resist, the pretention to U.S. military superiority in China's home waters. The strategy on which the United States has come to rely—the AirSea Battle strategy that calls, in the event of war, for strikes against China's military infrastructure and political leadership—poses a direct threat to China's national security. Americans should easily perceive that China has legitimate grounds to fear American power in the East and South China Seas, with its offensive war-fighting plans, considering how Americans would feel if a hostile foreign fleet should ensconce itself in the Caribbean Sea with similar offensive capabilities (while touting America's bad record in the neighborhood and the need for an impartial umpire to keep the United States in line). Not to be dismissed is the sentiment of the retired Chinese admiral who compared the U.S. Navy in East Asia to "a man with a criminal record 'wandering just outside the gate of a family home.'"[32]

This offensive strategy snuck up on little cat feet, eliciting hardly any adverse comment in Western security circles, but it is understandably opposed by China's officials and viewed with indignation by its populace. The United States can engage in this competition—a function of imagined military needs—only at enormous expense. It ought to be abandoned, and a true maritime strategy, one based on attrition rather than the annihilation of enemy armed forces, substituted in its stead. Such a policy would recognize that China has primary responsibility for maintaining the freedom of navigation in its inner seas, and adjust U.S. military dispositions accordingly. Under this revised policy, the United States would continue to support Taiwan's existing status, but would give up the threat to go to war with China in the unlikely event that China were to invade the island. Such a move would be met by economic sanctions, not war. To Philippine President Rodrigo Duterte's threat to evict the United States from its basing arrangements there, it would say: "Thank you very much. Good-bye."

The U.S. commitment to South Korea and Japan in Northeast Asia raises especially delicate questions. The seemingly maniacal character of the regime in North Korea makes the maintenance of peace a challenging objective. A U.S. withdrawal from its security commitments would in all probability lead South Korea and Japan to acquire a nuclear capability. That Japan is husbanding more nuclear material than it needs shows that this possibility has been deeply considered in Japan, though as the recipient of the only two atomic bombs ever used in war, its public does have deep pacifist inclinations that would make a decision to "go nuclear" a matter of agonizing debate. South Korea, with a population double the size of North Korea's and an economy 40 times larger, should be able to deter—and, deterrence failing, to defend against—a North Korean attack, but nuclear weapons complicate the picture enormously. North Korea's regime is also prone to blood-curdling threats and erratic pronouncements, making it seem the very model of the irrational actor.

One set of facts seldom put on the table in understanding the attitude of the North Korean regime is the devastation wreaked on the country during the Korean War. Forgotten in America, the air campaign against the North was one of great brutality, no different in character from the U.S. air war in Japan, only recently concluded, and stopping short only of the use of nuclear weapons. Most major towns were destroyed; airmen complained of the lack of suitable targets, having hit everything worth burning up. Famously insular, the once hermit kingdom remembers this as its Holocaust or its Nakba, seared upon the mind. That memory above all explains North Korea's desire to accumulate a fearsome nuclear arsenal, one that will make the U.S. think twice, thrice, ten times before committing aggression.[33]

The nuclear problem reveals its most tragic dimension in the Korean context, because weapons intended for deterrent purposes prey upon the minds of adversaries, tempting them to countermoves and putting preventive war on the table. It is, indeed, the propensity of nuclear weapons to elicit calls for preventive war that constitutes their most potent threat to peace—in Northeast Asia no less than the Greater Middle East today, but also on previous occasions in the nuclear age. Such rash expedients were considered in the late 1940s in response to the Soviet bomb, urged by many in the 1960s to contend with China's bomb, and counseled by Dick Cheney (after a 48-hour ultimatum) against North Korea in 1994. A U.S. withdrawal from South Korea—especially if attended by a U.S. pledge to help the South acquire nuclear weapons, or at least not obstruct its doing so—might raise those dangers. It would doubtless be viewed in the North as an insidious plot, with motives guaranteed to be malicious and with public rationales seen as lies issued from clenched teeth.

It is doubtful if the North, under those circumstances, would actually attempt to destroy South Korea's nuclear infrastructure, but it would be all but guaranteed to issue threats to do so, making for a state of continual tension.

China rather than the United States is the most important restraint on a potentially volatile North Korea, difficult though the Chinese find their old clients. North Korea's dependence on the Chinese makes it, despite fierce avowals, a paper tiger, with nowhere to go by way of offensive action. Given the ease of deterrence, and the potential dangers of total withdrawal, it seems advisable to continue with the U.S. commitment to security in Northeast Asia. These considerations also suggest, however, that U.S. threats to wage preventive war against North Korea, never fully taken off the table as a response to its nuclear program, are both unnecessary and provocative—threatening to do what no sane statesperson would do, given the potential for enormous destruction and retaliation, but also giving the North, with its historic paranoia, a reason to continue on its nuclearized path. The United States should abandon the war exercises that, as recently revised in OPLAN 5015, simulate the destruction of North Korea's nuclear capacity and political leadership. It should "un-deploy" the THAAD defense system, stationed in early 2017 in South Korea—a system threatening to China and indubitably dangerous to everybody's security, as it inevitably appears to the North as part of a first strike strategy. That threat, in turn, prompts North Korea to put its nuclear forces on hair-trigger alert or adopt launch on warning strategies, increasing the danger of accidental war.

Reducing the U.S. military presence in South Korea—and backing off the aggressive exercises and threatening deployments—would reduce the threat of war. Such reduction is also advisable on the principle that South Korea, with its far greater wealth than the North, should be able to handle its conventional defense, relying simply on the promise of U.S. reinforcement. As in other theaters, the U.S. would continue with its nuclear guarantee but adopt a "no-first-use" pledge, confining its threat to the first use of nuclear weapons by another power. Within these limitations, the U.S. commitment to the defense of South Korea should remain. The acquisition by South Korea and Japan of nuclear weapons would contribute nothing to Northeast Asian security, and might give a boost to proliferation elsewhere in the world. Efforts to cap that volcano remain a compelling interest for the United States and the world.

Threats to wage preventive war against nuclear proliferation during the early Cold War never made it into the upper echelons of American governance; the political leadership, from Truman to Johnson, saw the risks and never took that option seriously.[34] After the Cold War, however, this option immediately arose, and it was, in fact, implemented in the Gulf War of 1991. The war was provoked by Saddam Hussein's invasion of Kuwait in August 1990, but the Bush administration soon made clear that the resolution of the crisis required not simply Iraq's evacuation of Kuwait—economic sanctions could probably have accomplished that—but the abolition of Iraq's program for the development of nuclear weapons, an objective that could only be secured through war. The Bush administration greatly feared an outcome that left Iraq's nuclear program intact. It wanted the elimination of that capability (and the larger decimation of Iraq's military forces). The Iraqi spectacle gave a big boost to the North Korean program. What occurred in Iraq could easily occur in North Korea. On the one hand, getting nuclear weapons made you a target; on the other hand, they made you an unassailable one. So it looked to Pyongyang.

North Korea conducted its first underground nuclear tests on October 9, 2006, and had by the end of 2016 gone on to conduct four more. The decision to go nuclear arose out of the breakdown of the six-party talks among China, the United States, Russia, Japan, and the two Koreas. On September 19, 2005, their brief moment of success, North Korea committed "to abandoning all nuclear weapons and existing nuclear programs, and returning, at an early date," to the NPT and to supervision under International Atomic Energy Agency (IAEA) safeguards. In exchange, Washington affirmed (in much less categorical language than it might have used) that it had no intention to attack or invade North Korea. On the surface, it seemed that the United States was prepared to get security by giving it, but appearances proved deceiving. The nuclear accord was quickly followed by draconian sanctions against North Korea's financial sector, showing plainly that Washington remained determined to strangle the North economically. When nuclear talks resumed, North Korea objected vehemently to the U.S. financial sanctions. That proved a point of no return for the prospects of the Korean peninsula's denuclearization. Obstruct an agreement, force the other party into a submissive posture that you know he will reject, and then pass on the folly of your obstinacy to future administrations—such was George W. Bush's bequest in Northeast Asia.[35] Obama's decision to overthrow Qaddafi, who had surrendered his nuclear program in negotiations with the United States, was to North Korea just another confirmation that American assurances were worthless. From their vantage point, the North Koreans do have understandable reasons for a nuclear capability, provocative though their missile tests may be. Those motives center on self-protection, not aggression or conquest. When no one wants a war, it should not be beyond the wit of the regional concert—China,

U.S., Japan, Russia, especially—to keep the peace in Northeast Asia, but America's decades-long handling of the nuclear brief let slip serious opportunities for a negotiated settlement.

Concert versus Dominance

The larger justification for the U.S. role in the world, especially after the Cold War ended, was that it was necessary to keep the motors of history from revving up again, with the old problems of a remilitarized Germany and Japan creating momentum toward a revival of the competition that doomed the world in the twentieth century's first half. During the Cold War, it might be said, the great purpose was to avoid a repetition of 1939—that is, to forestall aggression; in the post-Cold War, the great purpose was to avoid a repetition of 1914—that is, to forestall the path by which multipolar systems become unstable and prone to war (with the secondary purpose also being present in each period). The post-1990 justification for the U.S. role was, in some official circles, deeply felt. In the absence of the American guarantee, Germany would again fall into conflict with its neighbors, as would Japan. Keeping them tied to the Americans would reassure both allies and enemies, defusing the logic that led multipolar systems to war. To complete this circle of reasoning, advocates of U.S. supremacy contend that unipolarity is a far surer route to peace than multipolarity, and cite the historic experience of the European system, with its evident proneness to war, as proof.[36]

International systems always have had, and probably always will have, the possibility of war within their anarchical structure. But it is also highly pertinent to note the differing material and geographical circumstances as between the nineteenth-century European system and the twenty-first-century global system. For one, the Rhine River is rather narrower in width than the Pacific or Atlantic Oceans; the assumption of inevitable conflict was a lot surer when such proud and confident powers were abutting one another so closely. It is also vital to remember that the attempt to solve this great nineteenth-century problem by one power bidding for dominance was, as the event showed, no remedy at all. The apologists of global U.S. military supremacy highlight as the cure the very phenomenon that brought down the old European system. But it is the comparison based on geographical factors and physical proximity that is most striking. The United States has a conflict with Russia and China because it wants to, not because it needs to.[37]

It is a distinguishing feature of the nuclear age that technological change—above all, the pairing of the ballistic missile and jet airplanes with atomic weaponry—brought close proximity despite oceanic distances. Internationalism was first aroused in the twentieth century by the implications of the military-scientific revolution. In the famous statement of H. G. Wells, arguing for world government, the marriage of science and militarism threatened to "so enlarge and intensify the scope and evil of war and of international hostility as to give what was formerly a generous aspiration more and more the aspect of an imperative necessity."[38] This was in 1919. Thirty years later, the development of nuclear weapons by the United States and the Soviet Union was now conjoined with a worldwide political rivalry. One of the implications was that the hypertrophy of power made global war highly improbable. At the same time, both superpowers kept their hands on the trigger and developed systems capable of instantaneous destruction. Alongside the new weapons lay the conviction, formed from the harrowing experience of the world wars, that aggression was a crime that could only be deterred by the threat of overwhelming force, or else it would acquire unstoppable momentum. The predominant attitude was well conveyed in a piece of popular culture early in the nuclear age: the speech that Klaatu, the visiting spaceman in *The Day the Earth Stood Still* (1951), gave in the final scene of the movie. We won't disturb you if you keep to yourselves, promised Klaatu, but commit aggression against other planets and total obliteration will follow. This message, presumably, was meant seriously by the film's *auteurs*— and was faithfully reflected in the war plans developed in the 1950s for the U.S. nuclear arsenal.[39] It also got a workout, as we have seen, in the use of American airpower against North Korea.

Even during the Cold War, a huge gap existed between the actual interests at stake in superpower squabbles and the danger of nuclear war, however slight, that attended these crises; in the post-Cold War, the gap became yet wider. However, the arsenals remain and, at least on the U.S. side, are scheduled to undergo a costly "modernization" and renewal. The general problem is that the weapons themselves—in theory, only a means—become themselves the key factor in generating fear on the other side and somehow leap above the more prosaic interests at stake. When means drive ends, a reconsideration is in order. Given U.S. technological dominance in conventional weaponry, the imperative of policy should be to marginalize nuclear weapons, declare "no first use" under any circumstances, aim to reduce further numbers of warheads and delivery systems, and remove the threat of obliteration from any foreign policy objective save retaliation in kind under absolute necessity.

But that is not the course the United States has adopted. Instead, it refuses to adopt a no-first-use policy. Its belief in the utility of nuclear weapons is attested by its massive investment program, which speaks more loudly than any doctrinal statement. The question to be raised about this program is that which U.S. hawks raised in the 1970s about the Soviet program. Yes, these massive investments would seem, to a rational person, to confer no advantage. Why then the massive investment? Those in charge of such programs obviously think otherwise. Is that not worrisome? For the United States, spending $1 thousand billion to secure its massive nuclear arsenal would not confer any advantage but would carry with it one signal disadvantage (apart from the wasted expense). It would not give the United States the ability to bully anyone, but it would foster the opinion elsewhere that the United States is indeed a bully.

Preventing a revival of a spiral into conflict and Great Power war should remain a fundamental objective of U.S. diplomacy. The proneness of the Westphalian system to war was its great deficiency. The principle invented to regulate the system, the balance of power, was intended to preserve its peace, as Burke said, but had only preserved its liberty. It had been "the original of innumerable and fruitless wars."[40] It is a great mistake to overcome these deficiencies, however, by combining "full spectrum dominance" in the military domain with an aggressive political push into the near abroad of other Great Powers. A concert strategy is far more eligible as a remedy for the ills of the Westphalian system than one that aims at dominance. As a matter of logic, and on the evidence before us, the U.S. effort has not stilled the rivalry of the Great Powers but instead has put the United States in the middle of it, often as the most provocative participant. That has to change.[41]

By recasting its strategic frontier, the United States would look toward a new structure of peace, to be achieved by dialing back the threats, not ratcheting them up, or abandoning them altogether. The key to a transformation is not instigating quarrels with friends but reconciling with enemies, by taking their vital interests into account in the formulation of U.S. policy. Such a step would contribute to both the U.S. national interest and the international order. Rather than withdraw from the international system, the United States would reach across the aisle for a concert among the Great Powers. Happily, there is an institutional vehicle for such a policy already extant: it is called the United Nations. There is also a normative framework already in place for this bold new course: it is called the United Nations Charter.[42]

Heart of Darkness

When the American alliance system was formed, it was the great transoceanic ties with Western Europe and Japan that were always deemed most important, but in the last generation, unlike the first two generations, the overwhelming preponderance of U.S. military effort has been in and around the Greater Middle East. Andrew Bacevich has dated the beginning of this with the Carter Doctrine of 1980—a reasonable marker—but it was the 1991 Gulf War that reflected the most dramatic change. Never before had the United States used force in the region on anything approaching the scale it did in 1991. The awesome display of power was meant to intimidate, and did intimidate. Americans have an idea of the use of force, drawn mostly from the movies, in which it all takes place in one heroic moment, after which the good guy goes home and gets the girl. What the war really meant was a shotgun marriage to the region. The U.S. got Iraq out of Kuwait, but it was now itself manifestly incapable of being anything other than the region's dominant power. Hannibal's saying, cited earlier, was duplicated in spirit: I have conquered Saddam in Iraq; send me more commitments. "Dual containment" followed. The great losses incurred by the Arabs in that spectacular display of American firepower also fueled in a certain Osama bin Laden—though not in him alone—a desire for revenge.

The U.S. alliance system that exists in the Middle East is riddled with paradox, and about as enigmatic and mysterious as Russia was back in the day. In its dominant features, the system has made a dramatic contrast with the pattern of interaction and influence in Europe and East Asia. It is in the Greater Middle East that America's position has been most "imperial," yet it is at the same time the venue that has most displayed a total lack of U.S. control over its supposed clients and dependents. It is from the Middle East that the demand to exit most fervently arises in the public, but it is to the Middle East that America has been inexorably drawn by equally potent, thus far more potent, domestic forces. It is the Middle East where the United States has invested by far the largest amount of military effort in the post-Cold War era, but in which its pretense of following the rules of a rule-based order is most hollow and even risible. A clutch of great problems—terrorism, nuclear proliferation, energy security—arise from the interstices of the Greater Middle East demanding solution, against a backdrop of the widespread sense at home that nothing attempted by the United States in the region ever goes as planned.

Understanding America's position in the Middle East must start from one outstanding fact, which is that the invasion of Iraq in 2003, and America's evident desire to install a new regime that would be the anchor of the U.S. position in the region, thrust it into an entirely new position with regard to its Arab allies in the Gulf. The U.S. was pursuing an ideological objective, the installation of a new democracy in the Muslim heartland that would show the viability of the U.S. model and become an inspiration to others. The Americans, listening to their own sweet music, reasoned that a new democracy would be pluralist, would respect the great principles of the free society, such as the separation of religion and state, would be based on parliaments rather than palaces, bottom up rather than top down, a bona fide democracy in a region of tyrants. They also expected great collateral effects on Iraq's neighbors, a domino effect that (with a little American help) might blow away the other autocracies as well.[43]

America's imperial masterminds neglected only to consider one important demographic fact, which was that the Shia constituted 60 percent of the Iraqi population and would inevitably emerge dominant if democracy was the rule. Once the U.S. figured this out—a revelation that occurred after the invasion, not before—America saw that it could not snuff out the Sunni voice without provoking more violence in Iraq and without disastrous consequences for its relations with the other Sunni powers—with the Saudis and the emirates, most obviously, but also with Jordan and Turkey. The U.S. military's objectives in the first few years of the war were all about "civilizing 'em with a Krag," in the expression of the U.S. soldiers in the Philippines a century ago. The discovery that this method provoked a universal loathing from the Iraqi population, plus the realization that a lot of this force was misaimed because enemies could make use of poor U.S. intelligence for their own purposes, led to a reconsideration. The great tactical improvisation of the war by the U.S. military (far more important than "the surge") was to separate the Sunni tribesmen from the crazed Al-Qaeda extremists, the forerunners of today's Islamic State, who threatened from 2004 to 2007 to take over the rebellion. The Americans had destroyed the Sunni state along with the hated leader of the Sunnis, Saddam Hussein; but the consequence of war was to make them the Iraqi Sunni's protector and voice, as Saddam had been previously.

The Saudis, especially, were appalled at the new political map they confronted, with the Shia axis ensconced all the way from Assad's Syria to Malaki's Iraq to Ahmadinejad's Iran. The Americans were also fairly appalled that every conceivable Shia government in Iraq was determined to have fully cordial relations with Iran, America and Israel's hated enemy, but the Iraqi Shia desire to do so arose imperiously out of their history and sensibilities. The Americans begged and begged the Iraqi Shia to reconsider their relationship with Iran, as also their attitude to their former oppressors, the Sunni, but any lasting reconciliation between Shia and Sunni eluded the occupiers. It was the main idea behind the reconstruction once the occupying forces began thinking in political terms—which took a while. Always beckoning as the only possible hope, the mirage of a grand coalition uniting Shia, Sunni, and Kurd—fairly dividing up the oil revenues, decentralizing administration as in the U.S. federal model—invariably receded in practice. Iraq was to be neither a barrier to Iran nor the anchor of U.S. military power in the region.

Out of its faith in democracy, America had thus brought to power a predominantly Shia regime allied with Iran, giving the Shia Crescent control of governments from the Mediterranean to Persia. The most important adjustment to that new fact came in response to the great revolts that swept over the Arab world in 2011. The U.S. government, as ever, was entirely evenhanded: it supported its allies, more or less, and sought to energize revolts against its adversaries. It voiced a bit of displeasure, but threatened nothing, when the Saudis used force to keep the Bahraini king in power in his rule over a majority Shia population (and where the U.S. headquarters its Fifth Fleet). In Egypt, it did abandon an old ally, Hosni Mubarak, but its role there was probably insignificant, far less so than Egyptians suppose. The deal was always going to be that Mubarak would go as a price of saving the army and the apparat, the "deep state" that obstructed Mohamed Morsi's brief rule and that never intended to go away.

The Arabs like to think that everything the United States does is all nicely worked out in advance, but, in fact, one of its biggest initiatives in 2011—the overthrow of Qaddafi—was unsupported by many of the U.S. national security elites. This hawkish project, as we saw earlier, was pushed by the humanitarian interventionists in Obama's national security team (Clinton, Rice, and Power, especially) over the opposition of the civilian and military leadership at the Pentagon. The purpose of the R2P enthusiasts was to prevent another Rwanda and also, perhaps, spread freedom by overthrowing a dictator, but the motives of U.S. policymakers were essentially unmoored from the larger commitment of U.S. policy in the region—the complex of interests that makes the U.S. an ally of the Sunnis and the Israelis against the Shia Crescent. The Saudis and the Qataris hectored the U.S. to get rid of Qaddafi, and by virtue of being paymaster of the Arab League got a lot of support from other Arab governments, but compliance with their wishes was a motive that seems not to have especially swayed the U.S. government—the Pentagon officials closest to these regimes opposed the intervention, and that was surely a secondary factor for Clinton, Rice, and Power.

Once Qaddafi was overthrown, attention turned to Syria, and many jihadists made transit to Syria immediately after Qaddafi's evisceration. When U.S. Ambassador Christopher Stevens was killed in September 2012, the U.S. Mission in Benghazi was closely monitoring the transfer of arms to the Syrian insurgents from Qaddafi's now-opened arsenals, and in all probability facilitating it.[44] In its consequences, the transfer of arms to the Syrian insurgents, much of which ended up in the hands of either ISIS or the Nusra Front, is a far greater scandal—apart, that is, from the destruction of Libya itself—than anything Secretary Clinton did or did not do to protect American personnel in the wee hours.[45]

In the well-known sequel, ISIS emerged as top dog of the Syrian resistance, first extracting ransoms from kidnappings to gain resources, then conducting a brutal internecine war against fellow jihadists to gain predominance, then seizing large swathes of territory and great caches of arms in 2014 in Syria and Iraq. Before its great victories, it had broken from Jabhat al-Nusra, or the Nusra Front, the local Syrian affiliate of Al-Qaeda and the preponderant military player in the resistance, lately rebranded as Tahrir al-Sham, to which both the Saudis and the Turks allocated tremendous resources. Somehow this didn't get our esteemed allies onto the State Department's list of state sponsors of terrorism. The American government maintained the fiction that the other forces in the Syrian resistance were moderates, and they were certainly more moderate than either ISIS or Al-Qaeda (who could not be?), but nearly all the soldiers (the Kurds apart) were Sunni fundamentalists and wanted a sectarian state.

American reporting on the Syrian crisis was 99 percent in agreement that the conflict was entirely Assad's fault and that he bore exclusive responsibility for all the suffering, but there is much in the story that disputes this narrative. Does it mean nothing that outside governments should throw such massive resources into support for the overthrow of an established government? Is that allowed under the rules of a rule-based order? Does it mean nothing that Assad should have on his side many denominations, whereas the armed resistance has on its side only one denomination? When Aleppo was taken in late 2016 in the Russian and Syrian offensive, Western opinion viewed it as the crime of the century, but the preponderant local sentiment experienced it as a liberation from the despotic control of crazed fanatics. The Western press conveyed the impression that the entire enclave stood in stout opposition to Assad, but after the fall, notes Patrick Cockburn, "only a third of evacuees—36,000—asked to be taken to rebel-held Idlib. The majority—80,000—elected to go to government-held territory in West Aleppo." Said one Aleppo professor in the aftermath, himself an opponent of the regime, "If there were an election today, [Assad] would get more than 70 percent of the vote." Undoubtedly, there are a great many Syrians who hate Assad, but there may be an even greater number who hate the rebels more.[46]

Despite America's historic attachment to "secularism" and its commitment to the principle that religious persecution is an evil, it put itself in Syria on the side of those most hostile to that very idea. The tears U.S. politicians have shed over the destruction of the Christian communities are especially notable, as no outside power has more responsibility for the state-wrecking enterprise in Iraq and Syria that made their position untenable than the United States of America. This responsibility goes unmentioned in their lamentations. A year before ISIS swept into Mosul, Michael Rubin reported after a trip to Iraq that "not only Iraqi Shi'ites, but also Iraqi Christians, Iraqi Kurds, and even many Iraqi Sunnis oppose American provision of arms to the Syrian rebels on the grounds that the Syrian rebels are either more radical than the Americans realize, or that nothing will prevent the so-called moderates whom the United States arms from selling or losing the weaponry to the radicals." The Iraqis deeply feared that they would be "the first victims of Sunni radicalism in neighboring Syria." And so they were.[47]

The disintegration of Syria is related to the disintegration of Iraq, as in the domino theory of old. In the dispensation that was overthrown, there was a kind of symmetry by which a minority-Sunni regime ruled over a majority-Shia population in Iraq, and a minority-Alawite regime, aligned with the Shia interest, ruled over a majority-Sunni population in Syria. The Iraqi breakdown contributed to the Syrian breakdown, especially in producing a felt want of Sunni representation from the Mediterranean Sea to Iran. It consequently fired the Saudis and eventually the Turks to see the overthrow of Assad as critical to their security. In the aftermath of the Arab Spring, the United States blindly signed on to that illegal and imprudent objective, oblivious to the catastrophe it was enabling.

I noted earlier the remarkable contrariety of aims between the United States and its allies. Saudi Arabia is fully engaged in a regional war against the Shia Crescent—Syria, Yemen, Bahrain—and sees this as vital to its security. It was furious with the United States when it did not act accordingly, though the United States under Obama opposed the Saudis nowhere and openly facilitated its military operations in Yemen. Such U.S. support came despite the clear illegality of the Saudi intervention and the devastating consequences for Yemen's civilian population. Saudi leaders called in 2016 for the overthrow of Iran's Islamic Republic. The kingdom has intervened with massive assistance to support groups, especially the Nusra Front, denominated as terrorists by the United States. These steps in the region are complemented by the Saudi abandonment of its role as "central banker for oil," a step inspired by its desire to inflict maximum pain on its immediate opposition (Iran and Iraq, especially), but that had as its announced target, gratuitously, the U.S. shale industry. Those steps had nothing to do with long-term price maximization or stability, and Saudi Arabia only began in 2016 to retreat from its price war when the self-inflicted pain became too great. From the standpoint of the way the U.S. conceived of the Saudi role in the past—a guardian of stability taking the long view and understanding that its interests could not be protected without protecting the consumers of its product—the Saudis have been entirely off the reservation. Their readiness to use force in Yemen and through proxies in Syria has shown an aggressiveness that is new and very different from the sleepy dispositions once prevailing in Riyadh. And now, spending five times as much on armaments as Iran, the Saudis have a gigantic cache of American weapons, courtesy of the prodigious arms sales authorized by Obama during his administration.[48] Instead of arms sales supporting U.S. foreign policy, the reverse dynamic has prevailed, with the tail very much wagging the dog in this instance. Trump seems determined to intensify the trend.

President Recep Tayyip Erdogan of Turkey is another "ally" with aims that raise alarm. He has fancied himself as a sort of sultan, a reincarnation of the Sublime Porte, and has been at work consolidating his power in Turkey in ways distinctly illiberal. This was so even before the abortive coup of July 2016; it is emphatically the case since that time. As of April 2017, 280,000 people—some perhaps guilty of participation in the coup, others emphatically not—were dismissed from their jobs or imprisoned. Before Erdogan's rapprochement with Israel, he spoke of the Jewish state in tones no different from—perhaps even more vehement than—the most radical rejectionist of the "Zionist entity." Baby-killers, he called them. He threatened in November 2016 to unleash hordes of refugees to Europe unless the Europeans tended to his wishes.[49] He told Iraqi Prime Minister Haider al-Abadi that he should "know his place," observing, "You are not my interlocutor anyway. You are not on my level, you are not of my quality. You ranting and raving from Iraq is not of any importance to us."[50] Turkey was the prime facilitator of the Islamist rebellion against Assad, opening its border to recruits from abroad, transiting arms, seeking the overthrow of its neighboring government. Despite getting in return the worst kind of blowback imaginable, in the shape of ISIS terror attacks, Erdogan has looked on the Kurdish insurgents—the PKK and their Syrian affiliates—as the primary threat to Turkey.

The great battle cry among Republican neoconservatives and Democratic hawks has been to "support our allies" 100 percent, everywhere in the world, but especially in the Middle East. Even Bernie Sanders wanted to hand things off to the Saudis, despite the Saudi support of jihadists a hair's breadth away in

doctrine and sentiment from ISIS. Supporting the Saudis means supporting
the increasingly virulent Saudi policy of deep participation in various revolutions and counterrevolutions throughout the region. Supporting the Turks
means supporting an increasingly autocratic and illiberal Turkey, an entirely
different country from what it was during America's long collaboration with
it in the Cold War and beyond, with the "indigenes" winning the old contest
between the modernizers and traditionalists.[51] Erdogan's significance lies in
his resolution to obliterate the vision of the secular elites that, out of Turkey's
"torn" condition, wanted to move it to the West. He wants it to be the head
of Islam. He is a supple politician, capable of executing impressive reversals, as
in his 2016 rapprochements with Russia and Israel. But his ideological complexion is not far from the Muslim Brotherhood and Hamas. After opening
promising negotiations with the PKK in 2010, he turned decisively against
any kind of peaceful solution to the Kurdish question and sought a resolution
by force. The United States should be extremely leery of supporting Kurdish
rebels against the Turks, but between Kurdish terror by the PKK, and state
terror by the Turkish government, there is not much to choose.

A different policy would not support our "allies" in their violent adventures, but seek to restrain them, and if they prove incapable of restraint, abandon them to their own good fortunes. This is not a call to subvert them, as
functioning states are indispensable in the suppression of anarchy and terrorism, but it is a call to separate U.S. purposes from theirs. Much of their utility, from the standpoint of the security establishment, consists of using their
territory as bases from which to project U.S. airpower, and the U.S. establishment seems terrified that it could lose this kind of access. A United States that
needs less of that from them acquires a greater ability to resist their demands
for support; at a minimum, it gets to define its own purposes. Is it a sign of
empire and great power that the U.S. government should slavishly tend to
their wishes?

Since the 9/11 attacks, the problem of terrorism has dominated U.S. policy in the Middle East, and much of the rationale for American involvement
is related in some fashion to combating terrorism. The Bush administration
sought to solve the problem of terrorism through regime change and nation-
building in Afghanistan and Iraq, though the result in both countries hardly
conformed to expectations. The Obama administration chose a different
tack. After the surge into Afghanistan, a major initiative of Obama's first term,
the U.S. diminished the presence of U.S. ground forces in the region, but it
also stepped up aerial attacks, mostly through drones. It greatly expanded
the geographical scope of these operations, conducting a campaign of aerial

assassination in Pakistan, Yemen, Somalia, and Libya. Once ISIS captured large swathes of western Iraq in 2014, the United States then re-engaged in Iraq and opened a new front in Syria.

Despite the expenditure of trillions of dollars, there is little evidence that fifteen years of Herculean effort have diminished the threat of terrorism either in the region or at home. Though operations against ISIS have been successful in retracting its territorial control, the problem of terrorism remains. Certainly, the fear of it remains in the public. But there is a mismatch between military operations and the prevention of terrorism. Nearly all perpetrators of domestic terrorism have sought to avenge U.S. attacks in the Muslim world. This was true of the 9/11 attack itself, just as it has been true of the lesser attacks that have followed. In the countries concerned, as General Stanley McChrystal has noted, drone attacks generate loathing "at a visceral level" in the population, hardly conducive to isolating terrorist groups from local sources of support.[52] They also generate visceral loathing among isolated malcontents in the West.

As a general matter, it is impossible to eliminate the threat of terrorism entirely. It is too easy for a single individual or small group of individuals to perpetrate an atrocity. But dealing with the danger, at home, is a function of police and intelligence agencies, not military force; abroad, it is the function of states with effective control of their own territory. Much of what the United States has done by way of force has been counterproductive, both because of its state-breaking policy of overthrow and the rage its attacks have induced, fostering the recruitment of jihadis. What has been counterproductive in large doses would be yet more counterproductive in extreme doses, which is the remedy often bruited about by a certain sort of right-wing nationalism in the United States, an outlook for which Trump seems to have great affinity. But solving the problem of terrorism by adopting terroristic methods, when such are certain to ricochet against you, is imprudent and immoral—worse than a crime, an error. Its key failure—a failure of imagination and of the capacity of empathy—is to not reckon on the immense strategic depth of a Muslim world encompassing 1.6 billion people, and of the sympathy and determination evoked in them by the unjust death of their brothers and sisters. America could never hope to make them tractable by overwhelming uses of force in their own lands, and only a misplaced faith in the efficacy of force has tempted it to try.

"Terrorism" as an object of U.S. foreign policy was a commanding feature of the U.S. approach to the region long before "the global war on terror" was announced in 2001. At its inception in 1979, the original state sponsors of terrorism list included Libya, Iraq, South Yemen, and Syria. Cuba was added in 1982 (and removed in 2015). Iran was added in 1984 and remains the foremost state sponsor of terrorism, according to the U.S. government. The activity that makes Iran a terrorist state consists partly in the support that Iran has given to Hezbollah, an authentic political movement representing the Shia of south Lebanon that arose in ferocious resistance to Israel's eighteen-year occupation of their homeland (from 1982 to 2000). Iran's support of Hamas (since greatly attenuated by the fallout of the Syrian conflict) also counts against it, though Erdogan's Turkey, our "critical ally," is much closer to Hamas than Iran's mullahs. Above all, Iran is a terrorist state because it has lent Assad's government in Syria much support in its struggle against Sunni jihadists, though such support to an existing government is a right of states under international law and has been exercised countless times by the United States itself. More widely, though perhaps less formally, Iran is seen as a terrorist state because it views Israel as an encroachment on the Islamic world, destined to disappear in time. Not mentioned in this indictment is that nearly all people among our principal Arab Sunni allies think the same. Where is the Saudi religious figure who accepts Israel's narrative of its necessary and just existence as a nation among nations in the Middle East? Where is the "moderate" Sunni jihadist in Syria, the object of America's futile recruitment efforts, who believes that? The American government's idea of terrorism is just an elevated form of mud-slinging that unfairly demonizes one group of Muslims, and absurdly absolves another group, when all the combatants are implicated in having thought or done things that would qualify as terroristic (as indeed have the United States and Israel as well). It is also a blanket declaration that Iran has no right to maintain protective relations with Shia communities in the Sunni Arab world and that all such support constitutes an intolerable encroachment on the Sunni Arab domain. On the ground of natural right, it is difficult to see the basis for this assumption.

In the longer run of history, the U.S. strategy of overthrow was most significant for having released the hounds of the Sunni-Shia conflict, inadvertently providing the formula for a new thirty years' war. There is no virtue, or any other kind of public good, in having done that. Having played so large a role in the unfolding of the disaster, the United States cannot simply walk away; it has an obvious duty to try to draw the fangs of this conflict. At the same time, it need not define its objectives in primarily military terms. A change for the better requires a reduction of its military role and a transformation of its political stance.

Though American security would be best served by U.S. military disengagement from the region, the emergence of ISIS did call for U.S. cooperation and collaboration in the fight against it. This was more an obligation of honor to the Iraqis than an expression of vital interest, but real and commanding nevertheless. What is remarkable about U.S. policy since 2014, however, is that it has subordinated the struggle against ISIS to its other enmities in the region. This was true under Obama; it is likely to remain true under Trump. Even when the Obama administration drew back in horror at the consequences of the civil war its own policies had encouraged, it was unwilling to rectify its original errors of calling for Assad's overthrow and funneling arms to the resistance, a course that solidified the Sunni violent resistance which spawned ISIS and the larger Syrian disaster. Obama's establishment critics had nothing better to offer, and, in fact, the consensus prescriptions for dealing with the Syrian imbroglio (reflected in the plans of former presidential candidates Hillary Clinton and Jeb Bush) were predicated on the idea that each of Syria's main factions—Assad, ISIS, and Nusra—was anathema to the United States, holding out the prospect that a successful war against ISIS would be followed by wars against Assad and Nusra. Given the self-limitation on U.S. ground forces that even the most hawkish proponents embraced, this was a project for wrecking Syria further and ultimately getting buried in the sand. It assumed a successful intervention despite being, in principle, opposed to 80 percent of the effectual armed forces in Syria and Iraq. Failure—and the need to escalate once failure was manifest—was written into its constituent articles.

Trump made a great show in his campaign of opposing "regime change," and he denounced Iran and Saudi Arabia alike, but the main appointments and first steps taken by his administration have indicated a much different posture. Trump and his national security coterie seem to have ingurgitated in toto the Saudi and Israeli worldview demonizing Iran. They have also defined the threat of "radical Islamic terrorism" so broadly as to make much of the Islamic world feel implicated in America's wrath, an outcome obviously in contravention to any sincere desire to mitigate the threat of terrorism. The most likely guess—halfway between a fear and a prediction—is that Trump sees a war with "radical Islamic terrorism" to be politically advantageous to him, a means of consolidating his power at home. That would be the rational deduction of republican security theory.

The evident need of the Islamic world is a Peace of Westphalia for their suffering peoples, a concordat by which all seek only peaceful means to propagate their faith. They are in the position of the Protestants and Catholics of the sixteenth century; their way out will have to bear comparison with Westphalian principles. Almost certainly, there will be a redrawing of the political map, new borders recognizing a different array of states, quasi-states, or in-limbo federal states, to replace the two unitary states of Syria and Iraq, formed from the debris of the First World War. A key principle will have to be that as few people as possible are ruled by their mortal enemies, with people who find themselves on the wrong side of the line allowed parole to enter the other. Sunnistan (embracing swathes of Syria and Iraq) was on T. E. Lawrence's maps; it is a real thing that has to have a political expression.[53] Truly, it was some kind of God-awful curse that gave this political expression to ISIS and the Nusra Front. No diplomatic objective in the region is more important than finding other less toxic voices for this long-suffering people.[54] A virtual precondition for mitigating the region's violence is that U.S. objectives are aligned with Russia's, as each could then exercise jointly restraint on their clients. Unfortunately, it is almost inconceivable to think that Washington would be attracted to such a change in policy. In the absence of constructive approaches, the obvious alternative is to get out and leave it to others to solve.[55]

Blood and Oil

We cannot leave this scene of destruction without noting the status of the great material interest—access to the oil of the Persian Gulf—that has been held to explain much of America's Middle Eastern policy over the last 50 years. Much has changed since the problem of oil dependency seized the public imagination during the two great oil crises of the 1970s, when it was so widely believed that growing dependence on the oil of the Gulf would render the West's position increasingly untenable. The invention of hydraulic fracturing, or fracking, has entirely transformed the reserves situation, as it has brought a much larger amount of oil potentially into play at the right price. Oil remains a weapon—Saudi Arabia used increased production levels to drive down the price and punish its enemies among the producers—but any attempt to use oil as a weapon to extract political concessions from consumers (as with the Arab oil embargo of 1973-74) would be virtually unthinkable today, as recoiling upon its authors. Also transformative, though in a different way, has been the emergence of global warming and climate change as a fundamental threat to humanity's prospects, requiring earnest efforts to move away from the intensive use of fossil fuels.

Anything like a long-term strategy is missing from the U.S. approach to these questions. No Davoisie is running things behind the scenes; it is just an incoherent mess, the product of domestic necessities (no taxes on energy, please) and entrenched institutional interests, especially the Navy's need to generate requirements for its indispensability. Back in the 1970s, the United States didn't venture to put an aircraft carrier in the Persian Gulf, much less establish a permanent station. The need for it today is difficult to fathom, as the United States could easily surge airpower to the region in the event of the expected contingency (a closure of the Straits of Hormuz or attacks on shipping in the Gulf). For any of the major states, any attempt to shut it down for others is just an obvious way of getting it shut down for themselves, and none of them want that in the least. Oil revenues are for them the very coin of the realm, without which expiration (of the regime, of their own necks) is made much more probable. If America is addicted to oil, as even George W. Bush conceded, the Persian Gulf states are into that particular dependency in a more profound way than even profligate Americans. As such, the desperate need of each for egress forms a profound barrier on the part of any of them to close the shipping lanes. The obvious regard that each of them has for its interest secures the Straits, not the U.S. Navy. An aircraft carrier battle group is needed only for the most improbable of contingencies, with even these requiring measured steps rather than instantaneous domination and an in-your-face presence. The United States could withdraw its naval presence easily, giving its responsibility to the regional states, and say goodbye to its Persian Gulf bases with no loss, and even gain.[56]

A different policy would have greeted Saudi Arabia's abdication of the role of "central banker for oil," which it claimed to disdain and repudiate, with a U.S. effort to take on that role. The price bust actually afforded a great opportunity to do so, as it would have enabled the U.S. government to purchase oil at a bargain rate, well below the cost of the "marginal barrel" of oil (storing it, to be released at a later time of exploding upward prices). Because a price of $40 to $50 is below the long-term marginal cost—the price of "the last and most expensive barrel" required to meet global demand—it also afforded a strong justification for the imposition of a variable protective tariff. In conjunction with Canada and Mexico, the United States might have enacted a variable tariff to protect domestic production from Saudi manipulation, paired with higher rates of taxation on oil producers whenever oil prices exploded upward. To dream a little further, this benefit to the oil industry might then have been paired with stringent environmental regulations over fracking, making an unlikely win-win outcome for oilmen and environmentalists.

To go from a net oil import deficit of 13 million barrels a day in 2006 to 5 million barrels a day in 2015-16 was a big deal, with important implications for energy security, the balance of payments, and the exposure of the financial system to crisis. (Exploding oil prices in the summer of 2008, at a time of enormous import exposure, played a now forgotten but critical role in the escalation of the financial crisis of that year.) But the Obama administration did nothing to preserve those gains, nor were they registered by a changing policy toward the Persian Gulf. Additional increases in the strategic petroleum reserve, carbon taxes, and a variable tariff would give the U.S. the capacity to influence the oil market by moderating its crazy booms and awful busts, the same sort of mission given to the Federal Reserve. The Fed can buy $3.7 trillion in debt securities as part of "quantitative easing," and nobody blinks, but effort on a far lesser scale is politically inconceivable for energy policy. Judging by its actual policies, the country would rather incur an annual $75 billion expense to ensure "stability" than make a one-time investment of $50 billion to double the strategic petroleum reserve, though the latter would make a much greater contribution to the avoidance of energy shocks and would actually make money for the government and nation in the future, unlike ongoing military expenditures.[57]

It is no sign of political maturity that such bargains have long been inconceivable in Washington, a sad commentary on its frequently touted claim to liberal and enlightened leadership. The political right wants undisputed military supremacy in the Gulf but rises up in indignation at the thought of taxes on energy. It supports a massive military subsidy to secure oil supplies while touting its faith in market-based solutions. It thinks climate change is a conspiracy. The political left demonizes the oil industry instead of enlisting its agency to reduce oil import dependence (a key step on the road to war avoidance). Our entire approach to the region is an instance of what Jefferson called "false arithmetic." The default option, since nothing serious can be done at home, is just to assign the problem to the U.S. Navy on the assumption that it must have a military solution. This is not a strategy, but domestic dysfunction and entrenched interest substituting for any serious strategic approach.

Israel and the Thrasybulus Syndrome

Ultimately, a new course in the Middle East rests on a new course with Israel—reputedly the anchor of the American position in the Middle East, the region's only democracy, the only country with whom the United States shares values "in the huge land mass from Gibraltar to the Khyber Pass," as Israeli Prime Minister Benjamin Netanyahu put it. For 35 years, since Reagan, the prime remedy for Middle Eastern troubles has been simply to support Israel, give her what she thinks she needs. The only exception to this rule—George H. W. Bush's attempt to hold up loan guarantees to Israel in 1991 and 1992 to force an Israeli accommodation with the Palestinians—actually served to confirm it, as Bush himself attributed his loss in the 1992 election to the ferocious opposition his actions aroused in the Israel lobby. Whether of primary or secondary significance, the political harm from the flap over loan guarantees was real and deeply felt. His sons George and Jeb surely took notice.

The loan guarantees ultimately were given, as were lots more guns, reconfirming Israeli's position as America's largest recipient of foreign aid. In the last decade, U.S. grants to Israel averaged over $3 billion per year; in 2016, in a concordat negotiated by the Obama administration, the amount was kicked up a notch, to $38 billion over a ten-year period, eliciting the immediate objection (from Senator Lindsey Graham) that it should be even higher. The aid package was in compensation for the indignity done Israel by seeking a peaceful settlement with Iran. U.S. assistance paid, at the old rate, 25 percent of Israel's military budget; that percentage is slated to go higher, too. The persistence of the Israel lobby's power is suggested by the parade of Republican presidential hopefuls that made their way to Sheldon Adelson's door in the 2016 presidential canvass (the other Republican primary) and the firm alliance Hillary Clinton struck with Netanyahu and Haim Saban, the Hollywood film producer.[58] Historically, such spending has been a rational distribution of funds for Israel's friends in America, giving bigger bang for the buck, corrosive though it may be to representative democracy when wealth deploys such power on behalf of a foreign state. Israel's hawkish friends in America want the United States to associate itself completely with Israeli ambitions and methods, with no "daylight" between the two countries. Instead, the United States needs to disassociate itself from the same, giving a commitment to Israel's security extending no further than its 1967 borders, and prepared to sever aid in certain circumstances. No more unconditional love.

Israel's credentials as a liberal democracy are, in fact, deeply suspect. It cannot be considered a fully fashioned democracy when Jews rule so completely over Arabs and deny to them the equality of national and political rights, all of which is accompanied by terrifying rituals of humiliation and second-class status. If it wishes to be considered democratic, Israel must divide its territory with the Palestinians (the two-state solution) or admit them to citizenship in a majoritarian state (the one-state solution). Israel wishes to do neither of these things, but either of them it must do if it wishes to be considered a liberal democracy. The same law of nature that gives the Jews the right of self-determination and self-defense gives it also to the Arabs.

In dealing with its neighbors, Israel has been profuse in its use of extraordinary and violent methods. Israel has fought four major wars in the last ten years, including the Lebanon War of 2006 against Hezbollah and three devastating wars against Hamas in Gaza from late 2008 to the present (not counting several smaller operations from 2006 to 2008). It assassinated Iranian nuclear scientists and bombed sites in Syria, Lebanon, and Sudan over the same time period, just as it continually agitated for U.S. military strikes against Iran's nuclear infrastructure. In its Dahiya doctrine, calling for the use of heavy firepower against civilian dwellings, it has enshrined disproportionality, brazenly so, as the essence of its approach to Gaza and Lebanon.

The regularity of Israel's perceived need to use force is illustrated by the notorious expression, "mowing the lawn," that one of its military officers used to describe strategy toward Gaza. It is reminiscent of the advice that Thrasybulus, ruler of Miletus, gave Periander of Corinth, recounted by the world's first great historian, Herodotus. Walking through a field, Thrasybulus broke off the tallest ears of grain by way of showing Periander's envoy the best way to rule violently. The envoy couldn't figure out his meaning, but Periander, the prototype of the ancient tyrant, understood immediately on hearing the envoy's report. The analogy showed that violence could not be a one-time affair. New stalks would grow up. It would remain necessary to keep lopping off the top ones—that is, mowing the lawn. That was a symbol of tyranny in antiquity; it is a symbol of tyranny today.

After Saddam was crushed, the Israelis quickly concluded that Hezbollah and the Shia Crescent, with Iran as its leader, were the main enemy. Israel wanted its main enemy taken down by an enemy less close. That put Israel on the side of the Sunni jihadists. Israel hardly stood alone in this determination, and contributed directly almost nothing to the result in Syria, far less than other states. Assad's overthrow was also sought by Paris, London, Istanbul, Riyadh—and, of course, Washington (who was looking out for Israel). Israel is vitally important in requiring opposition to the Shia Crescent—Hezbollah, Syria, and Iran—as a basic axiom in U.S. policy. That mattered and continues to matter in shaping the lines of the overall U.S. effort in the region (as does Israel's desire to use the Kurds as a lever against Turkey and Iran).

The prospects for a settlement of the Palestinian question look more remote than ever. Reconciliation might gain a footing if it arose from a common detestation among Jews and Arabs of where their hatred of each other had brought them, the bleak exhaustion after killing and being killed when the only way to save your own humanity is to recognize that of the enemy. It brought tears to people's eyes when Rabin, Arafat, and their peoples seemed to reach that moment 20 years ago, but since then just about every year has seen a further grim descent into violence. Kant's prophecy of perpetual peace rested on the assumption of no brief transit, but rather of terrible wars and much devastation, of utterly no respite save when, miraculously, moral awakening leads to reconciliation and deliverance. I pray for that, for Israel's Jews and Palestine's Arabs, despite my not believing in a God who fixes things for human beings, nor thinking that any such outcome is humanly possible today.

Barring insights prompted by a new revelation, Israelis might at least adopt a more cunning attitude toward force. Israel seemingly enters this ancient argument over the utility of force on the side of the Machiavellians, the ones who advised any means fair or foul to advance the interests of the state. Machiavelli's friend Francesco Guicciardini—a Florentine diplomat and the distinguished author of the *History of Italy*—took exception to Machiavelli's disposition, and on the same grounds should we criticize Israel. Guicciardini pointed to the weaknesses invariably incurred by force: "Violent remedies, though they make one safe from one aspect, yet from another . . . involve all kinds of weaknesses. Hence the prince must take courage to use these extraordinary means when necessary, and should yet take care not to miss any chance which offers of establishing his cause with humanity, kindness, and rewards, not taking as an absolute rule what [Machiavelli] says, who was always extremely partial to extraordinary and violent methods."[59] Valid though these criticisms are of Machiavelli, his thought—quite unlike Israel's today—also reflected an appreciation of "the economy of violence." "The indiscriminate exercise of force and the constant revival of fear," as Sheldon Wolin observed of Machiavelli's teaching, "could provoke the greatest of all dangers for any government, the kind of widespread apprehension and hatred which drove men to desperation."[60] This sense of the limits of force, even among one of its greatest partisans, is important to recall. Israel's strategy—seeking peace by periodically pummeling the Palestinians and the Lebanese, shedding the blood of numerous innocents—violates Machiavelli's injunction. It generates hatred as well as fear. It produces desperate men.[61]

The Israelis need to learn—or rather relearn—the rule of proportion in the use of force, and they need to employ more humanitarian methods. More Machiavellian economy in their approach to force, let us say, and more Guicciardinian kindness in their administration of the territories. Of course, the idea that Israelis might improve their relationship with the Palestinians by treating them with humanity, kindness, and rewards seems alien and even risible to Israeli opinion. The Palestinians, the Israelis think, hate them and will hate them unto eternity. It is worse than useless to take an interest in their well-being, because doing so has the fatal liability of demonstrating weakness. Much as this viewpoint must be regarded as a profound mistake, it is written all over the conduct of Israel toward Palestine and Lebanon over the last decade. Israel's belief that it can solve the issues with its neighbors by ever larger doses of the old medicine appears delusional—but there it is. Forget Machiavelli and Guicciardini, the reply is sure to come from Jerusalem. Israel wants to follow the method of Thrasybulus, and its own untroubled conscience is just about the only thing that stands in the way.

The Middle East hosts the most demonic and dangerous conflicts in the world. The wars that devastate it have deep roots. There seems no probable motive for a settlement save total exhaustion, at a time when none of the players are broke, all believe they have vital interests at stake, and most have plenty of resilience. America should try to help them out of that jam, rather than feed it, as it has done in the last decade and more. The parties themselves to these remorseless conflicts supply enough hatred and partiality for themselves. Outside powers have a duty, not to join in that, but to mitigate it; to cast back upon them any reasoning whereby the lives of their citizens are worth more than some outrageous multiple of the enemy's people, reminding them also that the mutual recognition of the equality of rights among their conflicting groups is the only real basis on which to construct a peace. "What doth the Lord require of thee, but to do justice, love mercy, and walk humbly with thy God?"[62]

Israelis will continue to reject that advice; Americans will doubtless continue to subsidize their policies. Nothing, surely, can or will change. Even if a settlement of the Palestinian issue is given up as hopeless, however, Americans need to be deeply wary of the larger implications of support for Israel's ferocious enmities, which span an area far larger than Israel itself. We cannot force it to do justice or show mercy in its immediate neighborhood, but we can and must resist its calls for a larger war on Iran and the Shia Crescent, an objective heartily embraced as well by the Sunni coalition centered on Saudi Arabia. The demand of these powers for aggressive actions against Iran, Hezbollah, Assad, and the Houthis, as evidence of American attachment and devotion, makes them a danger to American security.

Conclusion

OVER THE LAST 25 YEARS, the United States has defined itself in foreign policy by its commitment to a liberal world order. Embraced by both Democratic and Republican presidents, by liberal hawks and neoconservatives, liberalism was widely thought to define America's world position. Even the critics of American Empire agreed that liberalism lay at the core of it. America is liberal. America is the hegemon. America is the liberal hegemon. So went the inescapable syllogism. I have sought to dispute this view, arguing that America's world position, as it has entrenched itself over the past 25 years, has departed from the liberal tradition in critical respects. If the American-led world order has flaws, these should not be attributed to liberalism but to a flock of "neo-isms" parading in the guise thereof. In searching for a remedy, we must find it by rediscovering, not repudiating, the liberal tradition.

The election of Donald Trump threw the commitment to liberalism into very grave doubt. Whatever else he is, Trump is not a liberal. His rhetoric recalled the character traits that observers have imputed to demagogues since ancient Greece, with Trump outdoing even Cleon in unscrupulousness, though not in eloquence. Many of the things that Trump has done or threatened to do, such as demonizing the media, banning Muslims, or ordering the military to disobey statutory law, pose dangers to a government that prides itself on the rule of law. That he would prove cavalier in his attitude toward the constitutional order, the paladin of American liberties, has seemed since his election the only safe prediction.

Of all the institutions of American government that might admit a rogue, the presidency is least well suited to emerge from the experience unscathed. For generations, its powers have been stretched far by the perceived requirements of America's world role; at this late date, there seems no way to retract

them. Ominously, Trump shares and even outdoes the militarism of the establishment. He gives every sign of understanding the ancient phenomenon by
which external conflict becomes a club with which to beat down domestic
opponents and consolidate executive power. His administration seems destined to supply many leaves in the book wherein liberty acquires an empire by
which it is itself threatened.

Unfortunately, the American republic has been imperiled not only by
Trump but also by the security establishment that looked upon his rise with
horror. The sum of the conventional view—heralded by the security elites,
epitomized by Hillary Clinton and George W. Bush—is that it is impossible
to have a liberal world order unless America has hostile relations with Russia,
Iran, and China (together with a shifting cast of lesser states). A barrage of
elite opinion repeats daily, hourly, that hostile adversaries are inveterately trying to subvert the liberal world order.

These essentialist and demonizing views, dominant for so long, reflect a
studied incapacity of the hegemonists, arising from ideological hatred and
vested interests, to put themselves in the shoes of other nations. Those who
would lead us into battle with the RICs are precisely those who most threaten
a liberal world order, because they look to a competition that is to be settled
through dominance rather than reciprocity. Formed by ideology, greatly for-
tified by entrenched interests, the U.S. posture has put it into standing collision with other Great Powers. America forms military entrenchments around
them that it would never submit to being formed around itself, obstructing
the possibility of arms control and plainly in violation of the Golden Rule, the
central rule of all the liberal rules.

This state of affairs is more dangerous than most observers appreciate. It
has also produced a highly paradoxical situation, in which the nation entitled
by geographic position and superior power to be most secure, is yet the one
most constantly in danger of war. It is a function of contemporary interdependence that the injuries states can do to each other in war are magnified. It
should be a given, because obvious, that an American war with Russia, China,
or Iran is one that each side would lose, even if one lost more than the other,
and even if it did not proceed toward extremes (which, as Clausewitz said, it
is in the nature of war to do). Even "minor" wars—the proverbial "half wars"
of strategic planning—are deeply debilitating. The "opportunity cost" of the
Iraq and Afghan Wars, with their some $5 trillion price tag, was immense,
and appears the more glaringly so given an outcome so contrary to the initial promises and expectations. The capital that might have rebuilt America
was fruitlessly extended on unachievable objects, in the most inhospitable

environment imaginable, in pursuit of a phantom vision of American security, at great wastage of life.

A retrenchment of the U.S. strategic frontier against Russia and China, if undertaken in a friendly spirit, would not be destabilizing at all; it could rather be the formula of a new stability and "structure of peace." Russia and China have a need for minimally decent relations with their vast array of neighbors, just as they appreciate the obstacles and costs associated with the use of force even against relatively weaker states. They are most unlikely to respond to conciliation with conquest. It is worth remembering, too, that both Woodrow Wilson and Franklin Roosevelt found it necessary to acknowledge the special responsibilities of the Great Powers in their attempted reconstruction of international society, responsibilities duly registered in the League of Nations Council and the United Nations Security Council (with both Wilson and Roosevelt acknowledging the responsibility of those close by to keep the peace in their regions). Those concessions to the necessities of international governance did not make either man illiberal. On the contrary, the examples show that even these figures might often give a higher value to the perquisites of international peace than to the vindication of abstract right. Wilson, it is true, argued in his 1917 war address that "the right is more precious than peace," but he knew the other side of the argument (having accepted it for two and a half years before entering the war).[1] He might well agree today that the destructiveness of modern weaponry and the vulnerabilities of interdependence make the peace more precious than the right.[2] In the nuclear age, in the age of cyber-vulnerability, it remains the most vital responsibility of the great states to control this competition and keep it within bounds. America's doctrines of military supremacy and universal surveillance, combined with its forward deployments and revolutionary aspirations, evaded this responsibility over the last fifteen years. We are now reaping the whirlwind.

The aspirations that have guided the United States in the twenty-first century were framed in a period of universally acknowledged "unipolarity," in which all roads led to Washington. After victory in the Cold War, writers and politicians strove to describe the manifold ways in which America was superior in just about everything. Its awesome military prowess, prodigiously fertile economy, and unrivaled cultural appeal made for an exceptional and indispensable global role. These pretensions were maintained and extended in an era decidedly more multipolar and polycentric, setting up an inexorable clash between fading aspiration and new realities.

It is the role played by force in the American imaginary that is the root of the problem. Memory of the righteous use of force, even overwhelming force, has fed misconceptions about the real benefits it can achieve and the concrete purposes it can serve. America's participation in the Great Game, in its inimitable can-do spirit, has also fostered deeply illiberal practices (of subversion, propaganda, and surveillance) both at home and abroad. Instead of conceding the equality of national and political rights to others, as liberalism once did, the United States adopts toward its adversaries an uncompromisingly hostile attitude. One group of states is placed outside the human race and considered officially as terrorists (Syria and Iran today, Iraq, Afghanistan, and Libya yesterday). Another group of states, America's traditional rivals Russia and China, are portrayed as aggressive authoritarians who can only be tamed in their near abroad by the threat of overwhelming U.S. military power. The only thing they understand is force, in the often-repeated though insulting mantra. Those proclivities—the American way of defining its enemies and making them tractable—set up the possibility of, and even demand, armed confrontations that are dangerous to American security and international order.

There is a more modest conception of America's role available. I have attempted to sketch out its principal features. I have called it a new internationalism because it seeks not America's withdrawal from the world, but a redefinition of its purposes in the world. It would have America respond enthusiastically to proposals for international cooperation that address the manifold global challenges extant—of climate, oceans, disease, and development—but it would draw back from forcing ideological change on a reluctant and refractory world. Neither a militarized globalism, with its program of perpetual war for perpetual peace, nor aggressive nationalism, with its parochial myopia and selfishness, offers anything resembling an appropriate response to the contemporary world disorder. Rather than the militarized globalism to which we have become accustomed, and the belligerent nationalism that has offered itself as a false alternative, the United States needs a new internationalism that would restore the pluralist conception of international order, once an outstanding feature of the American approach to foreign affairs and an indispensable foundation for tackling common problems. Above all, the United States needs to base its policy toward other nations, and especially other Great Powers, on the Golden Rule. To do so would recall an older yet still compelling version of internationalism whose purpose in coming together was to stay apart—that is, to preserve the independence of the nations, not ride roughshod over their sovereignty. In this alternative conception, union and independence might yet be America's motto again.

To those schooled in the contemporary age, emphasizing the indispensability of American power and the intractability of our enmities, these ideas will appear heretical, but they are in keeping with older truths that once were central to the liberal tradition. The "doctrine that all men are equal," as William Graham Sumner once noted, "was set up as a bar to just this notion that we are so much better than others that it is liberty for them to be governed by us."[3] Sumner's pithy maxim, with its bow to the Declaration of Independence, gives the essential diagnosis of, and the indispensable remedy for, the ailments of contemporary U.S. foreign policy.

America's choice today, like that of Great Britain in the era of the American Revolution, is between dominance and reciprocity, superiority and equality, empire and independence. America, as Britain once did, measures its position among nations according to conventional indices of pride and power, and cannot bear the thought of the voluntary surrender of its advanced position, however untenable it may be to maintain that position.[4] Instead, the United States sees proposals for equality and reciprocity as "superpower suicide" and self-imposed decline. It wants to remain on top, with the most powerful military in the history of the world, a supplement and guarantor—or is it a substitute?—for unarmed truth.

The cure for this condition is not especially complicated; the nation has in its own best traditions a homemade brew that would do nicely. The most significant maladies of America's current posture in the world stem from a departure from liberal principles, rather than their embodiment. Given this confusion of words, or rather of a new thing parading under an old name, the temptation among many has been to condemn liberalism as such. This is a grievous error. The liberal tradition provides essential elements of wisdom that, if observed, might restrain the now greatly empowered American state and show a path to the reform of its international posture. The substitution of mutual interest and reciprocity for the ways of force, liberalism's great enemy; the equality of peoples and their possession in common of a right to carve out their own destiny; the privileging of the peaceful settlement of disputes; a zealous watchfulness against the abuse of power, acknowledging the need for checks and balances upon the exercise of governmental authority; the idea of an order based on the possession of right and the fulfillment of duty, for individuals and nations—all these themes are recognizably liberal, or used to be, and would be good maxims for any government committed to the cause of domestic reform and international peace.

THESE PROPOSALS ARE not put forward with any kind of expectation regarding their immediate political viability in the United States. Any hope that Trump would be attracted to them seems utterly forlorn. In gross and in detail, and all over the world map, they are totally inconsistent with the

Washington consensus, as previously championed by both Republican and Democratic administrations. They are emphatically contrary to the outlook of the national security bureaucracy, the Congress, and the media, each of which with few exceptions is devoted to the antagonisms that define the U.S. position in the world. The renovation called for here projects a dismantling of the empire; it is crystal clear that the empire is fully determined to stick around. We seek a reconfiguration of the relationship with both enemies and allies alike, whereas the configuration hitherto dominant—nothing too good for a friend, nothing too bad for an enemy—is supported by powerful interests, institutions, and ideologies, seemingly locked into place and controlling both the distribution of resources and the discourse. Reconciling with enemies, it would seem, is "not like us."

To call for change so contrary to contemporary political realities, in opposition to a bleating consensus, is not what one could call an entirely satisfactory conclusion. It is not, however, so atypical a stance as might be supposed. There are many examples in history of thinkers who, the closer they got to solving the puzzle, became yet more despairing as they contemplated how utterly inconsistent their remedy was with the temper of the times, how far it lay from the outlook of the dominant interests, how contrary it was to the hand that history had dealt. Such thoughts, in fact, come not only to the scribbler in his study but also to the statesperson on the hustings.

To no one did it come with more painful realization, and with such sense of the futility of all human endeavor, than to Woodrow Wilson, in the year he spent negotiating, with refractory allies and suspicious congressmen, the League of Nations and the Versailles Treaty. Wilson had come to Paris in early 1919 carrying the hopes of the world; no man, as Churchill recalled, stood more at the pinnacle of world leadership than did Wilson as he decamped from the USS *George Washington* and received the deliriously cheering crowds in France. This was in December and January. In August, we find Wilson complaining to his Secretary of State Robert Lansing that the allies in Wilson's great world venture were absolutely hopeless. In his heart of hearts, he wanted to pack it in: "When I think of the greed and utter selfishness of it all," he told Lansing, "I am almost inclined to refuse to permit this country to be a member of the League of Nations when it is composed of such intriguers and robbers. I am disposed to throw up the whole business and get out." Somewhat to his astonishment, Lansing noted that this was "the *third* time that the President has said to me that the present conduct of the nations makes him consider withdrawing from the League, though he never before spoke so emphatically."[5] Thus did the most powerful man in the world, once the carrier of a boundless optimism, assess the prospects for his transformative vision six months after setting it forth, all but concluding that the situation was beyond repair, the world too intractable, even, it may be, to hell with it. The arc of history has its own purposes, blind to true rationality, wedded to the satisfactions of bloodlust.

Wilson's flip-flop in sentiment (carried out very much in private) is symbolic of a larger dynamic in public opinion. He had wanted to change the world. The world having shown itself intractable to change, he wanted to withdraw from it. Lippmann had himself undergone a similar transformation in 1919, running from the League and its guarantees once he realized what was in the treaty, and differing mainly from Wilson, as with other of Wilson's friends, in coming to that realization earlier and with more vehemence. Lippmann, near the end of his life in 1967, found himself in a similar posture, wanting to go all-in for neo-isolationism as a deserved riposte to a militarized and fanatical globalism. Perhaps there is a lesson here for the stewards of American Empire. Push too hard on your grand ambition, and you will as the sun rises foster a reaction, even perhaps among yourselves, most probably among your children. Nothing is better calculated to produce neo-isolationists than imperial overstretch.

Confessedly, the alternative strategy proposed in this work faces in our own historical moment a very stiff wind; its time, if it has a time, is in the future or the past, not the present. But a day of reckoning, exposing the artificiality of America's world position, is surely coming. Then a foreign policy attuned to founding principles will look more attractive, beckoning as a safe harbor in a troubled world.

Acknowledgments

THE IMMEDIATE ORIGINS of this book, providing the skeleton of the manuscript, lay in a December 2014 seminar at Princeton University organized by John Ikenberry and Daniel Deudney on the theme of "America, Liberalism, and Empire." I thank them for inviting me and for the opportunity to participate in subsequent panels on the same theme at the International Studies Association and the American Political Science Association. Thanks also to Michael Lind, John Mearsheimer, and Tony Smith for their encouraging comments at these events.

On completion of my first draft in early 2016, I received the assistance of numerous friends and colleagues. Andrew Bacevich, Daniel Deudney, Vinnie Ferraro, Todd Greentree, Juan Lindau, Walter McDougall, Peter Onuf, Scott Sanger, and Jerry Slater were often profuse in their critical comments and suggested revisions. I had thought I was nearly done; they forced me to reconsider numerous themes. My hearty thanks to all of them, but especially to Dan and Jerry for their detailed and searching criticism.

I am grateful to Colorado College for providing a half-year sabbatical in the fall of 2016 that enabled me to complete the writing process in an expeditious fashion. I also extend thanks to old and new colleagues in the Political Science Department and to the staff assistants who helped me over the past three decades: Helen Lynch, Jane Stark, Georgia Moen, Jennifer Sides, and Jessica Pauls. Among Colorado College students who have assisted with my research over the years, I tip my hat especially to Arrow Augerot, Bradford Williams, and Luigi Mendez. To the now thousands of students I've taught at Colorado College for over three decades, I say fondly: you made it all worthwhile.

My manuscript was extensively revised in the fall of 2016. By a quirk of fate, much of this process of revision took place at the home, in Santa Fe, New Mexico, of Robert W. Tucker, my former professor in graduate school and long-time collaborator. My home in Colorado Springs was chosen out of the blue as one of the venues for a Netflix movie, *Our Souls at Night*. This chance development forced me out of my accustomed routines and into the direct supervision of Dr. Tucker, now 92 years of age but still, as ever, an agreeable companion and fast friend. We conquered Atalaya Mountain (well, three miles of it) on a daily basis for over two months. I am deeply appreciative to Judith and Bob for their hospitality and encouragement during that time.

The political earthquake represented by Trump's election, overturning previous estimations of the possible, forced further adjustments in the manuscript. It was put to bed in the spring of 2017. Thanks to David McBride and his team at Oxford for shepherding the book to publication, and to Patti Brecht for her expert copy-editing.

With the notes and bibliography, I seek to convey my debts to numerous scholars and past thinkers, but there is one class of writers whom it is impossible to cite adequately. These are the "ink-stained wretches" who generate tons of copy in reporting and commenting on the latest developments in international affairs and American foreign policy. Those who have meant the most to me over the past decade—all in some way belonging to America's "dissenting tradition," but a diverse lot withal—include Andrew Bacevich, Doug Bandow, David Bromwich, Pat Buchanan, James Carden, Ted Galen Carpenter, Patrick Cockburn, Tom Engelhardt, Chas Freeman, Philip Giraldi, Glenn Greenwald, Jacob Heilbrunn, Stephen Kinzer, Daniel Larison, Christopher Layne, Anatol Lieven, Michael Lind, Jim Lobe, Chase Madar, Scott McConnell, John Mearsheimer, Rajan Menon, Robert Parry, Ron Paul, Paul Pillar, Barry Posen, Christopher Preble, Gareth Porter, Justin Raimondo, David Rieff, Jeffrey Sachs, Nick Turse, Kelly Vlahos, Stephen Walt, and Micah Zenko. And these are just the old-timers; there are a host of new voices—Emma Ashford, Daniel L. Davis, Benjamin Friedman, John Glaser, Bonnie Kristian—whose work I avidly consume. Two-thirds of these writers I've never met, and most of the rest I don't know well, but I've learned something, often a lot, from each one. My advice to people who want to keep up with the subject is to read them.

This book is dedicated to the memory of my daughter Whitney, who died in a tragic accident in 2009, a casualty of the times, on behalf of her sister Marina, her brother Wesley, and her mother Clelia. We four loved that girl with something like religious faith, and miss her still.

David C. Hendrickson
Colorado Springs, Colorado
May 1, 2017

Notes

INTRODUCTION

1. For Obama's references to the "Washington playbook," see Goldberg, "Obama Doctrine," 76.
2. On the idea of an "official mind," see Ronald Robinson and John Gallagher with Alice Denny, *Africa and the Victorians: The Official Mind of Imperialism*, 2nd ed. (London, 1981).
3. John Maynard Keynes, *The General Theory of Employment, Interest, and Money*, chapter 24.
4. The best portrait is Bill Kauffman, *America First! Its History, Culture, and Politics* (Amherst, NY, 1995).
5. See the explication of "unseemliness" in Charles Murray, *Coming Apart: The State of White America, 1960-2010* (New York, 2013), 291–98.
6. James Madison, Eighth Annual Message, December 3, 1816.
7. To similar effect, see Mark Danner, "The Real Trump," *New York Review of Books*, December 22, 2016, 14.
8. Patrick Henry, Speech in Virginia Ratifying Convention, June 5, 1788.
9. Recounted in Hendrickson, *Union, Nation, or Empire*.
10. Representative David Trimble, March 28, 1822, *Abridgment of the Debates of Congress*, Thomas Hart Benton, ed. (New York, 1857-1861), 7: 298–99.
11. Edmund Burke, Speech on Conciliation with the Colonies, March 22, 1775. Elliot Robert Barkan, ed., *Edmund Burke on the American Revolution* (Gloucester, MA, 1972), 93.
12. David Armitage, *The Ideological Origins of the British Empire* (Cambridge, UK, 2000), 125, notes that "how to achieve empire while sustaining liberty became a defining concern of British imperial ideology from the late sixteenth century onwards."
13. Burke, Speech on Conciliation, 119–20.
14. Washington, General Orders, April 18, 1783, John Rhodehamel, ed., *George Washington: Writings* (New York, 1997), 513.
15. *Novanglus* No. VII (1774-75), Adams, *Works*, 4: 107.
16. Frederick Douglass, Oration in Memory of Abraham Lincoln, Freedman's Memorial, April 14, 1876.

17. Charles Sumner, *Are We a Nation?* (New York, 1867), 34.

18. Walter Lippmann, *U.S. War Aims,* 193–94.

19. Niall Ferguson's *Colossus: The Price of America's Empire* (New York, 2014), empha-
    sizes the "anti-imperialism of imperialism," a theme also developed from a different
    perspective by William Appleman Williams and Charles Beard. Giving primacy
    to empire in the American past are Fred Anderson and Andrew Cayton, *The
    Dominion of War: Empire and Liberty in North America, 1500-2000* (New York,
    2005), and William Weeks, *The New Cambridge History of American Foreign
    Relations: Dimensions of the Early American Empire, 1754-1865* (New York, 2013).

20. See Daniel Deudney and G. John Ikenberry, "America's Impact: The End of Empire
    and the Globalization of the Westphalian System," American Political Science
    Association, September 2015.

21. George Washington, Farewell Address, September 19, 1796.

22. On "international freedom," see Robert Jackson, *Global Covenant.*

23. J. G. A. Pocock, *The First Decline and Fall,* 310.

24. The argument, be it noted, is of ancient lineage, coeval with American political
    discourse, and rising in temperature in rough proportion to national folly. Fifty
    years ago, J. William Fulbright believed, writes his biographer, that "in their anxi-
    ety to be politically relevant, to play the anticommunist card, American liberals had
    embraced the military-industrial complex and had thereby placed the very things
    they worshiped—freedom, democracy, diversity—at risk." Woods, *Fulbright,*
    498–99. For the lessons of a lifetime, see Fulbright, *Price of Empire* (1989). Views
    of a similar tenor are advanced by Johnson, *Nemesis* (2007); Smith, *Pact with the
    Devil* (2007); Hoffmann, *Gulliver Unbound* (2005); and Tucker and Hendrickson,
    Imperial Temptation (1992). There are "left" and "right" versions of the jeremiad,
    with significant convergence between them on the central points. Among conserva-
    tives, most notable are Patrick J. Buchanan, *A Republic, Not an Empire: Reclaiming
    America's Destiny* (Washington, DC, 2002), and Ron Paul, *Swords into Plowshares*
    (Clute, TX, 2015).

25. *One Hundred Letters From Hugh Trevor-Roper,* Richard Davenport-Hines and
    Adam Sisman, eds. (New York, 2014).

26. Patrick Henry is cited in Henry Wheaton, *Elements of International Law,* 8th ed.,
    Richard Henry Dana Jr., ed. (Boston: Little, Brown, 1866), xix.

27. A proper introduction appears in Arnold Wolfers and Laurence W. Martin,
    *The Anglo-American Tradition in Foreign Affairs: Readings from Thomas More to
    Woodrow Wilson* (New Haven, CT, 1956).

28. Henry Kissinger, *World Order,* 3. In deference to contemporary understand-
    ings, I adopt the term "Westphalian" in this work, but it is a problematic usage,
    in that the "balance of power" did not appear in a European peace treaty until
    the peace of Utrecht in 1713, 65 years after the Westphalia settlement in 1648. The
    guarantees accorded to the rights of religious minorities, allowing for the inter-
    vention of outside powers (Sweden to protect the Protestants, France to protect

the Catholics), make "non-intervention" a problematic usage as well. (See David Trim, "Intervention in European History, *c.* 1520-1850," Recchia and Welsh, *Just and Unjust Military Intervention*, 39.) Probably the better historical term for the two objectives that Kissinger associates with the Westphalian peace is "Utrechtian" or "Vattelian," the latter after Emer de Vattel, the Swiss jurist whose treatise on the law of nations in 1758 summarized the principles of public international law for the old European system. (See discussion in Onuf and Onuf, *Federal Union, Modern World.*) For the publicists, the balance of power and non-intervention were indeed central. The best analytical term for these precepts—one I use indistinguishably from "Westphalian"—is pluralism, an idea richly developed by Martin Wight, Hedley Bull, and Robert Jackson, seminal figures in the English School of International Relations.

29. Jeffrey Sachs, "The Fatal Expense of American Imperialism," *Boston Globe*, October 30, 2016. The true costs of the national security establishment are radically understated in official figures, which then go on to form the basis of international comparisons that also understate the true U.S. percentage. Winston Wheeler has drawn attention to the true cost for many years, on unassailable grounds that the accountants—official and unofficial—somehow never recognize. See Wheeler, "America's $1 Trillion National Security Budget," *Counterpunch*, March 14, 2014. To the "baseline budget" so often used to estimate its size, at $495 billion in 2014, is to be added another $149.5 billion of Pentagon expenditures, mostly related to Iraq and Afghanistan, plus $20 billion for nuclear weapons, $52.1 billion in homeland security, $161 billion for veterans' affairs, and $39 billion for State Department and other activities. Add in another some $100 billion for interest on the national debt (taking simply the percentage of national security expenditures in relation to the total budget over time), and the total comes to about $1 trillion. With the U.S. GDP at $17.35 trillion in 2014, the security budget was 5.8 percent of GDP, not the 3.6 percent frequently touted.

CHAPTER I

1. Walter Russell Mead, *Special Providence.*
2. Cotton cited in Uri Friedman, "Why Would a Republican Hawk Support Donald Trump?," *The Atlantic*, July 3, 2016.
3. Mark Landler, "How Hillary Clinton Became a Hawk," *New York Times*, April 21, 2016.
4. Secretary of State Hillary Clinton, Address at the Council on Foreign Relations, May 15, 2009.
5. Ikenberry, *Liberal Leviathan*, xv.
6. See especially G. John Ikenberry, "The Myth of Post-Cold War Chaos," *Foreign Affairs* (May/June 1996).
7. Running in parallel with these views, though somewhat more unconventional, is foreign policy historian Elizabeth Cobbs Hoffman, *American Umpire.* In the

post-World War II period, she argues, the United States adopted "a role akin to the one that the nation's Founders had originally envisioned for the federal government: that of an umpire to compel acquiescence." The three fundamental values of access, arbitration, and transparency deeply informed the nation's foreign and domestic policy.

Among defenders of the U.S.-led liberal world order, liberal and neoconservative voices are not in unison. Liberal internationalists like Ikenberry and Francis Fukuyama opposed the Iraq War and developed a sharp critique of Bush's foreign policy. See Ikenberry, *Liberal Order and Imperial Ambition*, and Fukuyama, *America at the Crossroads*. By contrast, neoconservatives like Robert Kagan supported the Iraq War and developed a defense of the "liberal world order" much less principle-bound than those of Ikenberry, Fukuyama, or Hoffman. Kagan is anxious to avoid the hypothesis that the system rests on law, a separation that would have been surprising to America's post-World War II presidents. The aversion to law, of course, reflects the desire of Kagan and fellow neoconservatives to cross it. His liberal world order stands as an indispensable bulwark against a world that would otherwise spiral into massive disorder. Its maintenance requires not playing by the rules but playing to win.

8. The best account is Sakwa, *Frontline Ukraine*. More even-handed, though conscious of Western mistakes, is Samuel Charap and Timothy J. Colton, *Everyone Loses: The Ukraine Crisis and the Ruinous Contest for Post-Soviet Eurasia* (New York, 2017). For further elaboration of my argument, see my essays in *The National Interest* on Ukraine: "The West's Illusions about Ukraine," March 11, 2014; "The Democratic Values at Stake Ukraine," March 18, 2014; "Ukraine's Dangerous Drift Toward Chaos," July 11, 2014. For an account stressing NATO expansion, see John J. Mearsheimer, "Why the Ukraine Crisis Is the West's Fault," *Foreign Affairs* (September/October 2014). The post-Cold War record of antagonism to Russia is also detailed in Daniel Deudney and G. John Ikenberry, "The Unravelling of the Cold War Settlement," *Survival* (December 2009-January 2010): 39–62, Stephen F. Cohen, *Soviet Fates and Lost Alternatives: From Stalinism to the New Cold War* (New York, 2011), and Robert Legvold, *Return to Cold War* (New York, 2016).

9. Woodrow Wilson, Address to Congress, January 22, 1917.

10. On Stuxnet or "Olympic Games," the cyberattack on Iranian centrifuges at the Natanz nuclear facility in Iran, see Sanger, *Confront and Conceal*. On another cyberattack plan called "Nitro Zeus," far reaching in its penetration of and capacity to disable Iran's infrastructure, see David E. Sanger and Mark Mazzetti, "U.S. Had Cyberattack Plan If Iran Nuclear Dispute Led to Conflict," *New York Times*, February 16, 2016, and *Zero Days* (2016), a documentary film by Alex Gibney. The United States acted properly in seeking negotiations with Iran through a multilateral process (the P5+1), but it did not and does not have the sanction of international law or the support of the international community in putting preventive war or cyberwar "on the table."

11. As noted by Grant Smith, director of the Institute for Research: Middle Eastern Policy, U.S. law, under 1976 amendments to the 1961 Foreign Assistance Act sponsored by Stuart Symington and John Glenn, prohibits the United States from sending aid to clandestine nuclear powers. Smith filed a lawsuit on August 8, 2016, alleging an unlawful failure of U.S. government officials "to act upon facts long in their possession while prohibiting the release of official government information about Israel's nuclear weapons program." In his filing, *Grant F. Smith v. Central Intelligence Agency*, Smith documents that more than 330 kilograms of highly enriched uranium disappeared through 1968 from Pennsylvania-based Nuclear Materials and Equipment Corporation (NUMEC), with the CIA concluding that it was taken surreptitiously in an inside job by Israel. When President Lyndon Johnson was told of this by the CIA, he ordered the agency to not further discuss it. In July 1969, Kissinger wrote of the thefts of fissionable material in an internal memo, "This is one program on which the Israelis have persistently deceived us."

12. Remarks by Dilma Rousseff at the 68th UN General Assembly, *Voltairenet.org*, September 24, 2013; Ian Traynor and Paul Lewis, "Merkel Compared NSA to Stasi in Heated Encounter with Obama," *The Guardian*, December 17, 2013.

13. On the scale of the NSA's ambitions, see especially Glenn Greenwald, *No Place to Hide*.

14. For background, see Eyal Benvenisti, *The International Law of Occupation* (Princeton, NJ, 1993).

15. William Wordsworth, "Rob Roy's Grave," 1803, stanza 9.

16. James Madison, *Federalist* No. 10.

17. An incisive demonstration is Reinhold Niebuhr, *Moral Man and Immoral Society*, 91–97, 106–09.

18. See Ioannis D. Evrigenis, *Fear of Enemies and Collective Action*. The classic twentieth-century analysis of the friend/enemy distinction, emphasizing its essential antagonism to liberal constitutionalism, is Carl Schmitt, *The Concept of the Political* (Chicago, 2007).

19. John Adams to Abigail Adams, June 2, 1777, *Letters of Delegates to Congress, 1774-1789*, Paul H. Smith, ed. (Washington, DC, 1976-2000), 7: 160.

20. Ikenberry, *Liberal Leviathan*, 37.

21. Samuel P. Huntington, *Clash of Civilizations*, 53. Huntington called this compound republic "the emerging universal state of Western civilization," but he rightly rejected its pretensions to true universality. A cogent reconstruction of Huntington's perspective, often misinterpreted, is William S. Smith, "Samuel Huntington Was Not Like Steve Bannon," *The American Conservative*, May 2, 2017.

22. On the importance of "honor" as a foreign policy objective, see Lebow, *Cultural Theory of International Relations*. On the "transmission belt" by which allied interests become American, encouraging "reckless driving" in dependents, see Posen, *Restraint*, 33–35, and Layne, *Peace of Illusions*, 169. For U.S. doctrine of credibility,

see Daryl G. Press, *Calculating Credibility: How Leaders Assess Military Threats* (Ithaca, NY, 2005).

23. G. John Ikenberry, "The Rise of China and the Future of the West," *Foreign Affairs* (January/February 2008).

24. I consider this episode further in "Poland and America," *The National Interest*, July 8, 2014.

25. Jo Becker and Scott Shane, "The Libya Gamble," *New York Times*, February 27 and 28, 2016.

26. This instruction on how to treat allies was stated to me in 1981 by a State Department official in the Reagan administration, Charles Horner.

27. Target Tokyo, WikiLeaks, July 31, 2015, at https://wikileaks.org/nsa-japan/. See also Espionnage Élysée, WikiLeaks, June 29, 2015, at https://wikileaks.org/nsa-france/.

28. For an anguished German plea to this effect, see Markus Feldenkirchen, "Merkel Must End Devil's Pact with America, *Spiegel Online International*, July 7, 2015.

29. Stephen Schlesinger, *Act of Creation: The Founding of the United Nations* (Boulder, CO, 2003).

30. David E. Sanger, "U.S. and Germany Fail to Reach a Deal on Spying," *New York Times*, May 1, 2014. For subsequent revelations that Germany's spy agency cooperated with the U.S. and engaged in similar practices toward other EU countries, see "Intelligence Scandal Puts Merkel in Tight Place," *Spiegel Online*, May 4, 2015, and "Germany Spied on Friends and Vatican," *Spiegel Online*, November 7, 2015.

31. Figures available at the end of 2015 showed U.S. arms sales at $36.2 billion in 2014, compared with $10.2 billion for Russia, $5.5 billion for Sweden, $4.4 billion for France, and $2.2 billion for China. Nicholas Fandos, "U.S. Foreign Arms Deals Increased Nearly $10 Billion in 2014," *New York Times*, December 25, 2015. Total global arms sales, according to the Congressional Research Service, were $71.8 billion in 2014. For an overview of the dynamics, see William D. Hartung, "There's No Business Like the Arms Business," *TomDispatch.com*, July 26, 2016.

32. See discussion in Deudney, *Bounding Power*, 53–54. The scale effect seeks to understand how changes in size or quantity affect the relationship among the parts, allowing us to understand "how changes in quantity produce changes in quality."

33. These changes in the content of "economic liberalism" are examined in John Gerard Ruggie, *Winning the Peace: America and World Order in the New Era* (New York, 1996), and Lind, *American Way of Strategy*, 233–39.

34. Ambrose Evans Pritchard, "Ukraine Faces Economic Breakdown as War Returns," *The Telegraph*, November 14, 2014. On the IMF's shaky relationship to its own rules, see also Independent Evaluation Office, *The IMF and the Crises in Greece, Ireland, and Portugal* (Washington, DC, 2016).

35. See especially Mark Blyth, *The Austerity Delusion* (New York, 2013), for this ancient dispute, running all the way back to Hume and Smith. Blyth and other critics of austerity, like Paul Krugman, argue that austerity results in increased rather

than decreased debt-to-GDP ratios, making it self-defeating. In contrast, caution about going further into debt as a means of addressing a debt crisis is expressed in Carmen M. Reinhart and Kenneth Rogoff, *This Time Is Different: Eight Centuries of Financial Folly* (Princeton, NJ, 2011).

36. The more aggressive policies are described, by one of their advocates, in Juan C. Zarate, *Treasury's War: The Unleashing of a New Era of Financial Warfare* (New York, 2013).

37. Hillary Clinton, Council on Foreign Relations, May 15, 2009.

38. The BRICS acronym (Brazil, Russia, India, China, and South Africa) began life as a stock market projection by Jim O'Neill of Goldman Sachs in the late 1990s. Diplomatic convergence among the nations has lately given it a political significance.

39. See below, Chapter 3, for consideration of this theme.

40. See instructive chart in Ian Talley, "The U.S. Trade Deficit Excluding Oil Hit a Record High," *Wall Street Journal*, March 10, 2015.

41. Bureau of Economic Analysis, U.S. Department of Commerce, "U.S. Net International Investment Position, Fourth Quarter and Year 2016," March 29, 2017.

42. David Stockman, "The G-20s Big Fat Zero—Now Comes the Bubble's Demise!," *Contra Corner.com*, February 29, 2016.

43. Hendrickson, *Union, Nation, or Empire*.

44. Dwight Eisenhower, First Inaugural Address, January 20, 1953; Eisenhower, Second Inaugural Address, January 21, 1957; James A. Baker III, *The Politics of Diplomacy* (New York, 1995).

45. Obama quoted in Goldberg, "The Obama Doctrine," 78.

46. Odd Arne Westad, *The Global Cold War: Third World Interventions and the Making of Our Times* (New York, 2007); John W. Dower, *The Violent American Century: War and Terror Since World War II* (Chicago, 2017).

47. Lippmann, *U.S. Foreign Policy*, 132; Lippmann, *U.S War Aims*, 78.

48. Lenin's meaning in real historical time was about killing and being killed, whereas colloquial expressions of "using" and "taking advantage of" are more in keeping with my meaning. For Lenin's usage, see Paul Johnson, *Modern Times* (New York, 1983), 85.

49. Expletive deleted from Clinton's query.

50. Obama's journey to liberal Zionism is described in Beinart, *Crisis of Zionism*.

51. See, for example, Philip Weiss, " 'Forward' Columnist and Emily's List Leader Relate 'Gigantic,' 'Shocking' Role of Jewish Democratic Donors," *Mondoweiss.net*, April 19, 2016.

52. Helene Cooper and Somini Sengupta, "As Much of the World Frowns on Israel, Americans Hold Out Support," *New York Times*, July 23, 2014; "CNN Poll: Majority of Americans Side with Israel in Gaza Fighting," CNN, July 21, 2014; Jeffery M. Jones, "Americans' Reaction to Middle East Situation Similar to Past," *Gallup.com*, July 24, 2014; Shibley Telhami, "American Attitudes on the Israeli-Palestinian

Conflict," The Brookings Institution, December 2, 2016; Samantha Smith and Carroll Doherty, "Five Facts About How Americans View the Israeli-Palestinian Conflict," Pew Research Center, May 23, 2016.

53. Ahmed Rashid, "The Enemy's Enemy: How Arab States Have Turned to al-Qa'eda," *The Spectator*, July 18, 2015.

54. See the clarifying discussion in Forsyth, *Unions of States*, 206: "Hegemony is typically an unequal relationship established between a great power and one or more smaller powers which is nevertheless based on the juridical or formal equality of all the states concerned. It is not an empire. It is based not on 'ruler' and 'ruled' but on 'leadership' and 'followers.' It is held together not by command and obedience, but by influence, and what may be called 'allegiance.' "

Despite these clear distinctions, it is impossible in political speech to pin down a settled meaning for hegemony, which may signify leadership or domination as the writer so intimates. This double meaning also applies very much to Periclean Athens, the first great exemplification in international history of the *hegemon*. Athens was at the head of the Delian League, a little NATO in antiquity, which some classicists call the "North Aegean Treaty Organization." Athens rose to that position by virtue of its leadership role in the common cause of repelling Persia's advance on Greece, but later converted the league to an empire based on tribute.

CHAPTER 2

1. Charles Krauthammer, "Universal Dominion: Toward a Unipolar World," *The National Interest* (Winter 1989/90): 49.

2. One may call it the Engelhardt Gap, after Tom Engelhardt, editor of *TomDispatch. com*, who has most inventively described the great disjunction. See, for instance, Engelhardt, "Why Washington Can't Stop: The Coming Era of Tiny Wars and Micro-Conflicts," *TomDispatch.com*, October 22, 2013, and, Engelhardt, *Shadow Government*.

3. Andrew J. Bacevich, "Mr. Bush's Grand Illusion," *Los Angeles Times*, February 19, 2004.

4. Bacevich, *Short American Century*.

5. The world political system was never as "unipolar" as Americans thought. Even in the 1990s, Russia retained its strategic nuclear arsenals; even in the 1990s, states retained inherent powers of resistance to occupation. Nevertheless, all roads did lead to Washington in the 1990s; both Russia and China felt themselves dependent on U.S. goodwill in securing their own national interests (reconstruction for Russia after the collapse of Communism; entry into the world economy and the American market for China). Power can never be fruitfully considered apart from the purposes that it seeks to serve; a set of capabilities joined to extravagant and offensive purposes will invariably seem less powerful, that is, less capable of getting its way, than one joined to less extravagant and more defensive purposes. That makes all

such depictions of something-polarity to be fluid, not fixed. For further consideration, see Calleo, *Unipolar Fantasy*; Nuno P. Monteiro, *Theory of Unipolar Politics* (New York, 2014); and G. John Ikenberry, ed., *Power, Order, and Change in World Politics* (New York, 2014).

6. The reference is to Geico's iconic commercials in 2016.

7. As Daniel Deudney notes, *Bounding Power*, 137–38, Enlightenment observers saw Europe's resistance to universal empire as anomalous: "Other regions in Eurasia with comparable sizes, populations, and levels of material civilization were tending to consolidate into region-wide universal monarchies (the Ottomans in the Near East, the Moguls in India, the Manchus in China, and even the Romanovs in Russia)."

8. Wight, *Power Politics*, 37. Wight notes that each dominant power, though engaged in aggrandizement, "also appeals to some design of international unity and solidarity."

9. The idea of a polycentric system is an expression of Sergey Lavrov. See, for example, Speech by Russian Foreign Minister Sergey Lavrov, at meeting with members of the Russian International Affairs Council, Moscow, June 4, 2014.

10. See above, Chapter 1, note 28.

11. The relation of the UN Charter to previously existing conceptions of international law (reflecting both continuity and change) is explored in Jackson, *Global Covenant*. On affinities between the balance of power and collective security, see Edward Vose Gulick, *Europe's Classical Balance of Power* (New York, 1955).

12. A penetrating study is Anatol Lieven, *America Right or Wrong*. On the role and persistence of militarism, seen by its advocates as the highest form of nationalism, see Michael S. Sherry, *In the Shadow of War: The United States since the 1930s* (New Haven, CT, 1997), and Bacevich, *New American Militarism*. On misperception, see Pillar, *Why America Misunderstands the World*.

13. Kant used the term "unjust enemy" to "mean someone whose publicly expressed will, whether expressed in word or deed, displays a maxim which would make peace among nations impossible and would lead to a perpetual state of nature if it were made into a general rule." Kant's *Metaphysics of Morals*, section 60, cited in Andrew Hurrell, "Revisiting Kant and Intervention," Recchia and Welsh, *Just and Unjust Military Intervention*, 199.

14. Stout defenses of pluralism, with which I closely identify, are mounted in Jackson, *Global Covenant*, and Roth, *Sovereign Equality and Moral Disagreement*. For its identification with the broad middle ground of European thought, see Martin Wight, "Western Values in International Relations." An exposition of the central premises of a pluralist approach (abjuring the label "Westphalian") is Hurrell, *On Global Order*, 25–56; see also Anderson and Hurrell, Introduction to *Hedley Bull on International Society*, 1–73.

   Hurrell has constructed one of the best cases for pluralism but (oddly) doesn't buy it himself, insisting on its inadequacy for today's challenges. My subject in this chapter is pluralism as it relates to the rights of war and peace, not to the other questions (e.g., environmental sustainability or economic governance or global inequality) that might be considered under that rubric. I would argue, however, that a solidarist response to these planetary questions, which I favor, must rest on a pluralist foundation—that is, on the voluntary efforts of sovereign states. Do the Millennium Development Goals or the 2015 Paris Agreement on climate change show the contrary?

15. Tuck, "Grotius, Hobbes, and Pufendorf on Humanitarian Intervention," Recchia and Welsh, *Just and Unjust Military Intervention*, 98.

16. John Hale, *The Civilization of Europe in the Renaissance* (New York, 1994), 190.

17. Book 2, chapters 1–4, of the *Discourses on the First Ten Books of Titus Livius* contains Machiavelli's reflections on the "three modes of expansion." Christian E. Detmold, trans., *The Historical, Political, and Diplomatic Writings of Niccolò Machiavelli*, 4 vols. (Boston, 1882). For a more extended analysis, see David C. Hendrickson, "Machiavelli and Machiavellianism," in *Machiavelli's Legacy: "The Prince" After Five Hundred Years*, Timothy Fuller, ed. (Philadelphia, 2015).

18. See Anthony Pagden, *Lords of All the World: Ideologies of Empire in Spain, Britain and France, c. 1500-c. 1800* (New Haven, CT, 1995).

19. François de Salignac de la Mothe Fénelon, "On the Necessity of Alliances," in *Theory and Practice of the Balance of Power, 1486-1914*, Moorhead Wright, ed. (Totowa, NJ, 1975), 41. This section draws from David C. Hendrickson, "The Curious Case of American Hegemony: Imperial Aspirations and National Decline," *World Policy Journal* (Summer 2005).

20. Alexander Hamilton, "The Stand IV," April 12, 1798, *Hamilton Works*, 6: 282, 285.

21. David Hume, *Essays: Moral, Political and Literary*, Eugene Miller, ed. (Indianapolis, 1985 [1777]), 341; Montesquieu, *Spirit of the Laws*, book 9, chap. 7, 136; Jean-Jacques Rousseau, *Abstract of the Abbé de Saint-Pierre's Project for Perpetual Peace, Rousseau on International Relations*, Stanley Hoffmann and David P. Fidler, eds. (New York, 1991 [1756]), 62–64.

22. Montesquieu, *Spirit of the Laws*, book 11, chap. 17, 177–78.

23. Thomas Hobbes, *On the Citizen*, Richard Tuck and Michael Silverthorne, eds. and trans. (Cambridge, UK, 1998), 3.

24. William Robertson, *The Progress of Society in Europe: A Historical Outline from the Subversion of the Roman Empire to the Beginning of the Sixteenth Century*, Felix Gilbert, ed. (Chicago, 1972). The extract comes from the beginning of Robertson's *History of the Reign of the Emperor Charles V* (1769). An unfit model for international society, Rome's institutions and history also held lessons for constituting a republic. Deudney, *Bounding Power*, 93, defines what he calls "the two iron laws of polis republicanism" through Montesquieu's observation that a republic, if it remains small, is vulnerable to external conquest, whereas if it becomes too large—Rome was the unavoidable example—it would be "ruined by an internal

imperfection." Montesquieu's dilemma continues to express a vital tension within republican liberalism and is plainly relevant to the American predicament today.

25. The *Levée en Masse* for the French, precision-guided weapons and total battlefield awareness for the Americans.

26. Americus, "The Warning I," January 27, 1797, *Hamilton Works*, 6: 233–34. The parallel is explored in Claes G. Ryn, *America the Virtuous: The Crisis of Democracy and the Quest for Empire* (New Brunswick, NJ, 2003).

27. See Daniel H. Deudney, "'A Republic for Expansion': The Roman Constitution and Empire and Balance-of-Power Theory," in Stuart J. Kaufman, Richard Little, and William C. Wohlforth, *The Balance of Power in World History* (New York, 2007), 148–75.

28. The existence of these parallels is especially striking given the huge difference in material and technological circumstances—especially energy usage—between the ancients and the moderns. See on this point the contrarian view of Vaclav Smil, *Why America Is Not a New Rome* (Cambridge, MA, 2010). For contrasting views of Roman expansion, see William V. Harris, *War and Imperialism in Republican Rome* (New York, 1985) and Arthur M. Eckstein, *Mediterranean Anarchy, Interstate War, and the Rise of Rome* (Berkeley, CA, 2006). The parallels are more widely explored in Cullen Murphy, *Are We Rome? The Fall of an Empire and the Fate of America* (Boston, 2007).

29. Bass, *Freedom's Battle*.

30. Brendan Simms and D. J. B. Trim, eds., *Humanitarian Intervention: A History* (Cambridge, UK, 2011).

31. Adams to Jefferson, February 2, 1816, *The Adams Jefferson Letters*, Lester J. Cappon, ed. (Chapel Hill, NC, 1987), 2: 461–63.

32. This section draws from David C. Hendrickson, "Revolution and Intervention: A Delicate Balance, Destroyed," *The National Interest* (September/October 2014).

33. See Tuck, "Grotius, Hobbes, and Pufendorf on Humanitarian Intervention," Recchia and Welsh, *Just and Unjust Military Intervention*, on the relation between the rights of resistance and external intervention in early modern thinkers.

34. Hersch Lauterpacht, "The Grotian Tradition in International Law," 23 *British Yearbook of International Law* 1 (1946).

35. Speech of Richard Henry Lee, in Congress, June 8, 1776, *Principles and Acts of the Revolution in America*, Hezekiah Niles, ed. (New York, 1876), 397.

36. Emer de Vattel, *The Law of Nations, Or, Principles of the Law of Nature, Applied to the Conduct and Affairs of Nations and Sovereigns*, Richard Whatmore and Béla Kapossy, eds. (Indianapolis, 2009 [1758]), book 2, chapter 1, para. 7.

37. Vattel seemed to abandon his restrictive view in his commentary on intervention in civil war, writing that when a prince violates "the fundamental laws," obliging "the nation to rise in their own defence" against tyranny, "every foreign power has

a right to succour an oppressed people who implore their assistance" (ibid., book 2, chapter 4, para. 56; also book 3, chapter 18, para. 296). Colonial Americans were pleased that Vattel made an exception that fit their cause so nicely, but when France entered the war against Great Britain and signed a defensive treaty with the United States in 1778, Edward Gibbon wrote a furious denunciation of France's perfidy, in a highly charged and moralistic vein quite opposed to Gibbon's characteristically detached style. "Justificatory Memoir," in *The Miscellaneous Works of Edward Gibbon*, John, Lord Sheffield, ed. (London, 1837), 696–712. Then, as always, the legitimacy of intervention was a fundamental question for international society, of the utmost significance, but also never quite capable of commanding a consensus. The index of its inability to do so is the history of Europe's wars.

38. Tuck, "Grotius, Hobbes, and Pufendorf," 112. On Pufendorf, see also Ian Hunter, *Rival Enlightenments: Civil and Metaphysical Philosophy in Early Modern Germany* (New York, 2001).

39. Burke, "The Policy of the Allies," *The Writings and Speeches of the Right Honourable Edmund Burke* (Boston, 1901), 4: 434.

40. James J. Sheehan, *German History: 1770-1866* (New York, 1989), 214.

41. Albert Sorel, *Europe and the French Revolution* (New York, 1964), 457. As Hurrell demonstrates, Kant's subsequent disciples—the neo-Kantians—cross these balustrades, unaccountably belittling "Kant's opposition to revolutionary change domestically and his opposition to liberal or humanitarian intervention internationally." "Revisiting Kant and Intervention," Recchia and Welsh, *Just and Unjust Military Intervention*, 198–99.

42. James Madison to Richard Rush, July 22, 1823, *Letters of Madison*, 3: 330–31.

43. Castlereagh, "Memorandum on the Treaties of 1814 and 1815," Aix-la-Chapelle, October 1818, excerpted in Evan Luard, *Basic Texts in International Relations* (New York 1992), 431.

44. The classic text is Vincent, *Nonintervention and International Order*.

45. Daniel Webster, "The Revolution in Greece," January 19, 1824, *Webster Works*, 3: 67–68.

46. Ibid., 69–74.

47. "Resolutions on Behalf of Hungarian Freedom," January 9, 1852, in *The Collected Works of Abraham Lincoln*, Roy Basler, ed. (Rutgers, NJ, 1953), 2: 115–16. Lincoln's precise role in this resolution remains unclear, but a local newspaper reported that he spoke "in favor of sympathy but non-intervention" when responding to a resolution condemning British rule in Ireland. McDougall, *Tragedy of U.S. Foreign Policy*, 83.

48. The Destiny of America, September 14, 1853, *Seward Works*, 4: 128. Letter, March 15, 1844, *The Life of William Seward*, George E. Baker, ed. (New York, 1855), 230; Seward to the Marquis de Montholon, February 12, 1866, *Papers Relating to Foreign Affairs*, Part III (Washington, DC, 1866), 820. For numerous other utterances in the same vein, see Frank Tannenbaum, *The American Tradition in Foreign Policy* (Norman, OK, 1955).

49. Webster to Everett, The Case of the Brig Creole, January 29, 1842, *The Writings and Speeches of Daniel Webster*, Edward Everett, ed. (Boston, 1903), 14: 379.

50. Tyler to James S. Whitney, February 3, 1852, *Proceedings of the Massachusetts Historical Society* 47 (1914): 472–75. Speaking of satire, in both Kagan, *Dangerous Nation*, 156, and Anderson, *American Foreign Policy and Its Thinkers*, 4, the following statement of John Adams is quoted to show the sheer grandiosity of early American aspirations: "Our pure, virtuous, public spirited, federative republic will last forever, govern the globe and introduce the perfection of man." Yet the context of this famous letter to Jefferson shows Adams putting it that way so as to underline its evident absurdity and impossibility. The letter was part of a larger exchange with Jefferson on aristocracy, natural and artificial, and Adams was particularly concerned to show that even natural aristocracies could easily degenerate into oppressive structures, divorced from any true merit. Adams hated the aristocratic pretension, considering "the weakness, the folly ... [and] the unfeeling cruelty of a majority of those (in all nations) who are allowed an aristocratical influence," while lamenting also "the stupidity with which the more numerous multitude, not only become their dupes, but even love to be taken in by their tricks." Adams was a deep skeptic of overcoming these tendencies; the problem of aristocracy was ineradicable and universal, though good institutions could mitigate its worst excesses. This had been the lesson of his *Discourses on Davila* (1790); it remained a prized theme. Hence, when Adams wrote, "Many hundred years must roll away before we shall be corrupted" and spoke of America governing the globe and introducing the perfection of man, he was joking, going on to comment, archly, "his perfectability being already proved by Price, Priestly, Condorcet, Rousseau, Diderot, and Godwin"— that is, by philosophers Adams thought hopelessly utopian. Adams to Jefferson, November 15, 1813, Cappon, *Adams-Jefferson Letters*, 400. Adams wrote the following year to John Taylor, April 15, 1814: "We may boast that *we* are the chosen people; we may even thank God that we are not like other men; but, after all, it will be but flattery, and the delusion, the self-deceit of the Pharisee." Adams, *Works*, 6: 467.

51. Michla Pomerance, "The United States and Self-Determination: Perspectives on the Wilsonian Conception," *American Journal of International Law* 70 (1976): 1–27.

52. This understanding is emphasized in Lind, *American Way*, 28. See also David Armitage, *The Declaration of Independence: A Global History* (Cambridge, MA, 2007).

53. Welcome to Kossuth, December 9, 1851, *Seward Works*, 1: 177

54. Remarks by former Vice President Joseph Biden at Harvard's Kennedy School, Boston Massachusetts, October 23, 2014.

55. Alexander Hamilton, *Pacificus* Number II, July 3, 1793, *Hamilton Works*, 4: 454.

56. Thomas Jefferson to John Adams, May 17, 1818, Cappon, *Adams-Jefferson Letters*, 524.

57. Alexander Hamilton, *Federalist* No 1. On the subordination of universal human rights to Washington's global agenda, see the excellent study by James Peck, *Ideal*

Illusions: How the U.S. Government Co-opted Human Rights (New York, 2010). Samuel Moyn, *The Last Utopia*, emphasizes the novelty of the movement for universal human rights begun in the 1970s, one that over time became increasingly associated with external military intervention. He incisively distinguishes between "a politics of citizenship at home" and "a politics of suffering abroad." But Moyn goes too far in suggesting that the idea of universal human rights was novel; what was novel, and came increasingly to characterize the human rights movements in America and Europe in the last 20 years, was the assumption that external powers could impose such conceptions on other states and peoples, in violation of their "communal liberty." The prohibition against doing so, well understood in the long nineteenth century by American statesmen, did not mean that there were no individual human rights accorded by "the Laws of Nature and of Nature's God"—an expression of Jefferson's in the Declaration of Independence—but simply that the self-same laws of nature accorded priority to the right of every people to devise their own internal institutions and to find their own way to freedom. This insight required, not a repudiation, but an affirmation, of the idea of human rights belonging to man as such. The fundamental principle of the Republic was based on the freedom and equality "of not only men, but nations," as Daniel Dewey Bernard observed in opposition to proposals to revolutionize Mexico. "The Late Negotiations for Peace," *American Whig Review* 6 (November 1847): 446. For the Founders and their followers, imposing such conceptions on other peoples would be like trying to make a pyramid stand by inverting it. They didn't think it could be done. But they also saw it as a violation of natural right.

58. On the history of U.S. "regime-change," see Kinzer, *Overthrow*.

59. Lind makes a similar argument in "Case for American Nationalism." Also emphasizing the dramatic contrast between "Wilsonianism" and "neo-Wilsonianism" is Tony Smith, *Why Wilson Matters: The Origins of American Liberal Internationalism and Its Crisis Today* (Princeton, NJ, 2017).

60. See the classic evocation in Hans Kohn, *American Nationalism* (New York, 1957).

61. Sound Nationalism and Sound Internationalism, August 4, 1918, Theodore Roosevelt, *Roosevelt in the Kansas City Star* (Boston, 1921), 192. For Wilson's sorry record in Haiti, see Brenda Gayle Plumer, *Haiti and the United States* (Athens, GA, 1992), 86–100.

62. Wilson to Garrison, August 8, 1914, *Wilson Papers*, 30: 362. The discrepancy between Wilson's interventionist policy and his non-interventionist sentiments is highlighted in Robert W. Tucker, "Woodrow Wilson's 'New Diplomacy,'" *World Policy Journal* 21 (2004) 92–107.

63. Wilson in Betty Miller Unterberger, "Russian Revolution," *Woodrow Wilson and a Revolutionary World*, Arthur S. Link, ed. (Chapel Hill, NC, 1982), 73.

64. Remarks to foreign correspondents, April 8, 1918, *Wilson Papers*, 47:288.

65. Sumner Welles, February 16, 1942, *The World of the Four Freedoms* (New York, 1943), 45; Welles, *A Time for Decision* (New York, 1944), 198–99.

66. Welles, February 16 and May 30, 1942, *Four Freedoms* 45, 91–92.

67. Belair, "Roosevelt Warns," *New York Times*, April 16, 1940.

68. For Roosevelt's balancing act on these questions, see especially Lind, *American Way of Strategy*. Roosevelt's five principles of hemispheric order are virtually identical to the "five principles of peaceful coexistence" agreed upon by China and India on April 29, 1954, and today still touted as central by China's leadership: "(1) mutual respect for each other's territorial integrity and sovereignty, (2) mutual non-aggression, (3) mutual non-interference in each other's internal affairs, (4) equality and cooperation for mutual benefit, and (5) peaceful co-existence." *United Nations Treaty Series*, No. 4307, 299 (1958): 70.

69. Nicholas J. Wheeler, *Saving Strangers: Humanitarian Intervention in International Society* (New York, 2003); Menon, *Conceit of Humanitarian Intervention*.

70. See Edward Keene, *Beyond the Anarchical Society: Grotius, Colonialism and Order in World Politics* (Cambridge, UK, 1992); and Keene, *International Political Thought: An Historical Introduction* (Boston, 2004).

71. Sankar Muthu, *Enlightenment against Empire* (Princeton, NJ, 2003); for Smith, see *Wealth of Nations*, 626.

72. Smith, *Commonwealth or Empire*, 55.

73. Jackson, *Global Covenant*, 13–15.

74. Tim Weiner, *Legacy of Ashes: The History of the CIA* (New York, 2007), 109.

75. A Memorandum by Robert Lansing, August 20, 1919, *Wilson Papers*, 62:428–49; John A. Thompson, *Woodrow Wilson* (New York, 2002), 234.

76. See Bacevich, *America's War for the Greater Middle East*, 239–46, for an extended analysis in these terms.

77. Gareth Evans and Mohamed Sahnoun, co-chairs, *The Responsibility to Protect: Report of the International Commission on Intervention and State Sovereignty* (Ottawa, ON, 2001).

78. Joachin Gauck, Speech to Open 50th Munich Security Conference, January 31, 2014.

79. The classic study is William J. Bouwsma, *Venice and the Defense of Republican Liberty: Renaissance Values in the Age of the Counter Reformation* (Berkeley, CA, 1968). For discussion, see David C. Hendrickson, "Venice and the Liberty of States," *IR and All That*, December 13, 2013.

80. For various derogatory comments regarding international law, see Richard K. Betts, "Institutional Imperialism" (review of Ikenberry, *Liberal Leviathan*), *The National Interest*, May/June 2011. For an exposition and defense of the traditional legal perspective regarding intervention (consonant in policy implications with the outlook of Betts and other defensive realists), see Roth, *Sovereign Equality and Moral Disagreement*. By "traditional international law" in this context, I mean the "reformed Westphalianism" embodied in the UN Charter, as explicated by the post-World War II generation of international lawyers. A traditional "realist" objection to international law arises from its inefficacy—Morgenthau always

stressed that point—but, of course, the same thing may be said of realist prescriptions themselves. When, in the post-World War II period, did policymakers ever accept Morgenthau's recommendations, apposite though they may have been? Not all or even most realists, it should be emphasized, disparage international law. Daniel Larison of *The American Conservative*, commonly associated with a realist view, fully incorporates the law of nations in his outlook. See also Michael Lind, "Moynihan's Law," *The National Interest* (Winter 1990/91): 83–89.

81. Hedley Bull, "The State's Positive Role in World Affairs," Anderson and Hurrell, *Hedley Bull and International Relations*, 139–56.

82. See the discussion in Roth, *Sovereign Equality*, 138–42; Roth, *Governmental Illegitimacy in International Law* (New York, 2000), 136–49, 160–71; and Richard Falk, ed., *The International Law of Civil War* (Baltimore, 1971), 11–13.

83. Roth, *Sovereign Equality*, 12, 94.

84. Menon, *Conceit of Humanitarian Intervention*, 92–93. Anyone interested in humanitarian intervention should read Menon's book, the best in a vast and sprawling literature.

85. Letter dated November 9, 2011, from the permanent representative of Brazil to the United Nations addressed to the secretary-general, United Nations.

86. That these are the worst is attested by two of the most famous passages in Western political literature—Thucydides' depiction of the revolutions and civil wars in Corcyra, and Hobbes' depiction of the state of nature. Arabs also know the saying that "sixty years of tyranny is better than a single night of anarchy."

87. The best review of the evidence is Alan J. Kuperman, "Obama's Libya Debacle: How a Well-Meaning Intervention Ended in Failure," *Foreign Affairs* (March/April 2015). Both former President Obama and Secretary of State Clinton have insisted that the situation would be just as bad had the United States stayed out; Kuperman shows that the far greater likelihood is that Qaddafi would have rapidly repressed the rebellion. Kuperman also shows that Qaddafi's uses of force were targeted not against civilians, but against those who had taken up arms to oust him. See also the September 14, 2016, report of the Foreign Affairs Committee of the British House of Commons on these accusations, often invented out of thin air by Qaddafi's domestic opponents, *Libya: Examination of Intervention and Collapse and the UK's Future Policy Options* (London, 2016). One of the chief consequences of Qaddafi's overthrow has been the buildup of U.S. bases in Africa, for which see Nick Turse, "U.S. Military Is Building a $100 Million Drone Base in Africa," *The Intercept*, September 29, 2016, and Turse, *Tomorrow's Battlefield*.

88. For essential background, see Gareth Porter, "The Real U.S. Syria Scandal: Supporting Sectarian War," *antiwar.com*, August 31, 2016; James Carden, "How Libyan 'Regime Change' Lies Echo in Syria," *Consortiumnews.com*, September 25, 2016. The details of U.S. involvement in the Syrian resistance are hidden under a veil of official secrecy, but its complicity in the transfer of arms is well established. See Mark Mazzetti and Matt Apuzzo, "U.S. Relies Heavily on Saudi Money to Support Syrian Rebels,"

New York Times, January 23, 2016. Brad Hoff has accumulated valuable material on the subject at *Levant Report*, where he is managing editor. Clinton's analysis appears in Unclassified U.S. Department of State Case No. F-2014-20439 Doc. No. C05794498. The memo, incorrectly dated by the State Department, was written in late April 2012. It refers to a CNN interview "last week" (April 19, 2012) with Ehud Barak.

Objection may be taken to describing U.S. objectives in Syria as "state overthrow," in that the official position of the State Department has been that Assad should go but essential state institutions should remain. The idea has been roughly as follows: "The regime in question is a brutal tyranny, the very definition of top-down imposition. We propose to lop off the head of this construction, thus cleansing it of evil, and yet do request that all the institutions hitherto sustained by the regime should continue to function as previously, subject however to our orders rather than those of the deposed despot." The expectation was clearly absurd; it was not a policy but a prevarication, designed to disguise the real purport of U.S. policy.

89. Evans and Sahnoun, *The Responsibility to Protect*, 31–32.

90. A point illuminated by Betts, *American Force*.

91. A strong and convincing counterweight to the dominant tendency to award accolades to U.S. policy toward Yugoslavia—and to the principle of humanitarian intervention as carried out there—is David N. Gibbs, *First Do No Harm: Humanitarian Intervention and the Destruction of Yugoslavia* (Nashville, TN, 2008). See further discussion of the relation between territorial integrity and self-determination below in Chapter 5.

92. Philip Gordon, "The Middle East Is Falling Apart," *Politico.com*, June 4, 2015.

93. "Bind him down from mischief" is an expression of Thomas Jefferson's, referring to the purpose of constitutional rules. "In questions of power," Jefferson wrote, "let no more be heard of confidence in man, but bind him down from mischief by the chains of the Constitution." "Resolutions Relative to the Alien and Sedition Acts," November 10, 1798, Lipscomb and Bergh, *Writings of Thomas Jefferson* (Washington, DC, 1905), 17: 385–91.

Though critical of the humanitarian interventionists, I must myself also plead guilty to the same sin, having argued in the early 1990s, with Robert W. Tucker, that the United States ought to have conducted a humanitarian intervention in Iraq in the aftermath of the devastation wrought by the 1991 Iraq War (Tucker and Hendrickson, *Imperial Temptation*, published by the Council on Foreign Relations in 1992). Our larger argument was that the United States ought not to have gone to war against Iraq to liberate Kuwait, but that, having done so, and with such prodigious force, it was obligated to ensure a humanitarian outcome and could do so only by occupying the country. The United States had taken on an imperial role, but showed not the slightest inclination to take up the responsibilities of imperial rule. Tucker and I soon regretted the recommendation to occupy Iraq, and have argued over the years about who was most responsible for its inclusion in the manuscript—I graciously naming him for the dubious honor, and he reciprocating by attributing major responsibility to myself. In truth, we were both greatly affected by the arresting views of Kanan Makiya, the Iraqi expatriate author of a chilling study of Saddam in power (*Republic of Fear*), who argued in the aftermath of the war that Iraq had been shattered by the U.S. bombing and desperately needed a reconstruction that could only be provided by a U.S. occupation. Samir al-Khalil (a pseudonym for Makiya), "Iraq and Its Future," *The New York Review of Books*, April 11, 1991, 10–14. Tucker and I argued that if the multiple hazards of an occupation were as serious as observers contended, that bore out our larger claim that the war should not have been undertaken in the first place (150–51). Rather than recommending an occupation, however, what we ought to have said was that the Gulf War would set in motion forces that would keep the United States in Iraq for a generation, and that committing a second wrong (occupying the country) could never compensate for the first wrong—using force in so disproportionate a manner against an Arab state. It was the latter decision, of which Americans at the time were so proud and so jubilant, that created America's terrorism problem in its modern form.

94. For tensions between Al-Qaeda and the Taliban, see Robert Grenier, *88 Days to Kandahar: A CIA Diary* (New York, 2015).

95. For a revealing account, stressing U.S. incomprehension of Taliban motives, see Gopal, *No Good Men among the Living.*

96. This argument is elaborated in David C. Hendrickson and Robert W. Tucker, *Revisions in Need of Revising: What Went Wrong in the Iraq War* (Carlisle, PA, 2006). General James Mattis, the Marine commander in Iraq who became Trump's secretary of defense, nicely summarized U.S. rules of engagement there: "Be polite, be professional, but have a plan to kill everybody you meet." And this: "I come in peace. I didn't bring artillery. But I'm pleading with you, with tears in my eyes: If you fuck with me, I'll kill you all." Cited in Thomas Ricks, "Mattis as Defense Secretary," *Foreign Policy*, November 21, 2016.

97. For an instructive antidote to this essentializing thinking, see Zachary Karabell, *Peace Be Upon You: Fourteen Centuries of Muslim, Christian, and Jewish Conflict and Cooperation* (New York, 2007).

98. A key figure in the development of these ideas was Albert Wohlstetter, whose influence is traced in Bacevich, *New American Militarism*, 147–74. The "Costs of War" project at Brown University, relying principally on the research of Neta Crawford, estimates that, as of March 2015, "210,000 civilians have died violent deaths as a result of the wars" in Iraq, Afghanistan, and Pakistan, with civilian deaths from malnutrition and a damaged health system and environment far outnumbering deaths from combat. See http://watson.brown.edu/costsofwar/costs/human/civilians. On the theme that *jus in bello* became "less a restraint on lethal force than a license and a lubricant," see Chase Madar, "Short Cuts," *London Review of Books*, July 2, 2015.

99. The best account is Danner, *Spiral*. See also Ian G. R. Shaw, *Predator Empire: Drone Warfare and Full Spectrum Dominance* (Minneapolis, MN, 2016); Jeremy Scahill et al., *The Assassination Complex: Inside the Government's Secret Drone Warfare Program* (New York, 2016); Charlie Savage, *Power Wars: Inside Obama's Post-9/11 Presidency* (New York, 2015); and Brooks, *How Everything Became War*.

100. See the discussion in Jerome Slater, "Terrorism and the Israeli-Palestinian Conflict," *Middle East Policy* (2015). Over the last 35 years, from 1981 to the present, the Israelis have terrorized the Shia of southern Lebanon far more than the Shia of southern Lebanon have terrorized the Israelis. Hezbollah, though beyond the pale in bombing the U.S. Embassy in Beirut, committed an act of war, not terrorism, in bombing the U.S. Marine compound. Hezbollah's subsequent resistance was directed overwhelmingly at Israeli soldiers, not civilians.

     Israel's extensive bombing campaign in Lebanon in the summer of 1981 had a special effect on my political consciousness. The symbol of the raids was a collapsed apartment complex in Beirut housing PLO members, in which some 60 persons had died, most of them innocents, the carnage displayed on the front pages of American newspapers. I was then in the employ of Senator Daniel Patrick Moynihan and asked him in his office what he thought about the incident. He said to me, angrily: "It's an atrocity!" He then proceeded to lecture me on the subject of the United States and Israel. They are distinct countries with distinct interests and approaches, he told me. "You are not to confuse them." I was at that time a fledgling (and soon-to-be-fired) legislative assistant for foreign policy in the service of the esteemed senator. Moynihan employed a clutch of neoconservatives when he started out (Elliott Abrams, Charles Horner, Stephen Sestanovich, Abram Shulsky). For the previous decade, as an avid consumer of *Commentary* and *The Public Interest*—and a big fan of Alexander Bickel, Daniel Bell, Nathan Glazer, Charles Frankel, Lionel Trilling (and, of course, Moynihan)—I had felt myself to be a part of that intellectual movement. "I'm a neoconservative," I used to say.

     Moynihan entered the Senate in 1977 as junior senator from the State of New York, having previously wowed the Jewish vote with his bravura defense of Israel as U.S. ambassador to the United Nations. He ultimately broke free of the neoconservatives and the Henry Jacksonians, becoming a sharp critic of U.S. intelligence operations and the warfare state. He was a liberal internationalist in the old mode and couldn't quite believe in his later years that the U.S. political and security establishment no longer took seriously the great verities, an outlook given wise and eloquent expression in his *On the Law of Nations* (1990). Wistfully, I warm to the hypothesis that Moynihan would be pleased with the argument of my book. Too bad he didn't like me back then.

101. Indulging what Herbert Butterfield once called "the last insanities of unforgiving passion." For luminous reflection on these themes, see Rieff, *In Praise of Forgetting*.

102. Representative statements of the "new sovereigntist" position may be found in Jon Kyl, Douglas Feith, and John Fonte, "The War of Law," *Foreign Affairs* (July/August 2003); John Fonte, *Sovereignty or Submission: Will Americans Rule Themselves or Be Ruled by Others?* (New York, 2011); Jeremy A. Rabkin, *The Case for Sovereignty: Why the World Should Welcome American Independence* (Washington, DC, 2004); Rabkin, *Law Without Nations: Why Constitutional Government Requires Sovereign States* (Princeton, NJ, 2005); and John Bolton, *Surrender Is Not an Option: Defending America at the United Nations* (New York, 2008).

103. David Kaye, "Stealth Multilateralism," *Foreign Affairs* (September/October 2013). Kaye notes that there are dozens of multilateral treaties "pending before the Senate, pertaining to such subjects as labor, economic and cultural rights, endangered species, pollution, armed conflict, peacekeeping, nuclear weapons, the law of the sea, and discrimination against women."

104. On Hobbes' putative denial of international society, see Hedley Bull, *The Anarchical Society*, 25. On the identification of Hobbes with Mars, see Kagan, *Of Paradise and Power*. For a persuasive dissenting view, see Noel Malcolm, "What Hobbes Really Said," *The National Interest*, Fall 2005, and Malcolm, "Hobbes's Theory of International Relations," *Aspects of Hobbes* (Oxford, UK, 2002). Malcolm registers several cogent objections against this portrait of a bellicose and amoral Hobbes, but fails to give due weight to Hobbes' reconstruction of the laws of nature. A similar judgment applies to the portrait of a more pacific Hobbes in Donald W. Hanson, "Thomas Hobbes's 'Highway to Peace,'" *International Organization* 38 (1984): 329–54.

105. Constant, *Principles of Politics, Political Writings*, 179.

106. For Hobbes' elaborate discussion, see *Leviathan*, Michael Oakeshott, ed. (London, 1955 [1651]), chapters 14–15. Cf. Hans J. Morgenthau, *Politics among Nations: The Struggle for Power and Peace*, 4th ed. (New York, 1967), 540–50, who offers nine rules of diplomacy in the conclusion of his work. I am troubled by the fact that Hobbes' nine rules for peace-seeking, by virtue of my abridgment, seem to fall a bit short of the Ten Commandments and the Fourteen Points.

In Vattel's terminology, as summarized by Alexander Hamilton, the "necessary" or "internal" law of nations recognized by eighteenth-century publicists was "the law of Nature applied to nations: or that system of rules for regulating the conduct of Nation to Nation which reason deduces from the principles of natural right as relative to political societies or States." The Defense No. 20, October 23–24, 1795, *Hamilton Papers*, 19: 341. One of reason's deductions was that the rules could not be precisely the same for states and individuals; on the whole, however, it prescribed one code of morality for men and nations, founded in the law of nature.

The "necessary" law gained in authority when followed in customary practice or recognized in treaties, and by these routes, it entered into the basic foundation of international law. To call it "internal" is to say that it is morally binding on one-self and one's nation: the "external" law concerns the extent and limits of coercion in bringing others within the rules, if violated. The "necessary" or "internal" law, one might say, is also the law's substructure or infrastructure. The Golden Rule and the principle of reciprocity it enshrines sit at the base of this structure.

107. *Leviathan*, 103. Hobbes' posture here is quite similar to Adam Smith's idea of the Impartial Spectator.

108. Thomas Hobbes, *On the Citizen*, Richard Tuck and Michael Silverthorne, eds. and trans. (Cambridge, UK, 1998), 3–5.

109. Stephen Sestanovich, *Maximalist*.

110. Alexander Hamilton, Pacificus No. 4, July 10, 1793, *Hamilton Works*, 4: 463–65. In this essay, Hamilton dismissed Jefferson's idea (shared also by Benjamin Franklin and James Madison) that gratitude was owed to France, but affirmed the vital importance of justice and good faith. "Faith and Justice between nations," he wrote, "are virtues of a nature the most necessary and sacred. They cannot be too strongly inculcated, nor too highly respected. Their obligations are absolute, their utility unquestionable; they relate to objects which, with probity and sincerity, generally admit of being brought within clear and intelligible rules." In reject-ing gratitude, Hamilton did not mean "to advocate a policy absolutely selfish or interested in nations; but to show, that a policy regulated by their own interest, as far as justice and good faith permit, is, and ought to be, their prevailing one." To suppose otherwise was "to misrepresent or misconceive what usually are, and ought to be, the springs of national conduct." Lodge's rendering of this passage in his 1904 edition of Hamilton's writings is faithful to the meaning, but not to the exact wording, of the original. Hamilton did sometimes need a bit of help with punctuation.

111. Liberal realists of the postwar generation included Hans J. Morgenthau, Reinhold Niebuhr, George F. Kennan, Walter Lippmann, Arthur M. Schlesinger, J. William Fulbright, William Pfaff, and Robert W. Tucker. Anatol Lieven and John Hulsman have wisely distilled many of their precepts in *Ethical Realism*. Similar in sensibility, though not exactly in terminology, is T. J. Jackson Lears, "Pragmatic Realism versus the American Century," in Bacevich, ed., *Short American Century*, 82–120. In basically the same vein, see Duncan Bell, "Under an Empty Sky—Realism and Political Theory," in Bell, ed., *Political Thought and International Relations: Variations on a Realist Theme* (New York, 2009); Richard Ned Lebow, *The Tragic Vision of Politics: Ethics, Interests and Orders* (New York, 2003); and Owen Harries, "Power, Morality, and Foreign Policy," *Orbis* (Fall 2005).

112. Montesquieu, *Spirit of the* Laws, book 1, chapter 3, p. 7.

113. John Adams to Abigail Adams, June 2, 1777, Smith, *Letters of Delegates*, 7: 160; Adams to Secretary Livingston, January 23, 1783, Adams, *Works*, 8: 27.

114. John F. Kennedy, Commencement Address at American University, June 10, 1963.

CHAPTER 3

1. Jefferson to van Hogendorp, October 13, 1785, cited in Robert W. Tucker and David C. Hendrickson, *Empire of Liberty: The Statecraft of Thomas Jefferson* (New York, 1990), 32.

2. Robert D. Hormats, "A Foreign Policy for Main Street America," *Foreign Policy*, July 1, 2014.

3. The Pentagon dropped the ASB name in early 2015, rechristening it as the "Joint Concept for Access and Maneuver in the Global Commons (JAM-GC)." The announced reason was that the concept was missing "the land portion, basically how the land forces could be used to allow U.S. forces to gain access to a contested area," according to a spokesman. Sam LaGrone, "Pentagon Drops Air Sea Battle Name, Concept Lives On," *USNI News*, January 20, 2015.

4. "Beyond Air-Sea Battle: The Debate over U.S. Military Strategy in Asia," *Adelphi Papers*, 54 (2014): 73–104. See also the RAND report of David C. Gompert, Astrid Cevallos, and Christina L. Garafola, *War with China: Thinking through the Unthinkable* (Washington, DC, 2016).

5. See Richard N. Rosecrance and Steven E. Miller, *The Next Great War? The Roots of World War I and the Risk of U.S.-China Conflict* (Cambridge, MA, 2014).

6. Quoted in David Brunnstrom and Matt Spetalnick, "Tillerson Says China Should Be Barred from South China Sea Islands," *Reuters.com*, January 12, 2017.

7. A similar change in policy is set forth by Australian strategist Hugh White in *The China Challenge*.

8. On the classic objectives associated with maritime strategy, see Paul Kennedy, *The Rise and Fall of British Naval Mastery* (New York, 1976).

9. Posen, *Restraint*, 136.

10. Kurt Campbell, *The Pivot: The Future of American Statecraft in Asia* (New York, 2016), 160–63.

11. Mandelbaum, *Case for Goliath*, 155

12. William Kristol and Robert Kagan, "Toward a Neo-Reaganite Foreign Policy," *Foreign Affairs* 75 (July/August 1996): 26.

13. As part of an academic delegation led by Tom Farer of Denver University in 2002, I described to a group of high-ranking Chinese military officials recent talk in Washington suggesting that the United States had acquired nuclear superiority over China, meaning a first strike capability that would effectively disable China's means of retaliation, and asked: "How do you feel about that?" The answer, from an indignant Chinese official: "How would you feel?"

14. China's construction of artificial islands in the South China Sea has been environmentally destructive of coral reefs and was condemned in a 2016 award of a Hague-based tribunal, convened under the auspices of the United Nations Convention on the Law of the Sea. The Philippines brought the case; China refused the jurisdiction of the tribunal and did not participate in the proceedings. While lamentable,

China's refusal is not essentially different from the U.S. refusal to accept jurisdiction from the International Court of Justice for its mining of Nicaraguan harbors. Indeed, given the refusal of the U.S. Senate to ratify UNCLOS, the ideological fury directed at China for its attitude seems a stretch. Even good causes, it may be noted, can run afoul of the rules. The criteria that the Hague tribunal used to deny China's claim to artificial islands in the South China Sea also would forbid the United States from declaring a wide swath of protected natural reserves in the waters near Hawaii, as the Obama administration did a few months after the tribunal's ruling. When the rules stand in the way of a good cause, we violate them, too.

15. Michael Lind, "The Promise of American Nationalism," 17.
16. Trade in Goods with China, United States Census Bureau, at https://www.census. gov/foreign-trade/balance/c5700.html.
17. Clyde Prestowitz, "Free Trade Is Dead," *The Washington Monthly* (Summer 2016).
18. For these and other proposals, see Clyde Prestowitz, "The New Shape of Globalization," *American Affairs* 1 (Spring 2017): 50–61. On the market access charge, see also the blog maintained by former World Bank economist John R. Hansen, *Americans Backing a Competitive Dollar—Now!*
19. Lind has written with great eloquence and persuasiveness on this point—a key part of his republican security theory—in his three most significant works: *The Next American Nation* (1995); *The American Way of Strategy* (2006); and *Land of Promise* (2012). Lind and Clyde Prestowitz have been the leading voices for the past two decades in advocacy of a "national school" in American political economy. They have made many cogent points in their rather lonely critique, once nearly inaudible in Washington and still a definite minority in the academy, where the free trade gospel reigns, but wildly popular in the Rust Belt and elsewhere in the heartland, as Trump appreciated better than most. Prestowitz' views are summarized in *Rogue Nation* (2004) and *The Betrayal of American Prosperity* (2010). Among professional economists, Dani Rodrik has revived key teachings of the national school in his *Globalization Paradox* (2011). For the debate among economists, see Jagdish Bhagwati and Alan S. Blinder, *Offshoring of American Jobs: What Response from U.S. Economic Policy?*, Benjamin M. Friedman, ed. (Cambridge, MA, 2009). It is certainly true that trade policy cannot alone be blamed for the erosion of America's middle class; technological change also mattered. Nor can it be denied that other approaches (like a rational health-care system or changes in the tax code) might offer eligible ways of addressing the problem. But a different approach to trade does look like a necessary part of a coherent alternative strategy.

My partial embrace of nationalist approaches in political economy may seem terribly inconsistent with the larger appeal to the liberal tradition in this work, but the liberal tradition has plenty of thinkers who sought limits on an entire freedom in commerce. Even Adam Smith gave his blessing to England's Navigation Acts, which rested on a quite extensive web of vexatious trade restrictions. Nor did either side in America's first great debate over the political economy of trade accept "free trade" as such. The Jeffersonian Republicans supported commercial retaliation in the name of freer trade; their position (shared by John Quincy Adams) is most aptly characterized as one of "fair trade" or "commercial reciprocity." The Hamiltonian Federalists, by contrast, rejected Jeffersonian nostrums and saw the danger that commercial wars would beget real wars, but otherwise supported bounties and tariffs in support of American manufacturers. Both sides in the debate subordinated political economy to broader questions of national security and prosperity, and each saw a vital role for the federal government in securing those ends. These are not illiberal perspectives, though undoubtedly they may be pushed in an illiberal direction.

20. The True Greatness of Our Country, December 22, 1848, *Seward Works*, 3: 13.

21. Going far in hawkish prescriptions is Aaron Friedberg, *A Contest for Supremacy* (2012). Equally calculated to produce a state of overt hostility is Robert Sutter, "How to Deal with America's China Problem: Target Beijing's Vulnerabilities," *The National Interest*, July 22, 2014, and John Bolton, "The U.S. Can Play a 'Taiwan Card,'" *Wall Street Journal*, January 17, 2016. The disturbing precedent is analyzed in Christopher Clark, *The Sleepwalkers: How Europe Went to War in 1914* (New York, 2014), and Christopher Layne, "China and America: Sleepwalking to War?," *The National Interest* (May/June 2015).

22. Thucydides, *History*, 1.78.3. Cf. 6.24.4. The dynamic of acting before thinking, in matters of war, is not what analysts have in mind in referring to a "Thucydides Trap," but it does constitute a sort of corollary to it. (See Graham Allison, "The Thucydides Trap: Are the U.S. and China Headed for War?," *The Atlantic*, September 24, 2015.) Acting before thinking, in the U.S. context, takes the form of assuming commitments on the assumption that they will not lead to war, presenting them as a form of war-avoidance, when, in fact, they advance a claim that strongly conduces toward war. At various moments in American history—1812, 1844, 1916, 1941, much of the Cold War—the government took positions leading to war, while insisting that those self-same positions constituted the best means of avoiding it. That historic propensity is quite relevant to the danger, associated with Thucydides' explanation for the great war between Athens and Sparta, that reconciliation between a rising power and a declining power cannot be managed successfully, with the relationship instead succumbing in the end to relentless conflict and hegemonic war. How to avoid that trap is the problem; being careful about how far you extend your promissory notes is part of the solution.

23. National Iranian American Council, *Losing Billions—The Cost of Iran Sanctions to the U.S. Economy*, July 14, 2014.

24. For a skeptical view of U.S. commitments to the Persian Gulf, see Charles L. Glaser and Rosemary A. Kelanic, eds., *Crude Strategy: Rethinking the U.S. Military Commitment to Defend Persian Gulf Oil* (Washington, DC, 2016), and John Glaser, "Does the U.S. Military Actually Protect Middle East Oil?," *The National Interest*, January 9, 2017.

25. For the denouement, which saw the U.S. majors with a foothold in Kurdistan but virtually absent from Iraqi Shiastan, see Guy Chazan, "Iraq's Appeal Wanes for Oil Majors," *Financial Times*, March 17, 2013.

26. For supporting evidence on Israel's role, the best summation appears in Mearsheimer and Walt, *The Israel Lobby*, 229–62. Also bringing strong evidence to bear is James Petras, *The Power of Israel in the United States* (Atlanta, 2006), and Petras, *Zionism, Militarism, and the Decline of U.S. Power* (Atlanta, 2008). For a contrary view, emphasizing the significance of oil, see Andrew Price-Smith, *Oil, Illiberalism, and War: An Analysis of Energy and U.S. Foreign Policy* (Cambridge, MA, 2015). Several voices on the left—Noam Chomsky, Michael Klare, Tom Engelhardt—also emphasize the primacy of oil as a motivation for the war, but not all agree; see note 52 of this chapter on Perry Anderson. Contesting the significance of the Israel lobby is Jerome Slater, "Explaining the Iraq War: The Israel Lobby Theory," in *Why Did the United States Invade Iraq?*, Jane K. Cramer and A. Trevor Thrall, eds. (New York, 2012), 101–13 (a very useful compendium of diverse viewpoints). Downplaying Israel, but stressing U.S. militarism, is Jeffrey Record, *Wanting War: Why the Bush Administration Invaded Iraq* (Dulles, VA, 2010). Of all the arguments belittling Israeli influence, the least credible is the contention that the Israelis really favored war against Iran, not Iraq, and were therefore just spectators of U.S. decision-making. All this shows, however, is that there was a competition in lunacy among the neocons—between those who wanted to do Iraq first and Iran second, and those who wanted to do Iran first and Iraq second. The pro-Israel caucus in the United States, with very few exceptions, was in favor of the Iraq War, and exerted strong influence in that direction. See, for example, the review of the record in McConnell, *Ex-Neocon*, 43–47.

27. Marcus Weisgerber and Caroline Houck, "Obama's Final Arms-Export Tally More than Doubles Bush's," *Defense One*, November 8, 2016.

28. See Gareth Porter, "The War against the Assad Regime Is Not a 'Pipeline War,'" *antiwar.com*, September 24, 2016.

29. Hassan Rohani, "Iran's Nuclear Program. The Way Out," *TIME*, May 9, 2006.

30. The best background analysis of the Iran negotiations, challenging much of the Western narrative, is Porter, *Manufactured Crisis*. The solid character of Iran's legal position is shown in Daniel H. Joyner, *Iran's Nuclear Program and International Law: From Confrontation to Accord* (New York, 2016).

31. The case against preventive war has been widely developed. See William A. Galston, "The Perils of Preemptive War," *Philosophy and Public Policy Quarterly* 22 (2002): 1–6; Richard Betts, "Striking First: A History of Thankfully Lost Opportunities," *Ethics and International Affairs* 17 (2003); Betts, "Suicide from Fear of Death?," *Foreign Affairs* (January/February 2003): 34–43; John J. Mearsheimer and Stephen M. Walt, "An Unnecessary War," *Foreign Policy* (January/February 2003): 51–59; Jeffrey Record, "Nuclear Deterrence, Preventive War, and Counterproliferation," *Cato Policy Analysis*, July 8, 2004; and Scott Silverstone, *Preventive War and American Diplomacy* (New York, 2012).

32. Supporting Apple in a joint brief of amici curiae were Amazon, Box, Cisco, Dropbox, Evernote, Facebook, Google, Microsoft, Mozilla, Nest, Pinterest, Slack, Snapchat, WhatsApp, and Yahoo. The companies argued that backdoors for government inevitably create backdoors that can also be exploited by hackers, rendering the security of communication precarious. United States District Court, Central District of California, Eastern Division, Brief of Amici Curiae Amazon. Com *et al.*, March 22, 2016. The case was subsequently dropped by the government, with it having found another way into Apple's software.

33. See, for example, Jeevan Vasagar, "Berlin Drops Verizon over U.S. Spying Fears," *Financial Times*, June 26, 2014; Jeevan Vasagar and James Fontanella-Khan, "Angela Merkel Backs EU Internet to Deter U.S. Spying," *Financial Times*, February 16, 2014.

34. Ronald J. Deibert, *Black Code: Surveillance, Privacy, and the Dark Side of the Internet* (Evanston, IL, 2013).

35. On the importance of self-restraint for the provision of order, see Lebow, *Cultural Theory of International Relations*.

36. Henry Farrell and Abraham Newman, "The Transatlantic Data War," *Foreign Affairs* (January/February 2016). Threats to employ the SWIFT system of electronic payments as a foreign policy tool—successfully so in the case of Iran, and often-threatened though not yet employed against Russia—are the very definition of a wasting asset, an asset that once deployed is weakened. It is probable that the financial heavyweights in New York (along with the Europeans) drew the line at this exaction against Russia, saying "no way" and "you're out of your mind," but it is not difficult to imagine circumstances in which it would be employed, despite serious long-term costs to both the financial center banks and the economies of Western nations. The reductio ad absurdam in the deployment of U.S. financial penalties is the 2016 legislation allowing the families of 9/11 victims to sue Saudi Arabia in federal court, a clear demonstration that the U.S. Congress cares little for international law or basic principles of reciprocity.

37. The classic work is William Appleman Williams, *The Tragedy of American Diplomacy*.

38. Andrew J. Bacevich, *American Empire*.

39. Richard McGregor, "U.S. Business Groups Attack Russia Sanctions," *Financial Times*, June 26, 2014. Protesting the broad sanctions against Russia were the U.S. Chamber of Commerce and the National Association of Manufacturers.

40. Layne, *Peace of Illusions*, 201. For good overviews of the transformations in elite influence, see Geoffrey Hodgson, "The Foreign Policy Establishment," and Michael Lind, "Conservative Elites and the Counterrevolution against the New Deal," in *Ruling America: A History of Wealth and Power in a Democracy*, Steve Fraser and Gary Gerstle, eds. (Cambridge, MA, 2005), 215–85.

41. On the officer corps, see the portraits in Bacevich, *Breach of Trust*, and Bacevich, *Washington Rules*. According to a September 2016 poll conducted by *Military Times* and Syracuse University's Institute for Veterans and Military Families,

Trump (37.6 percent) held a slight lead over Gary Johnson (36.5 percent), with only 16.3 percent for Clinton among all military service members. The same poll showed a different breakdown among the officer corps, with 38.6 percent for Johnson, 27.9 percent for Clinton, and 26 percent for Trump. Leo Shane III and George R. Altman, *Military Times*, September 21, 2016. Post-election analyses show that the majority of service members attracted to Johnson ultimately went to Trump, but they liked Ron Paul over all other candidates in 2012.

42. George F. Kennan, *American Diplomacy: 1900-1950* (Chicago, 1951), 34–37.

43. Gerald W. Johnson, "The Ghost of Woodrow Wilson," *Harper's*, June 1941.

44. Layne, *Peace of Illusions*, 32.

45. Williams, *Tragedy of American Diplomacy*.

46. See Rodrik, *Globalization Paradox*. Accepting the rationality of national aims in economic policy, and accepting their value as an expression of democratic decision-making, as Rodrik urges, do not take us back to the closed world of the 1930s. Instead, they hold out the prospect of a more equitable and democratic capitalism. However we view the debate between "free traders" and the "national school," a move in favor of the latter's prescriptions would not—at least, it should not—mean a reversion to the autarchic schemes of yesteryear.

47. Mandelbaum offers an incisive summation of these contrasting experiences in *The Ideas That Conquered the World*.

48. For supporting analyses, stressing that U.S. military power does not underpin global commerce, see Preble, *The Power Problem*, and Preble and Mueller, *A Dangerous World?* Underscoring the irrelevance of military power in securing investor claims is the illuminating account in Noel Maurer, *The Empire Trap*. Even in the heyday of government support for imperiled overseas investors, when military power was brought into play especially in Central America, it was usually economic sanctions of various sorts that were hauled out when private interests convinced the government to go to bat on their behalf, in which cause they were usually quite successful. Today, as Maurer shows, the old pattern of private investors enlisting governments in their disputes has been displaced by a system of international tribunals allowing effective suits to proceed against expropriation, with enforcement available in national courts. Whatever the overall merits of the new regime—and they have had the salubrious effect, Mauer argues, of depoliticizing investment disputes—it is clear that military power has nothing to do with the efficacy of the system. When capital is king, gunboat diplomacy is passé.

49. Layne, *Peace of Illusions*, 30, is especially emphatic in insisting on continuity. He argues that "the goal of U.S. grand strategy has been to create an 'Open Door world'—an international system, or 'world order,' made up of states that are open and subscribe to the United States's liberal values and institutions and that are open to U.S. economic penetration." Such a world has required both maintaining an open international economic order and "spreading democracy and liberalism abroad."

50. Mauer, *Empire Trap*, 5.

51. Carl Oglesby, "Vietnamese Crucible," 73.

52. An insistence on economic motives continues to distinguish much radical historiography. The best statement of a contemporary New Left view comes from
Perry Anderson, *American Foreign Policy and Its Thinkers*. Anderson notes that
economic explanations have seldom been favored by U.S. historians of the Cold
War. For most historians, "Distortions of ideology and exaggerations of insecurity are the acceptable causes of American misjudgement or misconduct abroad.
The political logic of a dynamic continental economy that was the headquarters of
world capital is matter—at best—for evasion or embarrassment" (48). Anderson's
own account of the Iraq War, however, downplays the oil motive, accepting that for
many years (since 1967) the influence of the Israel lobby "became decisive in the
formation of regional policy" and installed "a supervening interest at odds with the
calculus of national interest at large, warping the rationality of its normal adjustment of means to ends" (124). The great problem with imputing too much power
to the capitalists in understanding America's policy in the Greater Middle East is
that so much of that policy is utterly inexplicable on conventional accountings of
profit and loss; if our titans of industry had run their companies as our governmental elite runs our Middle Eastern foreign policy, they would have fallen long ago
into bankruptcy.

53. Thomas L. Friedman, "A Manifesto for the Fast World," *New York Times*, March
28, 1999.

54. On the former danger, see Clive Cookson, "Scientists Warn of $2,000bn Solar
'Katrina,'" *Financial Times*, February 20, 2011; on the latter, see suggestive analysis
in Price-Smith, *Contagion and Chaos*.

55. The George Bailey Syndrome particularly afflicts Robert Kagan, *The World America
Made*. George Bailey is the lead character in Frank Capra's *It's a Wonderful Life*, the
classic holiday film from 1946. Courtesy of an angel, who averts his suicide, George
(played by Jimmy Stewart) gets to see what life in his hometown would have
been like had he never been born. Kagan uses the tale to describe a world without
America. But Kagan's defense of the American role has its peculiar elements, quite
opposed to the account of officialdom in crucial respects. He writes that the liberal
economic order is an "imposition," as in his reckoning all orders are; in fact, the system of exchange has flourished because it is a sort of necessity for nearly all states. Its
success is due not to being imposed on them, but in being accommodating to their
interests. Some rules of the WTO, to be sure, have been effectively imposed, with
very little in the way of consultation with weaker states—but it is odd to make this
feature part of the defense, as opposed to the critique, of "the liberal world order."

   Kagan's propensity to do such is key to his significance as a thinker. In
Dangerous Nation and other works, he has inverted the master symbols of
American civilization. Where once empire was derided as entirely untypical of
the American experience, such excursions being considered aberrational by liberals and conservatives alike, Kagan (though a bit skittish about the word) elevated

the imperial dimension to supremacy. "Once," as the late Jonathan Schell wrote, "the left had stood alone in calling the U.S. imperial and was reviled for defaming the nation. Now it turned out to have been the herald of a new consensus. Yesterday's leftwing abuse became today's mainstream praise" ("Jonathan Schell on the Empire That Fell as It Rose," *TomDispatch.com*, August 19, 2004). Whereas liberalism was once indelibly associated with reciprocity, Kagan associates it with dominance and imposition.

What Kagan has done—more subtly than any of his compeers among the neoconservatives—very much recalls Machiavelli's deliberate inversion of "the master symbols of Latin literature," a procedure that gave birth to Machiavellism. See Mark Hulliung, *Citizen Machiavelli* (Princeton, NJ, 1983), ix-x, 28. Also attesting to the debt to Machiavelli is the embrace by Kagan of the Roman method of finding peoples to liberate, enemies to fight, and protectorates to create—a package he has stoutly supported in fact, but that makes no direct appearance in *The World America Made*.

56. On what the Germans were taught, set to the music of the American Creed, see Ron Robin, *The Barbed-Wire College: Reeducating German POWs in the United State during World War II* (Princeton, NJ, 1995).

57. John Gray, *Enlightenment's Wake: Politics and Culture at the Close of the Modern Age* (London, 1997), and Gray, *False Dawn: The Delusions of Global Capitalism* (New York, 1999).

58. See discussion on this point in Robert Gilpin, *War and Change in World Politics* (Princeton, NJ, 1981), 44–49.

59. Timothy Fuller, "Hobbes's Idea of Moral Conduct in a Society of Free Individuals," in *Wealth, Commerce, and Philosophy: Foundational Thinkers and Business Ethics*, Eugene Heath and Byron Kaldis, eds. (Chicago, 2016).

60. Montesquieu's observation is highlighted in Albert Hirschman, *The Passions and the Interests* (Princeton, NJ, 1977). Kagan offers a good evocation of these early American and Enlightenment beliefs in *Of Paradise and Power*, 9–10, marred only by his intimation that they were not really believed but were instead simply thought useful as strategies for the weak.

61. James Madison, "Universal Peace," January 31, 1792, *Madison Writings*, 6: 88–91. Madison especially focused on whether a particular regime had internal institutions that created a profound disjunction between those who gained, and those who lost, from war. He condemned monarchies and aristocracies, as Paine had done, because they thrived on this disjunction, and a key aspect of early liberal thought is devising institutions whereby this disjunction is overcome, or at least mitigated. Madison's principal remedy was simplicity itself: "Each generation should be made to bear the burden of its own wars, instead of carrying them on, at the expence of other generations." Then the people would proceed more cautiously. "Were a nation to impose such restraints upon itself, avarice would be sure to calculate the expenses of ambition," eliminating a potent route to war.

CHAPTER 4

1. Thomas Knock, *To End All Wars: Woodrow Wilson and the Quest for a New World Order* (New York, 1992), 261.
2. The most evocative depiction is Tom Engelhardt, *Shadow Government*. See further Dana Priest and William M. Arkin, *Top Secret America: The Rise of the New National Security State* (Boston, 2011); David C. Unger, *The Emergency State: America's Pursuit of Absolute Security at All Costs* (New York, 2012); and Shane Harris, *The Watchers: The Rise of America's Surveillance State* (New York, 2011).
3. "Political Observations," April 20, 1795, *Letters of Madison*, 4: 491–92.
4. Speech of January 4, 1848, Richard K. Crallé, ed., *The Works of John C. Calhoun* (New York, 1888), 4: 411–12. On Calhoun's idea of "the constitution of the negative" as a model for international society, see Deudney, *Bounding Power*, 263. On minority rights, John L. Safford, "John C. Calhoun, Lani Guinier, and Minority Rights," *PS* 28 (1995): 211–16.
5. These issues are considered in broad historical perspective in Bruce D. Porter, *War and the Rise of the State: The Military Foundations of Modern Politics* (New York, 1994); Geoffrey R. Stone, *War and Liberty—An American Dilemma: 1790 to the Present* (New York, 2007), and Robert Higgs, *Crisis and Leviathan: Critical Episodes in the Growth of American Government*, 25th anniversary ed. (Oakland, CA, 2013).
6. Glennon, *National Security and Double Government*.
7. Turse, *The Complex*.
8. John Quincy Adams, July 4, 1821, *Niles Weekly Register* 20 (1821): 331. Glennon's assumption of basic continuity within the national security cadre, a key feature of the transition from Bush to Obama, has been thrown into grave question by the Trump administration. At one level, Trump is the very embodiment of movement from liberty to force, and of a militarism that discards diplomacy; at the same time, his administration has been deeply hostile to the existing cadre of national security experts, the heart and soul of Glennon's "Trumanites." The explanation for Trump's strange behavior—decimating the personnel as he is absorbing their ideology—is not fully clear, but these profound disturbances within the inner sanctum of the national security establishment have got to be highly significant. Around them vaguely hovers the air of constitutional crisis.
9. Alexander, Hamilton, *Federalist* No. 8.
10. Ibid.; Dwight Eisenhower, Farewell Address, January 17, 1961.
11. Tony Smith, *Foreign Attachments: The Power of Ethnic Groups in the Making of American Foreign Policy* (Cambridge, MA, 2000); Mearsheimer and Walt, *Israel Lobby*.
12. On these calculations, see Thorpe, *The American Warfare State*, and Hartung, *Prophets of War*. On inside influence, see James Risen, *Pay Any Price: Greed, Power, and Endless War* (New York, 2014.)
13. Robert A. Dahl, *A Preface to Democratic Theory* (Chicago, 2006). On the concentration of benefits and the diffusion of costs, explaining the political heft of

the security caucus, see the lucid explication in Benjamin Friedman and Harvey Sapolsky, "The Politics of Primacy and the Prospects for Restraint," Thrall and Friedman, *Case for Restraint.*

14. Constant, *The Spirit of Conquest, Political Writings*, 69.

15. Bolingbroke, Occasional Writer Number II, February 3, 1726-27, *The Works of Lord Bolingbroke* (New York, 1967 [1844]), 1: 221.

16. For misgivings among soldiers, see Ann Jones, *They Were Soldiers: How the Wounded Return from America's Wars: The Untold Story* (Chicago, 2014). On the costs, see David Philipps, *Lethal Warriors: When the New Band of Brothers Came Home* (New York, 2010).

17. John A. Thompson, "The Exaggeration of American Vulnerability: The Anatomy of a Tradition," *Diplomatic History* (Winter 1992), 23–43. The expansion of the American role, writes Thompson, "has reflected a growth of power rather than the decline of security. Yet the full and effective deployment of that power has required from the American people disciplines and sacrifices that they are prepared to sustain only if they are persuaded the nation's safety is directly at stake." For further development, see Thompson's illuminating treatise *A Sense of Power*. Exploration of this paradoxical situation—in which the United States risked its physical security over interests that, if lost, would not imperil that security—was a key theme in the investigations of Robert W. Tucker, especially *Nation or Empire?* and *A New Isolationism*. See further Robert H. Johnson, *Improbable Dangers: U.S. Conceptions of Threat in the Cold War and After* (Columbus, OH, 2009); and Preble and Mueller, *A Dangerous World?* Bacevich, *Washington Rules*, gives an expert tour of the security complex and its priorities, describing all the sacred liturgies and imperial axioms that have animated the cadres, alongside the corrupt and myopic special interests, snouts engaged, fighting for their fair share of the national security pie.

18. Alexander Hamilton, *Federalist* Nos. 7 and 15.

19. The classic reconstruction of "republican security theory," emphasizing its liberal lineage, is Deudney, *Bounding Power*. Its seminal statement was and remains the *Federalist*. Lind offers an excellent discussion of the terminological complexities in *American Way of Strategy*, 8–11, arguing persuasively that republican liberalism "is the most accurate shorthand description of the American Creed," with liberalism the noun and "democratic republican" the adjectival modifier. I give an assessment of the evolution of this paradigm of thought (using somewhat different terminology) in *Peace Pact* (2003) and *Union, Nation, or Empire* (2009). A good summing up is Karl Walling, "Toward an Old New Paradigm in American International Relations," *Orbis* (Spring 2011): 325–35. For the foundations, see Robbie J. Totten, "Security, Two Diplomacies, and the Formation of the U.S. Constitution: Review, Interpretation, and New Directions for the Study of the Early American Period," *Diplomatic History* 36 (January 2012): 77–117.

In addressing this issue, it is important to remember that "liberal ideology" and the "republican paradigm" were fused at the Founding. As Lance Banning has suggested, "Revolutionary thought—in 1787 as in 1776—is best conceived as an early modern *blend* of liberal and neoclassical [republican] ideas, that a coherent mixture of the two traditions was in fact its most distinctive feature." "The Republican Interpretation: Retrospect and Prospect," Milton M. Klein et al. *The Republican Synthesis Revisited* (Worcester, MA, 1992). The essays on these themes by Banning, who died in 2006, are collected in *Founding Visions: The Ideas, Individuals, and Intersections that Created America*, Todd Estes, ed. (Lexington, KY, 2014).

20. Joseph A. Schumpeter, "The Sociology of Imperialisms," *Imperialism and Social Classes* (New York, 1951), 25, 51; and discussion in the seminal essay of Arthur M. Schlesinger Jr., "America and Empire," *Cycles of American History*, 118–62, at 153. See also discussion of Schumpeter in Michael Doyle, *Ways of War and Peace* (New York, 1997). The classic study of the role of domestic coalitions in prompting expansion is Snyder, *Myths of Empire*. In a comment that remains highly pertinent, Snyder notes, 306, that the rationales for expansion were often contradictory: "Opponents were seen as unappeasably aggressive, yet somehow inert in resisting aggressive measures to contain their expansion"—an apt summary of hawkish approaches toward Iran, Russia, and China today.

21. Jean Jacques Rousseau, *Abstract and Judgement of Saint Pierre's Project for Perpetual Peace* (1756); Stanley Hoffmann and David P. Fidler, eds., *Rousseau on International Relations* (Oxford, UK, 1991), 91.

22. Hamilton, "Defense of the Funding System," July 1795, in *The Papers of Alexander Hamilton*, Harold C. Syrett et al., eds. (New York, 1961-79), 19: 56.

23. See discussion in Peter S. Onuf, "Anarchy and the Crisis of the Union," in *To Form a More Perfect Union: The Critical Ideas of the Constitution*, Herman Belz, Ronald Hoffman, and Peter J. Albert, eds. (Charlottesville, VA, 1992), and Hendrickson, *Peace Pact*.

24. Grotius, Prolegomena, *Rights of War and Peace*, 3: 1745.

25. Alexander Hamilton, *Federalist* No. 8.

26. Cf. Nisbet, *Present Age*, 39. "No nation in history has ever managed permanent war and a permanent military Leviathan at its heart and been able to maintain a truly representative character." The United States, Nisbet speculated, was not "the divinely created exception to this ubiquitous fact of world history."

27. Adams, July 4, 1821, *Niles Weekly Register* 20 (1821): 331.

28. Unsigned editorial [Oswald Garrison Villard], November 8, 1920, *The Nation* 111 (1920): 489. Lippmann to Newton D. Baker, January 17, 1920, in Steel, *Walter Lippmann*, 167.

29. For an enumeration of trends hostile to liberty, from A to Z, see John C. Whitehead, "The Tyranny of 9/11," *antiwar.com*, September 12, 2016.

30. Alexander Hamilton, *Federalist* No. 6.

31. For an eloquent statement of "how the national-security state threatens America's liberal political order," see John Mearsheimer, "The Burden of Responsibility," 27–29. Though welcome, Mearsheimer's argument here seems deeply inconsistent with

the prescriptions of offensive realism, as unfolded in his *Tragedy of Great Power Politics*. States, he wrote in *The Tragedy*, 11, "*should* behave according to the dictates of offensive realism, because it outlines the best way to survive in a dangerous world." But if "the overriding goal of each state is to maximize its share of world power," this inevitably puts in the shade the requirements of domestic liberty. In contrast with offensive realism, republican security theory places the control of power at home and abroad as the central problem reflection must solve, and sees these two questions as closely interrelated.

32. The primacy of security, prosperity, and liberty is directly advertised in the subtitle of Preble's *Power Problem: How American Military Dominance Makes Us Less Safe, Less Prosperous, and Less Free*.

33. Kagan, *World America Made*, 125. Kagan's general method in exculpating recent failures is to draw attention to an equally impressive number of failures during the Cold War. It is not clear why he believes that this establishes his case.

34. Alexis de Tocqueville, *Democracy in America*, Henry Reeve, trans. (New York, 1839), 1: 256; John Adams to Abigail Adams, March 17, 1797, *Letters of John Adams: Addressed to His Wife*, Charles Francis Adams, ed. (Boston, 1841), 2: 252. These strictures clearly remain relevant to an age of ever-expanding technological and military capabilities: in an age of "bounding power," binding power remains a crucial task of statecraft. The relevance of the old republican wisdom about restraint in politics to the new milieu of exploding technological possibilities is a key theme of Deudney, *Bounding Power*, and in his exposition a defining feature of American liberal internationalism in the twentieth century. I argue in the next section that U.S. military doctrines and deployments have fatally undermined this old aspiration, once central to liberal internationalism but now apparently headed to the dustbin of history.

35. Deudney, *Bounding Power*, 187.

36. James Madison, *Federalist* No. 41.

37. McDougall, *Promised Land, Crusader State*, 4–5. See also McDougall's splendid companion work, *Tragedy of U.S. Foreign Policy*. In the *Tragedy*, McDougall's explication of what he calls Classical American Civil Religion or the old orthodoxy is basically synonymous in substance with what he once called the Old Testament.

38. Grover Cleveland, First Inaugural Address, March 4, 1885. Van Buren, June 9, 1829, *A Digest of International Law*, John Bassett Moore, ed. (Washington, DC, 1906), 6: 14.

39. Calvin Coolidge, Message to Congress, December 7, 1926.

40. George Washington, Farewell Address, September 19, 1796.

41. Jefferson to Robert Livingston, September 9, 1801, cited in Robert W. Tucker, *Woodrow Wilson and the Great War: Reconsidering America's Neutrality, 1914-1917* (Charlottesville, VA, 2007), 61.

42. "An Examination of the British Doctrine . . . ," *Letters of Madison*, 2: 232; Charles Francis Adams, *The Struggle for Neutrality in America* (New York, 1871), 45–46.

43. Still incisive is Roland Stromberg, *Collective Security and American Foreign Policy: From the League of Nations to NATO* (New York, 1963).

44. Herbert Butterfield, "The Tragic Element in Modern International Conflict," *The Review of Politics* 12 (1950): 147–64.

45. Edwin Borchard and William Potter Lage, *Neutrality for the United States*, 2nd ed. (New Haven, CT, 1940), 237; Warren F. Kuehl and Lynne K. Dunne, *Keeping the Covenant: American Internationalists and the League of Nations* (Kent, OH, 1997), 180.

46. The significance of the nuclear revolution was especially emphasized by Tucker in his exploration of *A New Isolationism*, 45–51.

47. Jonathan Schell, *The Unconquerable World*.

48. These obstacles are recounted by Brooks and Wohlforth, *America Abroad* (2016) and *World Out of Balance* (2008), in support of the view that the conditions for U.S. primacy are likely to persist. But the conditions making for that persistence also show that the balance of power—that is, the prevention of a condition of dominance by other powers in Eurasia—would exist even were America to take a different geopolitical role. For an appreciation of the difficulties of conquest, see Jeffrey Record, *Beating Goliath: Why Insurgencies Win* (Dulles, VA, 2007). Describing the standoff between Napoleon Bonaparte and Toussaint Louverture, Henry Adams wrote of the Haitian leader: "He was like a rat defying a ferret; his safety lay not in his own strength, but in the nature of his hole." Henry Adams, *History of the United States of America During the First Administration of Thomas Jefferson* (New York, 2011 [1891]), 1: 388. That pattern is invariably on display in movements of nationalist resistance to external occupation.

49. James Madison, *Federalist* Nos. 18–20; Alexander Hamilton, *Federalist* No. 15.

50. The most systematic case is Mandelbaum, *The Case for Goliath*.

51. On the key importance of countervailing powers, see Gordon, *Controlling the State*.

52. Elizabeth Cobbs Hoffman, *American Umpire*.

53. The peace plans are intricately surveyed by F. H. Hinsley in *Power and the Pursuit of Peace* (Cambridge, UK, 1961), more approachably in John A. R. Marriott, *Commonwealth or Anarchy? A Survey of Projects of Peace from the Sixteenth to the Twentieth Century* (London, 1939).

CHAPTER 5

1. Cited in Steel, *Walter Lippmann*, 586.

2. See Albert K. Weinberg, "The Historical Meaning of the American Doctrine of Isolation," *American Political Science Review* 34 (1940): 539–47.

3. In a statement to the Senate on April 14, 1971, Fulbright held, "People who are now being called 'neo-isolationists' are by and large those who make a distinction between the new internationalism and the old, and who retain some faith in the validity and vitality of the United Nations idea." Quoted in Tucker, *New Isolationism*, 22.

4. Smith, *Commonwealth or Empire*, 36.

5. Sumner, *Conquest of U.S.*, 26.

6. Mahan is cited in Frank Ninkovich, *The United States and Imperialism* (Malden, MA, 2001), 37.

7. Andrew Kohut, "Americans: Disengaged, Feeling Less Respected, But Still See U.S. as World's Military Superpower," Pew Research Center, April 1, 2014. See also Daniel R. DePetris, "A New Poll Shows America's Reluctance for New Foreign Adventures," *The National Interest*, October 27, 2016.

8. On the Seminole War, January 1819, in *The Speeches of Henry Clay* (Philadelphia, 1827), 150–51.

9. Andrew Cockburn, "The New Red Scare: Reviving the Art of Threat Inflation," *Harper's Magazine* 333 (December 2016): 25–31.

10. The outlook of the armed forces is well summarized in Lieven, *America Right or Wrong*, 174: "The desire, and need, are for tension, not conflict; for large-scale military spending, not full-scale war." For evidence of military cautiousness in the past, see the nuanced scholarship of Richard K. Betts, *Soldiers, Statesmen, and Cold War Crises* (New York, 1991), and Betts, *American Force*. Robert Gates, in his memoir *From the Shadows* (New York, 1996), 275, counterpoises in the Situation Room civilians with "half-baked ideas for the use of military force" against the uniformed military, "the biggest doves in Washington." On the other hand, any president has numerous hawks within the services to promote to senior levels, if that is his inclination. Obama himself was more restrained than his generals, but no one can speak for the future. Of late, die-hard peaceniks have been reduced to hoping that a general nicknamed "Mad Dog"—Secretary of Defense James Mattis—will prove a restraint on the impulsive and errant ways of Donald Trump.

11. Oglesby, "Vietnamese Crucible," 165. See also Michael Lind, "The War Socialism of the American Right," *Salon*, September 14, 2010. "The U.S. economy," notes Lind, "increasingly resembles the dual economy of the Soviet Union, with an overfunded military sector and a chronically weak, dysfunctional civilian sector." But vote-seeking conservatives, as Lind insists, are not being irrational in "fostering a military economy that provides orders and jobs to many of their constituents. Theirs is the logic of Soviet-style conservatism."

12. Layne, *Peace of Illusions*, 7.

13. On "Jacksonian nationalism," see Mead, *Special Providence*.

14. If internationalists have often displayed the most barbarous insularity today, so-called isolationists in the past seldom advocated "cultural, economic, or complete political separation from the rest of the world," as shown by Christopher McKnight Nichols, *Promise and Peril: America at the Dawn of a Global Age* (Cambridge, MA, 2011), 352. Also incisive in the portraiture of figures frequently deemed isolationist are Robert David Johnson, *The Peace Progressives and American Foreign Relations* (Cambridge, MA, 1995), and David Mayers, *Dissenting Voices in America's Rise to*

Power (New York, 2007). As Robert W. Tucker noted in *A New Isolationism*, 12, "Isolationism is not to be identified with 'quitting the world,' something we have never done and will never do. It is not to be identified with the absence of all significant relationships but, rather, with the absence of certain relationships. As a policy, it is above all generally characterized by the refusal to enter into alliances and to undertake military interventions. This was the essential meaning of an isolationist policy in the past, and it remains the essential meaning of an isolationist policy today."

15. In a vast literature, see especially Elizabeth Kolbert, *The Sixth Extinction: An Unnatural History* (New York, 2014).

16. D. P. Chase, ed., *The Nicomachean Ethics of Aristotle* (Oxford, UK, 1861), 47.

17. Of Robert Art's "selective internationalism," with its worldwide bases and allowance for the use of U.S. power projection to "shape events" and "mold the environment" to "make them more congenial to U.S. interests," Perry Anderson comments: "In the vagueness and vastness of this ambition, open-ended with a vengeance, realism dissolves itself into a potentially all-purpose justification of any of the adventures conducted in the name of liberalism." Anderson, *American Foreign Policy*, 216–17. See Robert Art, *A Grand Strategy for America* (New York, 2003), and Art, *America's Grand Strategy and World Politics* (New York, 2008).

18. Micah Zenko and Michael A. Cohen, "Clear and Present Safety: The United States Is More Secure than Washington Thinks," *Foreign Affairs* (March/April 2012).

19. Irving Kristol, "American Intellectuals and Foreign Policy," *Foreign Affairs* (July 1967).

20. The term was coined by Samuel P. Huntington, "Coping with the Lippmann Gap," *Foreign Affairs* 66 (1987/1988): 453–77.

21. Congressional Budget Office, An Update to the Budget and Economic Outlook: 2016 to 2026, August 2016.

22. Richard Nixon, Second Inaugural Address, January 20, 1973.

23. See above, Chapter 2, section 5, "Pluralism and Liberal Internationalism."

24. Kissinger's legacy is not easy to assess, though reassessments—Niall Ferguson, Greg Grandin, Gary Bass—pour from the presses. Kissinger was hammered by Reagan and neoconservatives in the mid-1970s for the policy of détente. That left its mark. He became considerably more hawkish toward the Soviet Union in the 1980s, in a grand effort to make up with the neoconservatives, but he has usually been a voice of moderation in dealing with China; lately, to this author's great satisfaction, though without consequence, he has been a voice of moderation in dealing with Russia over Ukraine. But the modus operandi of his diplomatic outlook— be prepared to cut deals with Russia and China, but be ruthless toward smaller states elsewhere—continues to express itself. In his most recent book, *World Order*, Kissinger portrays Iran as a revolutionary state with whom no fruitful negotiation is possible. He was a big advocate and supporter of the war against Iraq in 2003. A relative dove toward Russia and China, and generally respectful of their claims, he has been a hawk toward many other states.

Kissinger's realism forms a striking contrast with that of Hans Morgenthau, another prominent realist of the post-World War II period. Morgenthau talked like a hard realist but acted like a soft one: he invariably opposed the use of U.S. military force and was a leading anti-interventionist critic of the Vietnam War. Kissinger, on the other hand, talked like a soft realist but acted like a hard one: he invariably supported the use of U.S. military force in the postwar era, especially in the Middle East but elsewhere in the Global South as well. Understandably, the left has no use for Nixon and Kissinger, but its casual demonization of them risks discrediting proven methods of softening the rigors of international conflict.

25. Nixon, Speech at NATO Summit, cited in McDougall, *Tragedy of U.S. Foreign Policy*, 312.

26. Warren G. Harding, October 1920, cited in Hendrickson, *Union, Nation, or Empire*, 339.

27. Elizabeth Knowles, *Oxford Dictionary of Modern* Quotations (New York, 2007), 163.

28. Philip Oltermann, " 'Europe's Fate Is in Our Hands': Angela Merkel's Defiant Reply to Trump," *The Guardian*, January 16, 2017.

29. Daniel Webster, "The Revolution in Greece," January 19, 1824, *Webster Works*, 3: 72.

30. See below, note 54, for my view of the relevant principles governing territorial integrity and self-determination.

31. Alexander J. Motyl, "Let It Go," *Foreign Policy*, August 12, 2016.

32. The retired Chinese admiral is cited in "Naked Aggression," *The Economist*, March 12, 2009.

33. See the account in Bruce Cumings, *The Korean War: A History* (New York, 2010), 147–61. The scale of the destruction, as Cumings shows, exceeded that which occurred in Japan. "The United States dropped 635,000 tons in Korea (not counting 32,557 tons of napalm), compared to 503,000 tons in the entire Pacific theater in World War II. Whereas sixty Japanese cities were destroyed to an average of 43 percent, estimates of the destruction of towns and cities in North Korea 'ranged from forty to ninety percent'; at least 50 percent of eighteen out of the North's twenty-two major cities were obliterated." Cumings cites an official American military history: "So, we killed civilians, friendly civilians, and bombed their homes, fired whole villages with the occupants—women and children and ten times as many hidden Communist soldiers—under showers of napalm, and the pilots came back to their ships stinking of vomit twisted from their vitals by the shock of what they had to do."

34. Jeffrey Record, "Nuclear Deterrence, Preventive War, and Counterproliferation," *Cato Policy Analysis*, July 8, 2004.

35. Chronology of U.S.-North Korean Nuclear and Missile Diplomacy, *Arms Control Association, www.armscontrol.org*, updated August 2016. On the role of the U.S. financial sanctions in fouling the six-party talks, see Leon V. Sigal, "Looking for Leverage in All the Wrong Places," *38 North*, May 2, 2010.

36. Kagan, *World America Made*, 84, especially emphasizes the vulnerability of the nineteenth-century European balance of power to war and argues, "There is no better recipe for great-power peace than certainty about who holds the upper hand" (90). On the role of equal as against unequal power in keeping the peace, see also Geoffrey Blainey, *The Causes of War* (New York, 1988), 113–14, and William C. Wohlforth, "The Stability of a Unipolar World," *International Security* 24 (1999): 5–41.

37. On the significance of the technological revolution, ostensibly shrinking distance, see Porter, *Global Village Myth*.

38. H. G. Wells [with others], *The Idea of a League of Nations* (Boston, 1919), 6.

39. The classic essay is David Alan Rosenberg, "The Origins of Overkill: Nuclear Weapons and American Strategy, 1945-1960," *International Security* 7 (Spring 1983).

40. *Annual Register* for 1760, 2–3, cited in Herbert Butterfield, "The Balance of Power," *Diplomatic Investigations*, Butterfield and Wight, eds., 144.

41. Michael Lind's 2006 work *The American Way of Strategy* makes a case for a "concert strategy" in-between "primacy" and "off-shore balancing." Rather than withdrawing from alliance commitments, he argued for their extension, inviting Russia to join NATO and extending the same U.S. guarantee to China as had long been offered to Japan. Lind's approach is generally quite sympatico with my own, but his proposals on this score are perplexing. Though the extension of guarantees to putative enemies would overcome the friend/enemy approach in theory—a valuable objective—it represents an ambiguous and potentially dangerous method of effectuating a more restrained U.S. grand strategy, as Lind otherwise urges. Lind's recent statement, "The Case for American Nationalism" (2014), seems less ambitious in the reach of the concerts to which the United States would be a party. Having previously distanced himself from "primacy," he argues here that the U.S. should embrace "primacy" rather than "global hegemony," becoming "primus inter pares in a world of multiple great powers." He has reconciled with "offshore balancing," which in 2006 he considered too recessed. Despite these shifts in terminology, the idea of a "concert-balance" strategy remains central to his outlook, and he has brilliantly articulated its logic as an alternative and antidote to both supremacy and withdrawal.

42. I differ from some non-interventionists in describing a political strategy of reconciling with enemies, but am generally in concord with their outlook and disposition. A fine exploration of a new policy that invokes Washington's Farewell Address but advises retention of America's "treaty alliances" is Daniel Larison, "Noninterventionism." Though non-interventionists tend to be united in their condemnations of interventions in the Greater Middle East, they are divided on what to do with America's treaty alliances in Europe and Asia. Some would withdraw from these treaty commitments altogether; others, like Larison, would retain them while seeking to effectuate a more equitable distribution of burdens.

   Important recent books describing a U.S. strategic retrenchment include Barry Posen, *Restraint* (2014); Christopher Preble, *The Power Problem* (2009);

and Christopher Layne, *The Peace of Illusions* (2006). Preble's work is an excellent study of how to approach this reconfiguration, especially good on how to approach defense cuts and allies, though he is noncommittal on the resolution of conflicts with adversaries. See also Preble, Ashford, and Evans, *Our Foreign Policy Choices* (2016), for an updating and extension of the approach of Preble and his collaborators at the Cato Institute (including Ted Galen Carpenter and Doug Bandow, two wise and incisive voices who have been prolific over many years). Posen and Layne engage productively with a range of historical and scholarly problems. Though both are "defensive realists," they differ in their remedies. Posen, fearful of nuclear proliferation, wants to remain in Northeast Asia; Layne advises disengagement, even at the cost of proliferation to South Korea and Japan, which he would be willing to facilitate if it allowed the U.S. to back out of its nuclear guarantee.

There is a substantial literature on "off-shore balancing" as the preferred U.S. strategy. The basic thrust of this literature is in keeping with the argument of this book; details aside, the offshore balancers make the case for retrenchment and restraint. The difficulty with offshore balancing as a concept is that the prospect against which it is to guard—an Axis-like bid to take over Europe, the Middle East, or Asia—is utterly remote; none of the candidates (Russia, Iran, China) has any intention or capability of doing that. A strategic posture in which interventionary forces remain at the ready for remote contingencies is also one that can be employed for different purposes. (See the discussion in Preble, *Power Problem*, 126–28.)

"Off-shore balancing" thus comes in different varieties, with the key ambiguity the status of America's treaty allies, but also with some regional variation in approach. A recent statement by Mearsheimer and Walt, "The Case for Offshore Balancing," takes toward China (though not toward Europe or the Middle East) a view almost indistinguishable from the U.S. security establishment: by working with regional allies, China is to be contained and prevented from achieving regional hegemony. Christopher Layne's version of offshore balancing (*Peace of Illusions*, 159–92) is much more restrictive about the positioning and threatened use of U.S. military power in Asia. Probably most self-described offshore balancers would have issues with Mearsheimer and Walt's latest formulation with regard to China. I do.

Earlier statements on behalf of offshore balancing are offered in Barry Posen, "The Case for Restraint," *American Interest* (November/December 2007), 7–17; Posen, "Pull Back: The Case for a Less Activist Foreign Policy," *Foreign Affairs* (January/February 2013), 116–29; Stephen Walt, "Offshore Balancing: An Idea Whose Time Has Come," *Foreign Policy*, November 2, 2011; Joseph M. Parent and Paul K. MacDonald, "The Wisdom of Retrenchment," *Foreign Affairs* (November/ December 2011); and Eugene Gholz, Daryl Press, and Harvey Sapolsky, "Come Home America: The Strategy of Restraint in the Face of Temptation," *International Security* (Spring 1997), 5–48. A similar strategy of restraint, anchored in the philosophy of Washington's Farewell Address, was urged in 1992 by Robert W. Tucker and myself in *The Imperial Temptation*. A cogent new entrée in this genre is Thrall and Friedman, *Case for Restraint*.

43. The expectation that the United States served revolutionary ends persisted under Obama. When the Arab Spring still looked a bit promising, Robert Kagan, *The World America Made*, 34–35, noted that "American power became a decisive factor shaping the regional and international environment in which the Arab political turmoil unfolded." In the absence of the United States, "it is unlikely the dictators in the region would have faced so much pressure and been compelled to give way or be overthrown."

44. Though vociferously denied in several government reports, a former government official acknowledged to Gareth Porter that "then-director of the CIA David Petraeus devised a plan, which Obama approved, to help move the small arms from Libyan government stocks in Benghazi to Turkey," then on to the Syrian rebels. Gareth Porter, "Behind the Real U.S. Strategic Blunder in Syria," *antiwar.com*, December 28, 2016.

45. The scandal of scandals was the intervention itself, an enterprise supported by many of Clinton's interrogators. Ben Norton, "The Real Benghazi Scandal That Is Ignored," *Salon*, October 26, 2015.

46. Patrick Cockburn, "Who Supplies the News?," *London Review of Books*, February 2, 2017. For the Aleppo professor, see the report of Turkish journalist Fehim Tastekin, "What Will Be the Cost of Aleppo Victory for Damascus?," *Al-Monitor*, January 16, 2017. The locals, writes Tastekin, hate the idea that this was a sectarian war. "At least six Sunni religious notables were killed in Aleppo because they rejected an armed uprising. Sunni religious figures were constantly under threat for not joining the war. The most annoying question you can ask soldiers on the Aleppo front is whether they are Sunni or Alawite. Nothing angers Syrians as much as this question." That the locals feel this way is a telling commentary on the one-sided Syrian narrative spun by the mainstream media since 2011.

47. Michael Rubin, "Arming Syrian Rebels Is Strategic Suicide," *Commentary*, June 23, 2013. Many Christian voices from Iraq and Syria attest to this interpretation.

48. Trita Parsi and Tyler Cullis, "The Myth of the Iranian Military Giant," *Foreign Policy*, July 10, 2015.

49. Rob Nordland and James Kanter, "Turkey and E.U. Near Breaking Point in Talks on Membership," *New York Times*, November 24, 2016; Patrick Cockburn, "Erdogan's 'Rigged Referendum,'" *Independent*, April 17, 2017.

50. Erdogan quoted in Tulay Karadeniz and Ercan Gurses, "Turkey Says Its Troops to Stay in Iraq until Islamic State Cleared from Mosul," *Reuters.com*, October 13, 2016.

51. For the great conflict in Turkey between the modernizers and the indigenes, making Turkey a classic instance of a "torn country," see Huntington, *Clash of Civilizations*, 144–49, 178–79.

52. Cited in Cole, "Drone Presidency."

53. For Lawrence's map, including a Sunnistan embracing parts of what subsequently became Syria and Iraq, see Scott Anderson, *Lawrence in Arabia: War, Deceit, Imperial Folly and the Making of the Modern Middle East* (New York, 2014).

54. The relation between territorial integrity and self-determination is complex. I think the right principle is to give a presumptive validity to territorial integrity but to recognize that self-determination (the right of a people to rule themselves and not be ruled by foreigners) may become morally imperative when a raging conflict has erupted. Its superior ethical basis in those circumstances rests not only on the principle of self-rule but also on the needs of a pacification. As the parties to these conflicts fear domination from powerful others, they will not accept peace if this prospect beckons. An insistence that conflicting peoples, nursing unfathomable injuries, be combined (according to some artful external solution) becomes a formula for further war rather than peace. In those circumstances, partition is the worst remedy except for all the others, and a vanished "territorial integrity" must give way to new facts.

55. For an especially constructive proposal, see Sharmine Narwani, "How Trump Can Defeat ISIS," *The American Conservative*, February 8, 2017.

56. On the empire of bases in the Greater Middle East, see David Vine, "Doubling Down on a Failed Strategy: The Pentagon's Dangerous 'New' Base Plan," *TomDispatch.com*, January 14, 2016.

57. Instead of building up the Strategic Petroleum Reserve, Congress is selling it off, a truly shortsighted step. The case for carbon taxes is laid out most recently by former Secretary of State James A Baker III et al., *The Conservative Case for Carbon Dividends* (Washington, DC, 2017.) This proposal from conservative leaders is a welcome intervention, but a better use of the proceeds from carbon taxes would be a reduction in taxes on labor, as Al Gore long proposed.

58. Andy Kroll, "The Billionaire Creator of the Power Rangers Has Invested Millions in Hillary Clinton. So What Does He Want?," *Mother Jones* (November/ December 2016).

59. Francesco Guicciardini, "Considerations on the 'Discourses' of Machiavelli," 1530, *Selected Writings*, Cecil Grayson, ed. and Margaret Grayson, trans. (New York, 1965), 92.

60. Sheldon Wolin, *Politics and Vision: Continuity and Innovation in Western Political Thought* (New York, 1960).

61. These paragraphs draw from David C. Hendrickson, "The Thrasybulus Syndrome: Israel's War on Gaza," *The National Interest*, July 29, 2014.

62. This quotation from the Book of Micah, which I listened to and spoke in prayer every week on Sundays growing up as a Unitarian, suggests that Judaism has within itself plenty of resources for the work of revelation. Peter Beinart shows why in *The Crisis of Zionism*.

CONCLUSION

1. Woodrow Wilson, Address to a Joint Session of Congress Requesting a Declaration of War Against Germany, April 2, 1917.

2. Vattel and Pufendorf, as we saw earlier, denied the right of any state to punish "enormous violations of the laws of nature" that do not affect its rights or safety. They held "that men derive the right of punishment solely from their right to provide for their own safety; and consequently they cannot claim it except against those by whom they have been injured." That distinction bears on when the right is more precious than peace.

3. Sumner, *Conquest of U.S.*, 12.

4. See the pertinent reflections of Adam Smith and Josiah Tucker, summarized in Hendrickson, *Peace Pact*, 92–100. Tucker's insight in 1774, later accepted by Smith, was to see that Britain could enjoy greater influence with its colonists in North America if it surrendered the pretension to exercise sovereignty over them, that it would lose from the attempt to exert dominion and gain from acceptance of Americans as equals, entitled to rule themselves. Such a resolution of the dispute would allow Britain to work with them on the basis of reciprocity, removing a thousand causes of antagonism arising from the claim to dominion. The resolution of the American crisis, according to Tucker's prophetic view, required not the military enforcement of Britain's authority, as Lord North proposed, nor a new way of exercising it, as Burke recommended, but its renunciation.

   Smith ultimately accepted Tucker's opinion, but was keenly aware of the potency of the opposing argument favoring the use of force to maintain the empire. Europe, Smith observed in 1778, would see American independence as dishonorable to Britain and signifying a decline in its national power and dignity. Worse, the people in Britain "would probably impute to mal-administration what might, perhaps, be no more than the unavoidable effect of the natural and necessary course of things." To give it up when you didn't have to, before stern necessity had left no other choice, was virtually unthinkable. A political administration that did so "would have every thing to fear from [the people's] rage and indignation at the public disgrace and calamity, for such they would suppose it to be, of thus dismembering the empire."

5. "A Memorandum by Robert Lansing," August 20, 1919, *Wilson Papers*, 62: 428–29.

Select Bibliography

Adams, John. *The Works of John Adams*. Edited by Charles Francis Adams. Boston, 1856.

Anderson, Perry. *American Foreign Policy and Its Thinkers*. London, 2015.

Bacevich, Andrew J. *American Empire: The Realities and Consequences of U.S. Diplomacy*. Cambridge, MA, 2002.

———. *The New American Militarism: How Americans Are Seduced by War*. New York, 2013 [2005].

———, ed. *The Long War: A New History of U.S. National Security Policy since World War II*. New York, 2007.

———. *The Limits to Power: The End of American Exceptionalism*. New York, 2008.

———. *Washington Rules: America's Path to Permanent War*. New York, 2009.

———, ed. *The Short American Century: A Postmortem*. Cambridge, MA, 2012.

———. *Breach of Trust: How Americans Failed Their Soldiers and Their Country*. New York, 2014.

———. *America's War for the Greater Middle East*. New York, 2016.

Bass, Gary. *Freedom's Battle: The Origins of Humanitarian Intervention*. New York, 2008.

Beard, Charles. *A Foreign Policy for America*. New York, 1940.

Beinart, Peter. *The Crisis of Zionism*. New York, 2013.

Betts, Richard. *American Force: Dangers, Delusions, and Dilemmas in National Security*. New York, 2013.

Brooks, Rosa. *How Everything Became War and the Military Became Everything: Tales from the Pentagon*. New York, 2016.

Brooks, Stephen G., and William C. Wohlforth . *World Out of Balance: International Relations and the Challenge of American Primacy*. Princeton, NJ, 2008.

———. *America Abroad: The United States' Global Role in the 21st Century*. New York, 2016.

Bull, Hedley. *The Anarchical Society: A Study of Order in World Politics*. New York, 2002 [1977].

Calleo, David P. *Follies of Power: America's Unipolar Fantasy*. New York, 2009.

Carpenter, Ted Galen, and Malou Innocent. *Perilous Partners: The Benefits and Pitfalls of America's Alliances with Authoritarian Regimes*. Washington, DC, 2015.

Clinton, Hillary. *Hard Choices: A Memoir.* New York, 2014.

Cole, David. "The Drone Presidency." *New York Review of Books,* August 18, 2016.

Constant, Benjamin. *Political Writings.* Edited by Biancamaria Fontana. Cambridge, UK, 1988.

Danner, Mark. *Spiral: Trapped in the Forever War.* New York, 2016.

Deudney, Daniel H. *Bounding Power: Republican Security Theory from the Polis to the Global Village.* Princeton, NJ, 2007.

Engelhardt, Tom. *Shadow Government: Surveillance, Secret Wars, and a Global Security State in a Single-Superpower World.* New York, 2014.

Evrigenis, Ioannis D. *Fear of Enemies and Collective Action.* Cambridge, UK, 2008.

Forsyth, Murray. *Unions of States: The Theory and Practice of Confederation* (New York, 1981).

Friedberg, Aaron. *A Contest for Supremacy: China, America, and the Struggle for Mastery in Asia.* New York, 2012.

Fukuyama, Francis. *America at the Crossroads: Democracy, Power, and the Neoconservative Legacy.* New Haven, CT, 2006.

Gates, Robert M. *Duty: Memoirs of a Secretary at War.* New York, 2014.

Glennon, Michael. *National Security and Double Government.* New York, 2014.

Goldberg, Jeffrey. "The Obama Doctrine: How He's Shaped the World." *The Atlantic* 373 (April 2016): 70–90.

Goodman, Melvin A. *National Insecurity: The Cost of American Militarism.* San Francisco, 2013.

Gopal, Anand. *No Good Men among the Living: America, the Taliban, and the War through Afghan Eyes.* New York, 2014.

Gordon, Scott. *Controlling the State: Constitutionalism from Ancient Athens to Today.* Cambridge, MA, 1999.

Greenwald, Glenn. *No Place to Hide: Edward Snowden, the NSA, and the U.S. Surveillance State.* New York, 2014.

Grotius, Hugo. *The Rights of War and Peace.* Edited by Richard Tuck. Indianapolis, IN, 2005.

Hamilton, Alexander. *The Works of Alexander Hamilton.* Edited by Henry Cabot Lodge. 12 vols. New York, 1904.

Hamilton, Alexander, James Madison, and John Jay. *The Federalist.* Edited by Jacob E. Cooke. Middletown, CT, 1961

Hartung, William D. *Prophets of War: Lockheed Martin and the Making of the Military-Industrial Complex.* New York, 2010.

Hendrickson, David C. *Peace Pact: The Lost World of the American Founding.* Lawrence, KS, 2003.

———. *Union, Nation, or Empire: The American Debate over International Relations, 1789-1941.* Lawrence, KS, 2009.

Hoffman, Elizabeth Cobbs. *American Umpire.* Cambridge, MA, 2013.

Hoffmann, Stanley, with Frédéric Bozo. *Gulliver Unbound: America's Imperial Temptation and the War in Iraq.* Lanham, MD, 2005.

Huntington, Samuel P. *The Clash of Civilizations and the Remaking of World Order*. New York, 1996.

Hurrell, Andrew. *On Global Order: Power, Values, and the Constitution of International Society*. Oxford, UK, 2007.

Hurrell, Andrew, and Kai Anderson, eds. *Hedley Bull on International Society*. New York, 2000.

Ikenberry, G. John. *Liberal Order and Imperial Ambition: Essays on American Power and World Politics*. Malden, MA, 2006.

———. *Liberal Leviathan: The Origins, Crisis, and Transformation of the American World Order*. Princeton, NJ, 2011.

Jackson, Robert. *The Global Covenant: Human Conduct in a World of States*. New York, 2000.

Johnson, Chalmers. *Blowback: The Costs and Consequences of American Empire*. New York, 2000.

———. *The Sorrows of Empire: Militarism, Secrecy, and the End of the Republic*. New York, 2004.

———. *Nemesis: The Last Days of the American Republic*. New York, 2007.

Kagan, Robert. *Of Paradise and Power: America and Europe in the New World Order*. New York, 2003.

———. *Dangerous Nation*. New York, 2006.

———. *The Return of History and the End of Dreams*. New York, 2008.

———. *The World America Made*. New York, 2012.

Kinzer, Stephen. *Overthrow: America's Century of Regime Change From Hawaii to Iraq*. New York, 2006.

Kissinger, Henry. *World Order*. New York, 2014.

Larison, Daniel. "Noninterventionism: A Primer: America's Alternative to War and Empire Is Not 'Isolationism.'" *The American Conservative*, June 11, 2014.

Layne, Christopher. *The Peace of Illusions: American Grand Strategy from 1940 to the Present*. Ithaca, NY, 2006.

Lebow, Richard Ned. *A Cultural Theory of International Relations*. New York, 2009.

Legvold, Robert. *Return to Cold War*. New York, 2016,

Lieven, Anatol. *America Right or Wrong: An Anatomy of American Nationalism*. 2nd ed. New York, 2012 [2004].

Lieven, Anatol, and John Hulsman. *Ethical Realism: A Vision for America's Role in the World*. New York, 2006.

Lind, Michael. *The Next American Nation: The New Nationalism and the Fourth American Revolution*. New York, 1995.

———. *The American Way of Strategy*. New York, 2006.

———. *Land of Promise: An Economic History of the United States*. New York, 2012.

———. "The Case for American Nationalism." *The National Interest*, May/June 2014.

Link, Arthur S. *The Papers of Woodrow Wilson*. 69 vols. Princeton, NJ, 1966-1994.

Lippmann, Walter. *U.S. Foreign Policy: Shield of the Republic*. Boston, 1943.

——. *U.S. War Aims.* Boston, 1944.

Madison, James. *Letters and Other Writings of James Madison.* Philadelphia, 1867.

——. *The Writings of James Madison.* Edited by Gaillard Hunt. 9 vols. New York, 1906.

Mandelbaum, Michael. *The Ideas That Conquered the World: Peace, Democracy, and Free Markets in the Twenty-first Century.* New York, 2002.

——. *The Case for Goliath: How America Acts as the World's Government in the 21st Century.* New York, 2005.

——. *Mission Failure: America and the World in the Post-Cold War Era.* New York, 2016.

Maurer, Noel. *The Empire Trap: The Rise and Fall of U.S. Intervention to Protect American Property Overseas, 1893-2013.* Princeton, NJ, 2013.

Mayers, David. *Dissenting Voices in America's Rise to Power.* New York, 2007.

McConnell, Scott. *Ex-Neocon: Dispatches from the Post 9/11 Ideological Wars.* New York, 2016.

McDougall, Walter A. *Promised Land, Crusader State: The American Encounter with the World Since 1776.* Boston, 1997.

——. *The Tragedy of U.S. Foreign Policy: How America's Civil Religion Betrayed the National Interest.* New Haven, CT, 2016.

Mead, Walter Russell. *Special Providence: American Foreign Policy and How It Changed the World.* New York, 2001.

Mearsheimer, John J. *The Tragedy of Great Power Politics.* 2nd ed. New York, 2014 [2001].

——. "The Burden of Responsibility: America Unhinged." *The National Interest* (January/February 2014).

Mearsheimer, John J., and Stephen M. Walt. *The Israel Lobby and U.S. Foreign Policy.* New York, 2007.

——. "The Case for Offshore Balancing: A Superior U.S. Grand Strategy." *Foreign Affairs* (July/August 2016).

Menon, Rajan. *The End of Alliances.* New York, 2007.

——. *The Conceit of Humanitarian Intervention.* New York, 2016.

Montesquieu, Charles de Secondat, baron de. *The Spirit of the Laws.* Edited and translated by Anne M. Cohler et al. Cambridge, UK, 1989.

Moyn, Samuel. *The Last Utopia: Human Rights in History.* Cambridge, MA, 2010.

Moynihan, Daniel Patrick. *On the Law of Nations.* Cambridge, MA, 1990.

Niebuhr, Reinhold. *Moral Man and Immoral Society: A Study in Ethics and Politics.* New York, 1960 [1932].

Nisbet, Robert. *The Present Age: Progress and Anarchy in Modern America.* New York, 1988.

Oglesby, Carl. "Vietnamese Crucible: An Essay on the Meanings of the Cold War." In Oglesby and Richard Shaull, eds., *Containment and Change,* 1-176. Toronto, 1967.

Onuf, Nicholas, and Peter S. Onuf. *Federal Union, Modern World: The Law of Nations in an Age of Revolutions: 1776-1814.* Madison, WI, 1993.

Pillar, Paul. *Why America Misunderstands the World: National Experience and Roots of Misperception.* New York, 2016.

Pocock, J. G. A. *Barbarism and Religion*, Vol. III: *The First Decline and Fall.* Cambridge, UK, 2003.

Porter, Gareth. *Perils of Dominance: Imbalance of Power and the Road to Vietnam.* Berkeley, CA, 2005.

———. *Manufactured Crisis: The Untold Story of the Iran Nuclear Scare.* Charlottesville, VA, 2014.

Porter, Patrick. *The Global Village Myth: Distance, War, and the Limits of Power.* Washington, DC, 2015.

Posen, Barry R. *Restraint: A New Foundation for U.S. Grand Strategy.* Ithaca, NY, 2014.

Preble, Christopher A. *The Power Problem: How American Military Dominance Makes Us Less Safe, Less Prosperous, and Less Free.* Ithaca, NY, 2009.

Preble, Christopher A., and John Mueller, eds. *A Dangerous World? Threat Perception and U.S. National Security.* Washington, DC, 2014.

Preble, Christopher A., Emma Ashford, and Travis Evans, eds. *Our Foreign Policy Choices: Rethinking America's Global Role.* Washington, DC, 2016.

Prestowitz, Clyde. *Rogue Nation: American Unilateralism and the Failure of Good Intentions.* New York, 2004.

———. *The Betrayal of American Prosperity.* New York, 2010.

Price-Smith, Andrew. *Contagion and Chaos: Disease, Ecology, and National Security in the Era of Globalization.* Cambridge, MA, 2008.

Recchia, Stefano, and Jennifer M. Welsh, eds. *Just and Unjust Military Intervention: European Thinkers from Vitoria to Mill.* Cambridge, UK, 2013.

Rieff, David. *A Bed for the Night: Humanitarianism in Crisis.* New York, 2003.

———. *In Praise of Forgetting: Historical Memory and Its Ironies.* New Haven, CT, 2016.

Rodrik, Dani. *The Globalization Paradox: Democracy and the Future of the World Economy.* New York, 2011.

Roth, Brad R. *Sovereign Equality and Moral Disagreement: Premises of a Pluralist Legal Order.* New York, 2011.

Sakwa, Richard. *Frontline Ukraine: Crisis in the Borderlands.* New York, 2015.

Sanger, David E. *Confront and Conceal: Obama's Secret Wars and the Surprising Use of American Power.* New York, 2013.

Schell, Jonathan. *The Unconquerable World.* New York, 2004.

Schlesinger, Arthur M., Jr. *The Cycles of American History.* New York, 1986.

Sestanovich, Stephen. *Maximalist: America in the World from Truman to Obama.* New York, 2014.

Seward, William. *The Works of William H. Seward.* Edited by George E. Baker. 5 vols. New York, 1884.

Smith, Adam. *An Inquiry into the Nature and Causes of the Wealth of Nations.* Edited by Edwin Canaan. New York, 1937 [1776].

Smith, Goldwin. *Commonwealth or Empire: A Bystander's View of the Question.* New York, 1902.

Smith, Tony. *A Pact with the Devil: Washington's Bid for World Supremacy and the Betrayal of the American Promise.* New York, 2007.

Snyder, Jack. *Myths of Empire: Domestic Politics and International Ambition.* Ithaca, NY, 1991.

Steel, Ronald. *Walter Lippmann and the American Century.* Boston, 1980.

Sumner, William Graham. *The Conquest of the United States by Spain.* Boston, 1899.

Thompson, John A. *A Sense of Power: The Roots of America's Global Role.* Ithaca, NY, 2015.

Thorpe, Rebecca U. *The American Warfare State: The Domestic Politics of Military Spending.* Chicago, 2014.

Thrall, A. Trevor, and Benjamin H. Friedman, eds. *The Case for Restraint: U.S. Grand Strategy for the 21st Century.* New York, 2017.

Thucydides. *History of the Peloponnesian War.* Translated by Benjamin Jowett. Oxford, UK, 1881.

Tucker, Robert W. *Nation or Empire? The Debate over American Foreign Policy.* Baltimore, 1968.

———. *A New Isolationism: Threat or Promise?* New York, 1972.

Tucker, Robert W., and David C. Hendrickson, *The Imperial Temptation: The New World Order and America's Purpose.* New York, 1992.

Turse, Nick. *The Complex: How the Military Invades Our Everyday Lives.* New York, 2008.

———. *Tomorrow's Battlefield: U.S. Proxy Wars and Secret Ops in Africa.* Chicago, 2015.

Vincent, R.J. *Nonintervention and International Order.* Princeton, NJ, 1974.

Walt, Stephen M. *Taming American Power: The Global Response to U.S. Primacy.* New York, 2005.

Webster, Daniel. *The Works of Daniel Webster.* Edited by Edward Everett. 6 vols. Boston, 1851.

White, Hugh. *The China Challenge: Why We Should Share Power.* Oxford, UK, 2013.

Wight, Martin. *Power Politics.* New York, 1981.

———. "Western Values in International Relations." In Martin Wight and Herbert Butterfield, eds., *Diplomatic Investigations,* 89–131. Cambridge, UK, 1966.

Williams, William Appleman. *The Tragedy of American Diplomacy.* 50th Anniversary ed. Edited by Andrew J. Bacevich. New York, 2009.

Woods, Randall Bennett. *Fulbright: A Biography.* New York, 1995.

Index

12/17